administrative
sciences

I0082455

Perspectives on Women's Higher Education Leadership From Around the World

Edited by
Karen Jones, Arta Ante, Karen A. Longman and
Robyn Remke

Printed Edition of the Special Issue Published in *Administrative Sciences*

MDPI

Perspectives on Women's Higher Education Leadership From Around the World

Perspectives on Women's Higher Education Leadership From Around the World

Special Issue Editors

Karen Jones
Arta Ante
Karen A. Longman
Robyn Remke

MDPI • Basel • Beijing • Wuhan • Barcelona • Belgrade

MDPI

Special Issue Editors

Karen Jones
University of Reading
UK

Arta Ante
Humboldt University
Germany

Karen A. Longman
Azusa Pacific University
USA

Robyn Remke
Lancaster University Management School
UK

Editorial Office
MDPI
St. Alban-Anlage 66
Basel, Switzerland

This is a reprint of articles from the Special Issue published online in the open access journal *Administrative Sciences* (ISSN 2076-3387) from 2017 to 2018 (available at: https://www.mdpi.com/journal/admsci/special_issues/WHEL)

For citation purposes, cite each article independently as indicated on the article page online and as indicated below:

LastName, A.A.; LastName, B.B.; LastName, C.C. Article Title. *Journal Name* **Year**, *Article Number, Page Range.*

ISBN 978-3-03897-264-8 (Pbk)
ISBN 978-3-03897-265-5 (PDF)

Cover image courtesy of shutterstock user Chinnapong.

Contents

About the Special Issue Editors

Karen Jones earned her Ph.D. from Bangor University, United Kingdom, and currently serves as Associate Professor of Educational Leadership and Management at the University of Reading's Institute of Education in the United Kingdom. A large part of her role involves the supervision of doctoral students, whose research in educational leadership and management encompasses a wide-range of socio-political, economic and cultural contexts, such as Saudi Arabia, Oman, Kuwait, Ghana, China, Turkey, and the UK. Karen is also Deputy Director of a professional doctoral degree in education—Ed.D., which has over 100 students from around the World, who are all working professionals in the field of education. She leads the Education Leadership and Management pathway on the MA Education, serves on the research ethics committee and the "Improving Equity and Inclusion through Education" Research Group. Karen previously served at the University of Plymouth, where she successfully directed a post-graduate program in Organizational Leadership, commissioned by the NHS Leadership Academy (South-West England). Prior to that, at Bangor University, she taught and researched a major £8m Leadership Development initiative for owner–managers of Small and Medium-sized Enterprises (SMEs), funded by the Welsh Government and the European Social Fund. Karen's primary research interest is women and leadership. Karen has published her research on this topic, most recently with a peer-reviewed journal paper that concerns the normalization of sexism in the workplace. She regularly presents her research at conferences, workshops, and events, and has designed and led initiatives to tackle gender stereotyping, unconscious bias, and sexism in the workplace and in the teaching and learning environment.

Arta Ante serves currently as Professor for Communication Management at design akademie berlin, SRH University of Applied Sciences in Berlin, and teaches courses in Communication Management, Gender, and Intercultural Communication. She earned her Ph.D. from the University of Vienna, Austria and was a Post-Doctoral Fellow at the Humboldt Universität Berlin. Her research topic was gender-focused communication in academic settings. Furthermore, she was also responsible for the management of a grant application for Horizon 2020, the EU Research and Innovation Programme (Value 2.3 Mio. Euros) with more than 11 partner academic institutions around Europe, focused on reducing gender inequalities in higher education. Arta additionally holds the office of Gender Equality Officer at design akademie berlin and her role consists partly of consulting the university leadership in issues related to communication and gender. Arta also has extensive experience in the management of the international non-profit sector, including the United Nations.

Karen A. Longman serves as Professor and Ph.D. Program Director in APU's Department of Higher Education. This program currently serves approximately 100 students, all of whom are working professionals in the field. She earned her Ph.D. from the University of Michigan and teaches courses in Higher Education Administration, Critical Issues in Higher Education, and Ethical Issues in Higher Education. Karen also holds the role of Senior Fellow with the 180-member Council for Christian Colleges & Universities (CCCU), where she worked for 19 years as Vice President for Professional Development and Research. In that role, Karen coordinated the design of an Executive Leadership Development Initiative, which has served over 400 participants (presidents, chief academic officers, and emerging leaders). Karen is co-editing a seven-volume book series focused on Women and Leadership. She was the lead editor on the first volume in the series, titled Women and Leadership in Higher Education (for details, see http://www.ila-net.org/communities/ag/WomenAndLeadershipV1.pdf). She also co-edits the journal *Christian Higher Education: An International Journal of Research, Theory and Practice*, and she has served on several national and international boards over the past 20 years.

Robyn Remke is a Lecturer in the Department of Leadership and Management, within the Lancaster University Management School of Lancaster University (U.K.). She has published numerous articles, focused primarily on the use of a critical/feminist lens to explore the gendered nature of leadership, organizations, and organizing. In particular, Dr. Remke has researched the ways that organizational members embody practices such as leadership, diversity management, and parental leave policies through communication. Additionally, her scholarly work has focused on alternative forms of workplace organizational structures and gendered identity in the workplace. Dr. Remke is the Past-President of the Organization for the Study of Language, Communication, and Gender. She also serves as Associate Editor of the journal *Women & Language*.

administrative
sciences

MDPI

Editorial

Perspectives on Women's Higher Education Leadership From Around the World

Karen A. Longman

Department of Higher Education, Azusa Pacific University, 701 East Foothill Blvd., Azusa, CA 91702, USA;
klongman@apu.edu; Tel.: +1-626-387-5706

Received: 5 July 2018; Accepted: 5 July 2018; Published: 19 July 2018

Numerous studies in recent years have tracked dimensions related to the status of women both within specific countries and from an international perspective. For example, the Millennium Development Goals (MDGs) in eight specific areas that were established by the United Nations for the period from 2000–2015 included targets for improving gender equality and the empowerment of women, including improved access to education (United Nations New Millennial Goals 2017). The UN subsequently established 17 Sustainable Development Goals for the period of 2016–2030, one of which focuses on providing "women and girls with equal access to education, health care, decent work, and representation in political and economic decision-making process"(United Nations Sustainable Development Goals 2017). Similarly, the World Economic Forum's Global Gender Gap Report (World Economic Forum 2017), which draws data annually from 177 countries, serves as "a framework for capturing the magnitude of gender-based disparities and tracking their progress over time" (p. vii). Data are organized into four subindexes for analysis: Economic Participation and Opportunity, Educational Attainment, Health and Survival, and Political Empowerment. Over the past decade, the Nordic countries have ranked highest in terms of a minimal gender gap in these areas, with Iceland, Norway, and Finland achieving the most favorable ratings.

For example, a review of the status of women leaders within politics and the business sectors around the world by Goryunova et al. (2017) documented that only 22.7% of parliament positions and 9% of CEO positions were held by women. Within the US context, the non-profit organization Catalyst has annually tracked the percentage of women within the S&P 500 corporations—a combination of 500 large companies that have common stock in one of the American stock market indexes; Catalyst's most recent report found that women made up only 5.0% of CEOs, 21.2% of Board seats, 26.5% of Executive/Senior-Level Officials and Managers, 36.9% of First/Mid-Level Officials and Managers, and 44.7% of total employees (Catalyst 2018).

This underrepresentation of women in leadership has detrimental ripple effects across communities and countries. In fact, scholars have repeatedly documented the benefits of having diverse perspectives around the leadership table (Catalyst 2013; Page 2007; Woolley et al. 2010). In addition, numerous others have emphasized the importance of having women's voices present in decision-making (Eagly 2015; Kezar 2014; Sandberg 2013; Madsen et al. 2015) as part of bringing that desired diversity.

Notably, recent research in various countries seems to indicate movement toward greater support for women in leadership, which may relate to the growing dissatisfaction not only with economic conditions but also with the attitudes and behaviors of those holding government offices. Survey research involving 64,000 participants in 13 countries that was conducted by Gerzema and D'Antonio (2013) identified widespread dissatisfaction regarding the male-normed models of those currently in power. In response to a survey item worded: "I'm dissatisfied with the conduct of men in my country" (p. 6), a majority of all three subgroups of respondents indicated agreement (global average of adults = 57%; men = 54%; and millennials = 59%). In summarizing key findings from their survey data, the researchers concluded:

Universally, it seemed that people had grown frustrated by a world dominated by codes of what they saw as traditionally masculine thinking and behavior: codes of control, competition, aggression, and black-and-white thinking that have contributed to many of the problems we face today, from wars and income inequality to reckless risk-taking and scandal. (p. 7)

At this particular time in world history, it is interesting to note that scholars have emphasized the importance of having greater diversity in leadership, and specifically for greater representation by women in leadership. Similar to the importance of increasing the rates of educational access and school completion by girls as reflected in the UN's New Millennium Goals (2000–2015) and the follow-up U. N. Sustainable Development Goals (2016–2030), access by women to higher education—and having role models by women in higher education leadership—has ripple effect benefits, given that postsecondary institutions shape the lives of future generations.

This special issue focuses on the topic of "Perspectives on Women's Higher Education leadership from Around the World," offering research and narratives of women in academic leadership from the United States, the United Kingdom, Australia, India, China, and Saudi Arabia. The opening article, "How Organizational Culture Shapes Women's Leadership Experiences (Longman et al. 2018)," presents the findings of a grounded theory study involving 16 participants working in faith-based institutions regarding the role of "organizational culture" and "organizational fit" in their leadership aspirations and experiences. Given that certain theological traditions within Christianity have historically limited the role of women in leadership, the study resulted in the identification of four subgroups of participants ranging from those who did not perceive that gender issues in the culture influenced their work or roles within the institution to participants who offered explicit criticism regarding the gendered dynamics evident in the culture in their institutions and in Christian higher education more broadly. The resulting theory and model reflected that various influences represented either a "push" (i.e., diminishing aspirations or willingness to move into or remain in leadership) or a "pull" (i.e., increasing the desire to become or remain a leader in that context) and had implications for anyone considering leadership opportunities vis-à-vis the realities of the organization's culture.

The second article, "Ascending: An Exploration of Women's Leadership Advancement in the Role of Board of Trustee Chair," (Scott 2018) presents the findings of a phenomenological study involving five women who had held of role of chair of the board of trustees of a private institution in a Southeast state in the U.S. Given that the board of trustees has the responsibility of hiring the president, who then is responsible for hiring senior-level leaders, the role of board chair is significant in shaping the future direction of these private institutions. The researcher conducted an in-person interview (with the opportunity for a second follow-up interview) with each participant to explore the experiences of these women board chairs, along with any perceived barriers or obstacles they reported encountering in their leadership role. In describing what had contributed to achieving the role of the board chair, certain skills or "skill sets" were identified, such as the ability to organize and lead an effective meeting, being held in high esteem by their peers, and having served in a variety of other leadership positions that provided knowledge related to effective board leadership.

Turning to the role of women's leadership development programming as an important strategy for preparing and equipping greater numbers of future women leaders in higher education, autoethnographic reflections about one institution's model program are presented in an article titled "Rethinking Women's Leadership Development: Voices from the Trenches." (Selzer et al. 2017). The program, which operates through the provost's office, was designed to identify and prepare mid-career faculty and staff women for senior-level leadership roles. Components of the curriculum include leadership skills such as visioning and strategic alignment, finance and operations, and understanding and building culture. Three former participants based their self-reflection of this seven-month program on the leader identity work of Ely et al. (2011), which emphasizes the importance of three related components: "(1) considering topics in light of gender bias; (2) supporting women's identity work; and (3) focusing on leadership purpose." In addition to the benefits gained through the use of the self-reflective process that was used in the collaborative autoethnography, the authors reported two key findings: "(1) to effectively develop women leaders, work must be done at the personal, interpersonal, and organizational levels, as these levels are interrelated and interdependent; and (2) women's multiple identities must be engaged." This article offers a full-orbed overview of the literature related to women and leadership and a helpful analysis of specific components of one institution's leadership development programming; it can also serve as an example of the benefits of collaborative autoethnography as a research methodology.

Another autoethnographic research project, this time from the UK context, is found in the article titled "The Implications of Contractual Terms of Employment for Women and Leadership: An Autoethnographic Study in UK Higher Education" (Vicary and Jones 2017). It offers a touching first-person perspective—yet a perspective that is well-grounded in related theory and research—on the experiences of individuals who lack the permanency and status of full-time employment within a university setting. The author notes that employment under a short-term or non-permanent contract has become common practice in higher education; such contracts are often referred to as "sessional" or "zero-hours" (meaning that no specific hours of work are guaranteed) and typically are renewed each term or each year. This autoethnographic study is grounded in the recognition that more than half (54%) of all academic staff and 49% of teaching staff in UK universities are employed under this type of non-permanent contract, 48% of whom are women. With courage and transparency, the author reveals how the lack of permanent and respected employment within academe can contribute to professional isolation, lowered self-esteem, and can dampen leadership aspirations due to lack of career progression opportunities.

Also written from the context of the United Kingdom, yet on a topic relevant to the higher education scenario of many other countries, is the article titled "Increasing Gender Diversity in Senior Roles in HE: Who Is Afraid of Positive Action?" (Manfredi 2017). Here, the author directly addresses the controversial topic of whether postsecondary institutions should adhere to "positive action" (referred to as "affirmative action" in other cultural contexts) as a constructive means of addressing the underrepresentation of certain groups (including women) in senior-level leadership roles. Referencing the UK context in specific, the author draws attention to section 159 of the UK Equality Act 2010, whereby employers are allowed to give preference to an applicant from an underrepresented group in tie-breaking situations. Yet the fairness of that approach has been challenged for a variety of reasons, including perceptions of reverse discrimination and tokenism. Citing both UK and European aspirational targets for advancing more women into senior-level leadership roles of postsecondary institutions, the author provides five compelling arguments for adhering to the practice of positive action in the recruitment and promotion of individuals from underrepresented groups.

Drawing data from two studies that focused on women in leadership (one based in the United Kingdom; the other from Australia), the article entitled "Fixing the Women or Fixing the Universities" (Burkinshaw and White 2017) addresses the gendered power relations at play in universities that often hold women back, despite efforts implemented to support their advancement. Using different methodologies—one study involved qualitative interviews with 18 senior women (e.g., vice chancellors); the other drew data from a quantitative survey—this project emerged from the experiences of two women representing different generations, both of whom had been negatively impacted in terms of their leadership aspirations by increasing job insecurity and continuous organizational restructuring that affected gender power relations at work. The precariousness for women having a career involving academic leadership was explored through the lenses of previous studies that have identified women as "the problem" rather than recognizing how organizational culture often contributes to the barriers faced by women in university settings.

Another interesting study from the context of higher education in Australia that takes a constructive tone is represented by the article titled "Frank and Fearless: Supporting Academic Career Progression for Women in an Australian Program" (Parker et al. 2018). When a 2009 analysis of data at a large Australian university identified that gender parity at the level of lecturer and senior lecturer did not translate to gender parity at more senior levels, a targeted program (a "Career Progression for Women" course) was developed to support the advancement of more women from senior lecturer to associate professor rank. Because applicants for this promotion were expected to demonstrate leadership abilities in the domains of teaching, research, engagement, and/or clinical service, various aspects of leadership development were central to the program's design. This article contains helpful descriptive material and an evaluation of various aspects of the course (e.g., guest speakers, development of a portfolio, the women-only structure) that could prove beneficial to other campuses seeking to initiate related supportive programming.

Three additional articles add rich international perspectives to this special issue of *Administrative Sciences*. The first, titled "Towards Social Justice in Institutions of Higher Learning: Addressing Gender Inequality in Science & Technology through Capability Approach" (Kameshwara and Shukla 2017), analyzes qualitative data from 40 interviews with faculty and staff at a university in South India to identify socio-cultural barriers faced by women studying in the fields of science and technology. Among the 30 respondents who were women, self-reported concerns were expressed regarding the "hard attitude" they had experienced, particularly within the male-dominated disciplines (i.e., science and technology). Historically and culturally, the authors report a private-public divide in India that has been associated with notions of gender; women's work has been viewed within the private domain of household, whereas men's work has been associated with authority and productivity. Also contributing to the underrepresentation of women in science and technology have been limitations on resources such as funding and educational opportunities, despite efforts by the government to address these concerns. While recognizing that discrimination and marginalization are present, the authors call for a capability approach to be advanced in addressing the status quo; in other words, women must be equipped with the identified capabilities (e.g., self-esteem, motivation levels, administrative and decision-making posts) that can be instrumental in tackling gender disparity and inequality in the Indian higher education context.

Similarly, revisiting the earlier themes of how organizational culture and/or socio-cultural influences shape the leadership aspirations and experiences of women in various settings, the perspective of Chinese academics is represented in the article entitled "Women and Leadership in Higher Education in China: Discourse and the Discursive Construction of Identity" (Zhao and Jones 2017). Noting that only 4.5% of the higher education senior-level leadership roles in that country have been held by women, the authors present the findings of qualitative interviews with nine women from two Chinese universities to examine "how women construct multiple identities, the interplay of identities, and the influence of broader societal Discourses of gender and leadership."

The findings revealed the extent to which the participants viewed the interplay of various identities (e.g., mothers, teachers, managers) in ways that were consistent with Confucian thought and societal norms (e.g., being supportive of the husband, tending to household chores, fulfilling duties); notably, all nine participants distanced themselves from leadership as a professional identity.

The concluding article in this special issue, titled "An Overview of the Current State of Women's Leadership in Higher Education in Saudi Arabia and a Proposal for Future Research Directions" (Alsubaie and Jones 2017), turns the reader's attention to an area of the world where relatively little is known about women's leadership. Similar to several other articles that preceded it, these authors address the concern expressed by Eagly (2015) that much of the literature related to leadership has been written from a Western orientation, reflecting assumptions that are inaccurate for other cultural contexts. The authors note that despite stereotypical images of Saudi women and culture, the status of women in the Kingdom of Saudi Arabia has been modified and improved in social, political, and economic life over the past two decades. Describing the methodology that led to this article as a "desk-based study," the work of these authors represents a helpful contribution to the literature both by synthesizing the available literature on women and leadership in higher education in Saudi Arabia and in proposing specific directions that future related research might take.

In conclusion, the full participation of women in leadership of postsecondary institutions is critical both for wise decision-making and for numerous other financial, organizational culture, and relational reasons, as articulated by Madsen in a synthesis of the literature titled: "Why Do We Need More Women in Leadership of Higher Education?" (Madsen 2015). Interestingly, a key finding of the international research project of Gerzema and D'Antonio that involved 64,000 participants was the significant level of agreement by adult respondents (66%) and by male respondents (65%) with the statement: "The world would be a better place if men thought more like women" (Gerzema and D'Antonio 2013, p. 8). While working toward that goal, increasing the visibility and engagement of women in higher education leadership also merits urgent focused attention and energy.

References

Alsubaie, Azzah, and Karen Jones. 2017. An Overview of the Current State of Women's Leadership in Higher Education in Saudi Arabia and a Proposal for Future Research Directions. *Administrative Sciences* 7: 36. [CrossRef]

Burkinshaw, Paula, and Kate White. 2017. Fixing the Women or Fixing Universities: Women in HE Leadership. *Administrative Sciences* 7: 30. [CrossRef]

Catalyst. 2013. Why Diversity Matters. Available online: http://www.catalyst.org/system/files/why_diversity_matters_catalyst_0.pdf (accessed on 5 July 2018).

Catalyst. 2018. Pyramid: Women in S&P 500 Companies. June 1. Available online: http://www.catalyst.org/knowledge/women-sp-500-companies (accessed on 5 July 2018).

Eagly, Alice H. 2015. Foreword. In *Women and Leadership around the World*. Edited by Faith Wambura Ngunjiri, Karen A. Longman and Cynthia Cherrey. Charlotte: Information Age Publishing, pp. ix–xiii.

Ely, Robin J., Herminia Ibarra, and Deborah M. Kolb. 2011. Taking gender into account: Theory and design for women's leadership development programs. *Academy of Management Learning & Education* 10: 474–93.

Gerzema, John, and Michael D'Antonio. 2013. *The Athena Doctrine: How Women (and the Men Who Think Like Them) Will Rule the Future*. San Francisco: Jossey-Bass.

Goryunova, Elizabeth, Robbyn T. Scribner, and Susan R. Madsen. 2017. The current status of women leaders worldwide. In *Handbook of Research on Gender and Leadership*. Edited by Susan R. Madsen. Northampton: Edward Elgar Publishing, pp. 3–23.

Kameshwara, Kalyan Kumar, and Tanu Shukla. 2017. Towards Social Justice in Institutions of Higher Learning: Addressing Gender Inequality in Science & Technology through Capability Approach. *Administrative Sciences* 7: 22.

Kezar, Adrianna. 2014. Women's contributions to higher education leadership and the road ahead. In *Women and Leadership in Higher Education*. Edited by Karen A. Longman and Susan R. Madsen. Charlotte: Information Age Publishing, pp. 117–34.

Longman, Karen, Jessica Daniels, Debbie Lamm Bray, and Wendy Liddell. 2018. How Organizational Culture Shapes Women's Leadership Experiences. *Administrative Sciences* 8: 8. [CrossRef]

Madsen, Susan R. 2015. Why do we need more women leaders in higher education? HERS Research Brief, No. 1. Available online: http://hersnet.org/wp-content/uploads/2015/07/HERS-Research-Brief-No.-1-Susan-Madsen-.pdf (accessed on 5 July 2018).

Madsen, Susan R., Faith Wambura Ngunjiri, Karen A. Longman, and Cynthia Cherrey, eds. 2015. *Women and Leadership around the World*. Charlotte: Information Age Publishing.

Manfredi, Simonetta. 2017. Increasing Gender Diversity in Senior Roles in HE: Who Is Afraid of Positive Action? *Administrative Sciences* 7: 19. [CrossRef]

Page, Scott E. 2007. *The Difference: How the Power of Diversity Creates Better Groups, Firms, Schools, and Societies*. Princeton: Princeton University Press.

Parker, Polly, Belinda Hewitt, Jennifer Witheriff, and Amy Cooper. 2018. Frank and Fearless: Supporting Academic Career Progression for Women in an Australian Program. *Administrative Sciences* 8: 5. [CrossRef]

Sandberg, Sheryl. 2013. *Lean in: Women, Work, and the Will to Lead*. New York: Alfred A. Knoph.

Scott, Heather Inez Ricks. 2018. Ascending: An Exploration of Women's Leadership Advancement in the Role of Board of Trustee Chair. *Administrative Sciences* 8: 7. [CrossRef]

Selzer, Robin, Amy Howton, and Felicia Wallace. 2017. Rethinking Women's Leadership Development: Voices from the Trenches. *Administrative Sciences* 7: 18. [CrossRef]

United Nations New Millennial Goals. 2017. Available online: http://www.un.org/millenniumgoals/ (accessed on 5 July 2018).

United Nations Sustainable Development Goals. 2017. Available online: https://www.un.org/sustainabledevelopment/gender-equality/ (accessed on 5 July 2018).

Vicary, Anne, and Karen Jones. 2017. The Implications of Contractual Terms of Employment for Women and Leadership: An Autoethnographic Study in UK Higher Education. *Administrative Sciences* 7: 20. [CrossRef]

Woolley, Anita Williams, Christopher F. Chabris, Alex Pentland, Nada Hashmi, and Thomas W. Malone. 2010. Evidence for a collective intelligence factor in the performance of human groups. *Science* 330: 686–87. [CrossRef] [PubMed]

World Economic Forum. 2017. The Global Gender Gap Report. Available online: http://www3.weforum.org/docs/WEF_GGGR_2017.pdf (accessed on 5 July 2018).

Zhao, Jiayi, and Karen Jones. 2017. Women and Leadership in Higher Education in China: Discourse and the Discursive Construction of Identity. *Administrative Sciences* 7: 21. [CrossRef]

administrative sciences

MDPI

Article

How Organizational Culture Shapes Women's Leadership Experiences

Karen Longman [1,*], Jessica Daniels [2], Debbie Lamm Bray [3] and Wendy Liddell [4]

[1]   Department of Higher Education, Azusa Pacific University, Azusa, CA 91702, USA
[2]   Higher Education Leadership Graduate School, Bethel University, St. Paul, MN 55112, USA;
     j-daniels@bethel.edu
[3]   Salem Campus, Northwest University, Kirkland, WA 98033, USA; debbie.lammbray@northwestu.edu
[4]   Department of Leadership Studies, Great Northern University, Spokane, WA 99207, USA;
     wliddell@greatnorthernu.org
*   Correspondence: klongman@apu.edu

Received: 21 December 2017; Accepted: 17 March 2018; Published: 22 March 2018

Abstract: This article presents the findings of a grounded theory study that examined the role of organizational culture and organizational fit in the leadership aspirations and experiences of 16 women working in faith-based colleges and universities in the U.S. Specifically, the researchers sought to understand what aspects of organizational culture at the home institutions of these participants influenced their employment experiences, including their considerations and decisions related to aspiring to and/or advancing into leadership. Analysis of the interview data indicated that the participants clustered into four subgroups: (1) participants who did not perceive that gender issues in the culture influenced their work or roles within the institution; (2) participants who reported that they did not perceive gender issues to be an institutional problem; however, they cited examples of problematic systems and cultures; (3) participants who identified gender inequalities at their institution, but indicated that such problems impacted them only minimally, if at all; and (4) participants who offered explicit criticism regarding the gendered dynamics evident in the culture in their institutions and in Christian higher education more broadly. Influences on leadership aspirations or experiences were identified as either being "push" (i.e., propelling the participant away from the organization and thus diminishing aspirations or willingness to move into or remain in leadership) or "pull" (i.e., drawing the participant into further engagement with the organization, thus increasing the desire to become or remain a leader in that context), with particular attention to the context of faith-based higher education. The article concludes with a brief discussion of implications for practice for individuals and postsecondary institutions.

Keywords: organizational culture; institutional leadership; women and leadership; leadership aspirations

1. Introduction

A Harvard Business Review article by Watkins (2013) carries the provocative headline: "What is Organizational Culture? And Why Should We Care?" Watkins opened the article by noting "universal agreement" (par. 1) that organizational culture exists and that "it plays a crucial role in shaping behavior in organizations" (par. 1); however, the author also noted that there has been limited consensus on exactly what organizational culture is. Hofstede et al. (2010) offered a practical description of culture as "[consisting of] the unwritten rules of the social game. It is the collective programming of the mind that distinguishes the members of one group or category of people from others" (p. 6).

Although a degree of ambiguity exists regarding the nature and definition of organizational culture, researchers have identified helpful characteristics of the nature of culture within a defined context. For example, Schein (2010) offered a clear description of an organization's culture based on his research in the field of business:

> ... [a] pattern of shared basic assumptions learned by a group as it solved its problems of external adaptation and internal integration, which has worked well enough to be considered valid and, therefore, to be taught to new members as the correct way to perceive, think, and feel in relation to those problems (p. 18).

The present study is informed by Schein's definition of culture as assumptions, behaviors, and perceptions that guide decisions and behavior within an organization. Additionally, previous researchers (e.g., 1; 38) have observed that organizational cultures (and even formal staffing structures) tend to be gendered, meaning that assumptions about leaders and the contributors to effective leadership are typically male-normed. Helgesen (2017), for example, has described the "inhibitory environment [in which] women often struggle, particularly in the formative years of their careers, to find and use their voices" (p. 4). Earlier research by Helgesen and Johnson (2010) within the corporate sector had focused on reasons that highly talented women were choosing to leave well-paying jobs; these scholars observed that over the previous two decades, there had been "increasing recognition that the structure of work was designed to reflect the realities of an all-male workforce whose constituents had few, if any, domestic responsibilities beyond supporting their families" (p. 58), contributing to a "mental mismatch between what the marketplace assumes people will value in their work and what women ... most deeply value" (p. 58). The perception of a mismatch is enhanced, according to Helgesen and Johnson (2010), "because organizations still offer reward, recognize achievement, build incentive, and decide promotion using definitions of worth that reflect an all-male industrial leadership culture" (p. 58). Such cultural expectations and structures influence the beliefs, behaviors, and experiences of people within an organization in regard to expectations and evaluation of leadership.

As Hofstede et al. (2010) research on cultures around the world documented, patriarchal systems have influenced (and continue to influence) issues of access and equity in all spheres of life, including the workplace culture and its influence on climate (i.e., the environment as experienced by employees). With particular attention on the influence of organizational culture reflected within participants' institutions, this article presents the findings of a qualitative study that examined the leadership experiences and aspirations of 16 women who had been identified as "emerging leaders" at faith-based colleges and universities in the United States. Colleges and universities often operate on the assumptions of a male-normed workplace culture, requiring women to "navigate their own leadership preferences (e.g., being collaborative) within a world of hierarchical and top-down organizations and structures" (32, p. 126). Specifically related to the workplace environment of postsecondary institutions that are aligned with evangelical Christian faith , the complexities may be informed and amplified by a theological understanding that has been characterized by Gallagher (2004) as reflective of a "hierarchically ordered universe" (p. 219). These male-normed leadership structures and theological commitments that influence dominant views of gender roles in faith-based institutions combine with the multiple cultures that function within a college or university (2). The result is deep, even if unseen, currents of cultural forces that need to be recognized and named if they are to be addressed or even considered for possible change. Thus, faith-based higher education provided a complex cultural context for this study.

Influences on leadership aspirations or experiences were identified as either being "push" (i.e., propelling the participant away from the organization and thus diminishing aspirations or willingness to move into or remain in leadership) or "pull" (i.e., drawing the participant into further engagement with the organization, thus increasing the desire to become or remain a leader in that context), with particular attention to the context of faith-based higher education. Collectively, the findings of this study are illustrated in a model (see Figure 1 below) that visualizes the variety of relationships that were identified between the institutions where these women were employed and the participants themselves. This research contributes to the development of theory on women in leadership, particularly regarding women's motivation to accept or vacate positional leadership. The findings, which have implications for leadership development programming and institutional leaders who contribute to shaping organizational culture, centered on the themes of organizational fit, the power of choice, and personal confidence.

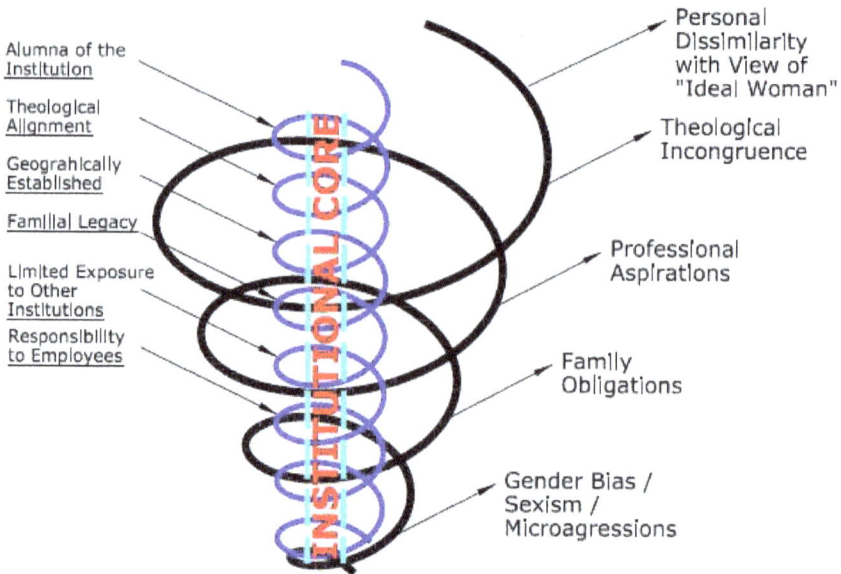

Figure 1. "Push" and "pull" influences related to organizational culture and women's leadership aspirations and experiences in Christian higher education.

2. Literature Review

As a leading scholar of organizational culture, Schein (2010) contributions to the literature have noted the interdisciplinary nature and use of the term, spanning business, sociology, leadership, and other fields. According to Schein, an organization's culture is influenced by historic events, religion, and group decisions, contributing to a type of organizational identity. Further, Schein offered a helpful distinction between: (1) the visible organizational structures and processes; (2) the strategies, goals, and philosophies or espoused justifications of the organization; and (3) the unconscious or taken-for-granted beliefs, perceptions, thoughts, and feelings that ultimately shape the values and actions of an organization.

For the purpose of this study, we also noted the distinction made by Schein (2010) between the concepts of organizational culture and climate. The latter term was described by Schein as "an artifact of the deeper cultural levels, as is the visible behavior of its members" (p. 26). Schein also observed that culture implies organizational structure and operates as a stabilizing and defining force. This integrated definition of culture, which "somehow implies that rituals, climate, values, and behaviors tie together into a coherent whole" (41, p. 15), is used expansively in reference to the institutional culture and climate encountered by participants in this study.

A variety of external, interpersonal, and internal factors that can hinder women's advancement into leadership have been identified by researchers, with many of those factors related to organizational culture. As summarized by Ely and Rhode (2010) in a chapter titled "Defining the Challenges" in the Handbook of Leadership Theory and Practice, women aspiring to leadership face a litany of behavioral and attitudinal barriers in many organizational settings. These scholars summarized: "Women leaders clearly navigate a different societal and organizational terrain from their male counterparts, a terrain deeply rooted in cultural ambivalence" (p. 379). The variety of subtle organizational influences that shape women's experience actually "disrupt the learning cycle at the heart of becoming a leader" (27, p. 62), negatively influencing the experiences of women considering or moving into leadership roles. In part, the cognitive association of leadership and maleness challenges women's advancement, whether that association is held subconsciously or overtly (14; 33).

To offset the powerful influence of individual and organizational biases, Egan, Shollen, Campbell, Longman, Fisher, Fox-Kirk, and Neilson (15) have advocated for the adoption of a more capacious model to explain women's leadership experiences and development. Building upon the "mature" model of Bronfenbrenner (2009) Ecological Theory of Child Development, the theory offered by Egan and colleagues explores the interplay of influences at five levels: chrono, macro, exo, meso, and micro. Using a somewhat similar framework to examine influences that hinder women's leadership advancement, Diehl and Dzubinski (2016) offered descriptions of 27 types of gender-based leadership barriers, organizing them according to "the level of society in which they generally operate: macro (societal), meso (group or organizational), and micro (individual)" (p. 187). Notably, Diehl and Dzubinski observed that the challenges facing women in leadership cannot be targeted in isolation; rather, "the first step is to recognize that women encounter barriers at all three levels, and that macro and micro barriers impact women's ability to see themselves as leaders, as well as others' ability to consider them for leadership roles" (p. 199).

2.1. Organizational Culture and Higher Education

Although the institutional culture of colleges and universities tends to reflect "an amalgam of institutional subcultures" (34, p. 129) with both vertical and horizontal cross-cutting dynamics (39), the senior-level leadership of most institutions is predominantly male. This fact was documented by Gangone and Lennon (2014), who conducted an analysis of demographic trends of ten sectors of U.S. society, one of which was higher education; findings were reported in the "Benchmarking Women's Leadership in the United States 2013" report (8). Trends across the ten sectors in terms of the under-representation of women in leadership were fairly consistent; in higher education as of 2010, only 23% of chief executive officers were women, 38% of chief academic officers, and 36% of the academic deans. The American Council on Education (ACE) found the pattern of under-representation of women in postsecondary leadership to be sufficiently troubling that an initiative titled "Moving the Needle: Developing a 21st Century Agenda for Women's Leadership" was launched in 2010, calling together presidents and organizational leaders to strategize how to address this concern (42). A 2017 ACE report noted slight improvement over time, as reflected in the fact 30.1% of U.S. university presidents at that time were women (18).

Further explaining the complexities of higher education institutions, Bergquist and Pawlak (2008) describe six cultures that are present in most academic settings: (1) collegial, (2) managerial, (3) developmental, (4) advocacy, (5) virtual, and (6) tangible. Although women who are considering leadership must navigate these various cultures effectively, it is notable that Bergquist and Pawlak (2008) described the collegial culture as being aligned with the "values and perspectives that are decidedly male-oriented" (p. 33). These scholars further added: "Quite clearly, the traditional collegial culture is a world of the blade, with a strong emphasis on often subtle but nevertheless quite powerful competition and striving for prestige and dominance" (p. 33). These cultural dynamics can create challenges for women who aspire or advance into leadership, including the problem of wage inequities and lack of supportive workplace priorities, policies, and reward structures (30), second generation bias embedded in stereotypes or organizational practices (27), the need for more targeted mentoring (31) and leadership development programs oriented toward women (17).

2.2. Institutional Fit

Related to the dynamics that flow from organizational culture, the concept of organizational fit also must be taken into account when considering the workplace environment for women. In institutions where the structures, systems, environment, traditions and interactions are created and sustained primarily by men, the culture that develops tends to be defined and understood in terms that reflect male norms (1; 25; 38). Lindholm (2003) identified two ways in which "fit" can either work comfortably for the individual involved or contribute to misalignment or dysfunction. First, the person-organization fit theory relates the interests, values and abilities of an individual to associated features of an organization (34). Thus, in the person-organization model, fit reflects a high degree of similarity or compatibility between an organization and an individual. In contrast, the person-environment models of organizational fit refer to dimensions of the relationship between individuals and vocations, specific jobs or work teams (34). Both models can be helpful when considering whether an individual is compatible with the culture of a higher education institution.

Given the variety of cultural influences (macro, micro, etc.) that shape the day-to-day environment of a college or university, individuals may find themselves experiencing numerous complexities in the workplace. Strengthening an alignment with an institution for which there is apparent affinity and learning to navigate an institution's cultural complexities can be challenging for individuals considering whether to remain and invest fully. As described in the section that follows, this challenge may be compounded for women considering leadership in faith-based higher education, particularly in cases where the theological commitments of the institution and its senior-leadership may be somewhat out of sync with that of women who aspire to leadership, particularly in relation to, the role of women in the church and broader society.

2.3. Theological Commitments and Women's Leadership

The faith-based institutions that were represented by the 16 participants in this study were employed at institutions that are members of a Washington DC-based organization, the Council for Christian Colleges & Universities (CCCU), which serves more than 180 postsecondary institutions around the world. Within the U.S., the CCCU institutions, represent one subset of just over 1000 religiously-affiliated institutions; they are affiliated with more than 30 Christian denominations (ranging from Mennonite and Evangelical Friends to Presbyterian and Southern Baptist). Binding the CCCU membership together is a commitment by institutional leadership to a shared purpose of "Advancing faith and intellect for the common good" (6). The CCCU institutions, education a total enrollment of 460,000 annually and collectively have served over 3.5 million alumni; additionally, 64,000+ faculty and staff are employed by the CCCU membership (6).

Although CCCU institutions share many commonalities, they differ in the nature of each institution's relationship with a sponsoring group of churches or denomination (22). Regardless of whether or not a CCCU member institution retains a formal denominational relationship, its theology typically is at least somewhat consistent with that of the founders or its sponsoring denomination. Although these colleges and universities are not churches, this partnership relationship may include the expectation that the institution operates according to the denomination's commitments and structures (22; 28). Thus, the theology of a founding or sponsoring denomination is often important in understanding the culture of many CCCU institutions.

Many, if not most, of the CCCU member institutions self-identify with Evangelical Protestantism. An analysis of this subset of private colleges and universities by Dahlvig and Longman (2016) in relation to women's leadership development identified that "individuals adhering to an evangelical worldview may view leadership—either consciously or subconsciously—through a set of presuppositions that is detrimental to women's advancement into leadership roles" (p. 244). Although it is clear that evangelicalism in the U.S. (let alone worldwide) is not monolithic, some streams of thought within evangelicalism understand there to be God-ordained gender roles in marriage, the church, and (in fewer cases) society in general. In a major study funded by the Pew Charitable Trusts, Gallagher (2004) concluded that "gender persists as a central, salient and effective element of the boundary work that maintains evangelical subculture and identity" (p. 216). Specifically related to the appropriate roles for men and women in the church and in society, Gallagher described the dominant view of evangelicals as being "organized by the principles of hierarchy and subordination" (p. 218). Such conditions have implications for women's leadership aspirations and experiences within the context of denominationally-owned or -sponsored colleges and universities.

3. Research Methodology

Our study used a constructivist grounded theory approach to explore how women leaders at CCCU institutions perceive and experience the gender climate at their institutions; relatedly, the research examined the relationship of the perceived gender climate to the participants' considerations about advancing in leadership. Creswell (2007) described grounded theory as one of five qualitative research methodologies; within each, a variety of research approaches has emerged. Early work by Glaser and Strauss (1967) popularized grounded theory as a qualitative methodology in which data are gathered through open-ended, emergent, and probing questions to explore the experiences of participants. Charmaz (2006) subsequently advocated a constructivist grounded theory approach, which acknowledges the role of the researchers' and participants' context in the way knowledge is understood and constructed. Given that the cultural context of the participants was a key dimension of this research focus, constructivist grounded theory was used to obtain an understanding of the participants' individual and collective perceptions of leadership vis-à-vis institutional culture.

Data collection involved an initial face-to-face interview of approximately an hour in length with each of the 16 participants; the protocol questions focused on participants' understanding of leadership, various aspects of participants' leadership journey, future aspirations, and sources of encouragement and discouragement on the leadership journey. Follow-up interviews, conducted in person or by telephone a year later, further explored the denominational/theological orientation of each participant and her institution, as well as perceptions of the influence of organizational culture on the participant's leadership experiences. The second set of interviews served as the primary data source for the analysis that follows; the researchers coded each transcript individually, then confirmed the themes that seemed to be emerging through group dialogue and analysis, using constant comparative methods to establish "analytic distinctions" (7, p. 54). Comparisons were subsequently made across the entire dataset to identify similarities and differences. Contextual information was drawn from a review of participants' application materials to participate in a four-day Women's Leadership Development program, transcriptions from the first set of interviews, and comparison of these themes with the transcriptions of four related focus groups that were arranged at approximately the same the time as the second interviews. The co-authors of this article, who conducted the research, all work at CCCU institutions; from that framework of shared experiences, we sought to enter into the lived experiences of the participants in order to accurately represent their voices in the findings presented below.

3.1. Participants

The participants were 16 women who had been identified by their home institutions as emerging leaders and nominated to participate in a four-day Women's Leadership Development Institute (WLDI) offered through the CCCU. Each of the participants met several criteria for inclusion, as components of the application process for the WLDI: (1) held a doctorate or was nearing completion of a doctorate; (2) was recognized institutionally as an emerging leader with demonstrated leadership skills and the potential for future cabinet-level service; and (3) provided evidence of increasing levels of leadership responsibility within and/or beyond higher education.

At the time of the initial set of interviews, the participants ranged in age from 30–59; 13 of the 16 were married; 11 of the 16 were mothers; and 15 were Caucasian (one self-identified as Hispanic). Eleven of the participants held roles as academic administrators or faculty chairs; two served within student development; and three held other administrative roles (alumni, business/finance); all but one worked at a CCCU institution at the time of the interviews. Denominational membership of the participants represented a spectrum of Christian denominations including Southern Baptist, Roman Catholic, Nazarene, Assemblies of God, Missionary Church, Presbyterian Church USA, Wesleyan,

United Methodist, and Mennonite. Seven of the participants were employed by the institution they had attended as an undergraduate student; four had attended another CCCU institution for their undergraduate education.

3.2. Findings and Discussion

Many of the themes common in the literature related to women and leadership were corroborated by findings in the present study. However, the participants frequently referenced that their work within an evangelical Christian culture, in particular, influenced certain inequities they had experienced. One participant made the point that such experiences were not atypical elsewhere (institutionally and/or in other professional environments); however, she went on to explain, "I think specifically in CCCU schools, that's why we can't seem to make progress. It is the religious, the biblical issues."

Common themes that emerged in our findings, consistent with earlier research findings, included expressed concerns regarding inequality in compensation, tenure, and workload. Other common gender discrepancies present in our findings were more difficult to measure, such as the micro-inequities that seemed to be related to prejudices and precedent, especially when justified by an institution's theological orientation. The patriarchal history of the church, gender-related denominational doctrines, and scriptural interpretations all impact gender-role understanding (28; 40). One participant explained, "I think the biggest barrier is the 'good old boys' club, it's the informal networking to which women have no access." Another participant explained that some male Christian leaders, in an attempt to avoid the appearance of impropriety, adopt a policy of not socializing or meeting alone with the opposite sex. Such a policy actually restricted women's access to mentoring and informal networking, thus disadvantaging women by limiting professional development opportunities.

The participants frequently emphasized sensing a struggle related to work and family balance, in part due to perceived assumptions that women would (or should) hold the majority share of parenting duties. One participant described her perception of a key reason for women's underrepresentation in leadership at CCCU institutions: "I really think it's the child-rearing question. I think if you are in a Christian institution, it's much more acceptable, encouraged, and maybe even expected that you'll be a little bit more domestic." A few participants reported that they had experienced discrimination as a working mother. One participant stated, "I simply was viewed as an oddity. I should be home taking care of my children. I mean I got openly very, very rude comments and I know it hindered my time at [institution] ..." An early study by Moreton and Newsom (2004) had reported that cultural expectations related to children and marriage were exacerbated for women working within the context of CCCU institutions. One participant in the present study concluded, "So, I think ... we're back to evangelical rhetoric ... Evangelicalism is the barrier. It's the problem ... the stuff that is happening is so *not* Jesus. It's pathetic."

During the process of data analysis, a pattern gradually emerged that related to a variety of "push" and "pull" factors; awareness of this pattern was helpful in understanding the participants' leadership aspirations and experiences in relation to their organizational culture. As described below and visualized in Figure 1, the participants' interview responses and subsequent leadership paths could be clustered in four distinct groups.

In the first group (Group 1), participants did not perceive that gender issues influenced their work or roles within the institution. In addition to reporting their perceptions that gender equity was the campus norm, these participants provided examples to support the accuracy of their perception. Notably, the participants in this group remain employed within the CCCU, with half having progressed further into broader leadership roles.

Participants in the second group (Group 2) also reported that they did not perceive gender issues to be an institutional problem. However, the participants' responses included examples of seemingly problematic systems and cultures related to balance and family, policies practices, and evangelical culture and patriarchal systems. All of the participants in this category remain at their

CCCU institutions, with some choosing to limit their involvement due to family responsibilities and others advancing in various leadership positions.

Participants in the third group identified gender inequalities at their institution, but indicated that such problems impacted them only minimally, if at all. Although these participants articulated that gender issues had not influenced their own careers, the pattern of their career progression following the interviews seemed to contradict these statements. All but one of the participants in Group 3 have moved to positions outside the CCCU; the participant who remains was serving in a non-cabinet level position at the time of the interviews.

Finally, the women in the fourth group had the most explicit criticism for their institutions and of Christian higher education more broadly. The participants in Group 4 reported having had the most painful or challenging experiences, which they attributed to cultural and individual gender bias and gender role expectations that were inconsistent with their own. Of the four participants in this group, two subsequently had been terminated from their positions, one had been demoted, and one sought employment at a university outside of the CCCU. Characteristics of the participants in each of these four subgroups are described in the sections that follow.

Group 1: "I think it's a very fair playing field."

The four women in Group 1 reported that they did not perceive gender issues to be problematic at their institutions; accordingly, they expressed that they had not felt any gender-related negative impact on their employment experience or perceived opportunity to progress in leadership. The participants in this category were employed at institutions that were either non-denominational or aligned with Anabaptist theological traditions that tend to be supportive of women in all levels of leadership (e.g., Mennonite, Brethren in Christ).

Two participants, one a faculty member and one an administrator, expressed enthusiasm regarding the many opportunities afforded them at the nondenominational university at which both worked. The administrator spoke of programs and structures she had created and cited no negative experiences regarding gender and leadership. The faculty member corroborated this perception, stating: "I felt like I was offered a lot of opportunities. I never felt that gender either gave me a disadvantage or an advantage." She expressed having appreciation for the "fair playing field" of her workplace, in which she felt encouraged and supported.

A participant from an institution aligned with a charismatic theological tradition perceived her university to be "proactive" in advancing women to positions of leadership. Specifically, she reported: "I don't think that there has been a limitation or a roof or a barrier at the upper levels." This participant noted that women held administrative and board positions in the institution and that a woman held the role of associate dean in the university's theology department.

Another participant, speaking from her experience at a CCCU institution, stated, "I really have had very little experience that I would say has been discrimination based on my gender, even within mathematics . . . It seems to me a pretty positive environment for women and leadership." A list of previous and current female leaders on that campus was offered as evidence of her institution's openness to promoting women into leadership roles: interim president, provost, deans, and department chairs.

These four women indicated high levels of institutional satisfaction and remain employed and/or have advanced in leadership positions at CCCU institutions. Notably, all four participants in this group reported an interest in leadership progression, with most of them explicitly expressing confidence (and having received encouragement from institutional leaders) regarding their ability to successfully manage increased responsibilities.

The three CCCU institutions represented by the four participants in Group 1 appeared to cultivate a female-friendly environment. The lack of a denominational affiliation in two of the institutions and the Anabaptist tradition of the third seemed to fuel a campus climate that was supportive of women's leadership aspirations.

Group 2: "It's just sort of life in early 21st century United States culture."

Most of the five participants in Group 2 did not perceive gender issues to be an institutional problem; however, examples they provided seemed to indicate that gender was, in fact, an issue to at least some degree. The participants in this category were employed at institutions with varying theological orientations, including Wesleyan Holiness, non-denominational, and two from baptistic traditions.

These five women expressed generally positive experiences at their institutions of employment. One participant noted, "I really don't see a big . . . difference with how women and men are treated here on campus. You'll get all of the support you need as a woman here to grow, and expand, and . . . just really excel professionally." Most of the participants self-reported having high job satisfaction and a commitment to their field and/or to Christian higher education more broadly. Additionally, the significance of these participants' contributions on their home campuses was documented by the supportive reference letters submitted by their supervisors that were influential in the women's selection to participate in the four-day Women's Leadership Development Institute.

Many of the participants in Group 2 did, however, express concerns about the patriarchal tone of evangelicalism more broadly. A faculty participant spoke of the impact of evangelical systems and culture on women and leadership: "I don't know that we nurture women professionally in the same way. I look at the majors that women on our campus go into and how big our education and nursing [programs] are . . . We tend to socialize women into those fields in theologically conservative Christianity." According to this participant, the socialization can be attributed to "a broader cultural set of understandings . . . that derive from the theological pool that we happen to be swimming in." She clarified, "Maybe . . . the ecclesiastical pool . . . [is] church culture. It might be just more generalized church culture stuff." Another participant stated, "It's subtle and I don't know that I can attribute it to organizational culture as much as . . . it's just sort of life in early 21st century United States culture."

Although the participants in Group 2 characterized their employment experiences as positive, they did reference problematic systems related to gender, although typically not personalizing the issues. Still, the responses regarding a lack of family-friendly workplace policies, hiring and promotion practices, cultural expectations, and evangelical/patriarchal systems suggested that gender issues did, in fact, exist on their campuses, although not emphasized as being problematic to the participants.

Although the reasons for the contradiction between the explicit description of their campuses as being supportive of women and their contrasting stories of experience were not clear in the data, two possibilities seem viable. First, the women may have not labeled their experiences as gender inequity given that they had become accustomed to the environment and did not expect anything more from it. Alternatively, the women's comfort with the gender climate may be congruent with their own views of gender roles. If so, these four women may not have chosen to identify current beliefs and practices as being problematic because doing so might identify them with ideologies outside the accepted norm on campus (e.g., as "radical" feminists). Regardless of the reason, the outcome is interesting: The five participants in this category continue to be employed at their CCCU institutions, with some limiting their involvement due to family responsibilities and others advancing in various leadership positions.

Group 3: "There's been a real awakening of the awareness of lack of women in leadership, and a lot of angst about it. Probably more angst than actual solutions, unfortunately."

The three participants in this group identified gender issues as being problematic at their institution; however, they perceived the impact to be minimal or nonexistent for them personally. Women in Group 3 were employed at institutions from three different theological orientations: Nazarene, Church of God, and non-denominational. The experiences of the participants were similar: All reported having had opportunities to advance in leadership despite what the participants perceived as obvious gender inequities.

One participant was able to create a culture in her area of responsibility that she believed encouraged equality and developed women's leadership potential. Yet this participant indicated that the organizational culture, as a whole, was not as supportive of women as some of the subcultures within the institution. Ultimately, the participant left the institution to accept a senior-level position outside of the CCCU membership. After another administrator had commented on the absence of women in cabinet level-positions in her institution, she expressed concern about the status quo: "I'd put it [my university] pretty much in the mainstream of the Christian institutions, but there's been a real awakening of the awareness of lack of women in leadership and a lot of angst about it. Probably more angst than actual solutions, unfortunately."

The employment outcomes for participants in Group 3 suggest that the participants may have been more influenced by campus gender issues than they perceived to be the case. One participant indicated satisfaction with the support she experienced at her institution. After her contract had not been renewed, the institution's senior leadership had affirmed her talents and created a director-level position for her. However, she was then terminated a year later due to institutional downsizing. In fact, only one participant from Group 3 remains employed at a CCCU institution; she serves in a non-cabinet level position.

Group 4: "The real danger for Christian higher education is that they're using Scripture to back their prejudices."

The four participants in Group 4 identified gender issues as being a significant problem at their institutions and provided clear personal and institutional examples. The women were employed at institutions that embrace a variety of theological perspectives, including differences in how gender roles are understood. These participants, who perceived that the gender climate negatively impacted their employment experience, described the culture at their institutions as "inhospitable" and "hypocritical." The participants in this fourth group attributed their negative experience to cultural and personalized gender bias and gender role expectations inconsistent with their own convictions.

Cultural and individual gender bias within institutions was identified by some participants as the reason for the lack of support for women in leadership. An administrator at a nondenominational college referenced the report of a consultant who had been hired to conduct a gender audit; the report concluded that the institution "definitely" perpetuated gender inequities. Describing gender bias within the leadership of the institution, this participant noted, "There are some people on campus who are definitely not big fans of women in leadership, and there are other people who are very supportive." This participant also perceived that the theologically-conservative views held personally by the president, vice president, and board were potential barriers to the leadership advancement of women. Another administrator critiqued what she perceived a hypocrisy between the rhetoric and actions of leaders at her institution. Although senior leadership spoke about "diversity and progress" regarding women, their actions conveyed a different message: "I don't think that they want women and I don't think that they are willing to actually say that." This participant concluded, "It's worse than it was for women when the spoken policy was one of oppression, because now it's transitioned into an unspoken policy of oppression."

The word "hostility" was offered as a descriptor of the way participants experienced the environment created, at least in part, by the organization's cultural expectations of women. These participants perceived that there was a commonly-held ideal regarding female employees on campus; women who did not fulfill the ideal face challenges regarding institutional fit. Within the context of her theologically conservative institution, one participant who held an administrative role commented that women who garner respect at her university needed to be quiet, competent, smart, likable, and not prone to "rocking the boat." Another participant noted that even the idea of a working woman could be questioned within her institution. "Women are supposed to manage the home," the participant said. "Women are supposed to support the husband. And women are supposed to raise the kids." Deviating from this ideal caused the participants to sense they did not fit with the culture of the institution.

Confusion regarding the appropriate roles for women in leadership also arose in relation to the purpose of a Christian college and how that purpose intersects with the theological position of the sponsoring denomination in terms of gender roles. One participant framed this question as it had arisen at her institution: "Is this a church? Or, is this a business, or a school?" Such lack of clarity about the relationship of church and college is consistent with other research that has identified a lack of clarity on the part of many Christian higher education institutions regarding whether the institution is an extension of, or separate from, the church (28; 40).

Perceptions of the relationship between the institution and the church seemed to be further complicated by deeply-embedded cultural influences. At one non-denominational institution that had been strongly influenced by a theologically-conservative founder, disparaging comments about women leaders reportedly had been made by male colleagues. The participant from this institution commented: "I've had someone say to me, 'I've never had to report to a woman before. I just don't think I could do that.'" At the same institution, a female colleague was told that she had "no business being in charge of men at all." The justification for such comments was summarized by one participant: "The real danger for Christian higher education is that they're using Scripture to back their prejudices . . . "

Of the four groups, those in Group 4 had experienced the most difficult experiences, conveyed the most explicit criticism for their institutions, and expressed the greatest level of concern about Christian higher education in general. Only one of the four participants remained at the same institution at the time of the writing of this article, yet she had experienced a demotion due to a campus closure. Of the other participants in Group 4, two had been terminated from their positions; one of those two now works outside of higher education, and the other has moved to a senior-level leadership position at a large public institution.

Perhaps more than the denomination affiliation, the participants in Group 4 indicated that the conservative theological orientation of these institutions was the source of the cultural resistance to women in leadership. However, it is also important to consider the idea of institutional fit. Although the women in Group 4 may have experienced gender prejudice, participants' negative experiences may have been exacerbated by a poor fit between the participant and the culture of the institution. For instance, the idea that an "ideal woman" will have specific characteristics would be a difficult expectation for some women who think otherwise. It is impossible to fully identify all the factors impacting these situations, but the outcome is clear: These women perceived that they were not valued at their institutions.

The findings of the present study, in which the responses of 16 participants were divided into four subgroups, corroborate the findings of previous research by Billing (2011). Billing interviewed 20 women managers in male-normed organizations in Denmark and Sweden, seeking to understand the management experiences of the participants. The participants' stories were found to be represented by four categories of relationship between the participant and organization, or the employee's sense of whether she "fit" within her organization: "(a) congruency, (b) congruency and ambivalence, (c) adjustments and resistance, and (d) conditional assimilation" (p. 306). In the present study, participants' relationships with their campus environment also could be divided into four categories, representing increasing levels of dissatisfaction. The similarity between the two studies indicates that personal congruity with the organization or institution is an important consideration for women employees who are serving in or aspire to leadership roles.

3.3. Grounded Theory Model

To illustrate findings from this study in a visual representation, the researchers developed a model (see Figure 1) regarding the relationships between the culture of higher education institutions and the experiences of aspiring or experienced women leaders.

In the model, the college or university is represented as a solid, cylindrical core with a porous exterior shell. This solid core represents the dominant institutional culture, or the core culture. Although the cultures of higher education institutions are complex, the core culture in the model includes the distinctive and influential components of Christian higher education: the macroculture of Christian theology, denominational subcultures, historic theological underpinnings, and male-normed structures reflective of church governance. To visually represent the possibility of cultural changes within organizations, the porous exterior represents the possible influence of individuals, circumstances, or other change agents.

Helgesen and Johnson (2010) noted that women's career paths tend to take the form of a spiral rather than a straight line of progression. Similarly, in the model, the lives and career paths of women are represented as an upward spiral. The length of the line represents the personal and professional journey of the women leaders, including their experiences related to leadership. Finally, to reflect the variety of responses about future leadership aspirations, the blue spiral reflects individuals who remain aligned with the institution and experience institutional fit; in contrast, the black spiral widens and gradually becomes more distant and removed from the institutional core.

To illustrate the theoretical relationship between a higher education institution and women leaders, the model identifies various factors that influence women's decisions to continue at an institution and, in some cases, to pursue additional leadership opportunities. In such cases, we suggest that women leaders were pulled toward greater engagement with their institutions by a variety of influences. For example, some women were alumnae of the institution and exhibited a deep sense of loyalty even in the face of occasional discouragements; others were very committed to the mission or were bound geographically to that area. In contrast to the pull factors, some of the women were pushed out of the institution by a range of influences (e.g., personal theological incongruence with their college and university). In some cases, participants struggled to reconcile the institutional view of an "ideal" woman with their own identities. The push and pull factors represent aspects of the literature of gendered leadership (12; 15; 27; 30), as well as circumstances unique to Christian higher education (11; 28; 40).

3.4. Limitations

Our findings provide helpful insight into the role of "fit" with organizational culture, particularly as related to women's leadership experiences in male-normed organizational cultures. These experiences clearly influenced the participants' leadership aspirations and opportunities for professional mobility. However, as with the findings of all qualitative studies, the findings may not be generalizable to other contexts. Additionally, although the research involved two rounds of interviews with each of 16 participants, additional data sources such as visits to the home campuses of these participants would undoubtedly have yielded more nuanced understanding of their workplace contexts.

One specific limitation of this study is the racial and ethnic homogeneity of the participants. Of the 16 participants, 15 self-identified as Caucasian. Although not entirely disproportionate to the overall CCCU employment demographics (the underrepresentation of ethnic diversity among CCCU employees has been a longstanding problem; see McMurtrie (2016), a more diverse participant group would likely have affected the findings due to the intersectionality of race, gender, and culture. This limitation relates to a recommended area for further related research.

Additionally, the participants represented 13 colleges or universities that varied theologically, geographically, and structurally. Although the broader literature indicates that women in higher education leadership face challenges that are similar to those in other work contexts, the specific results of this study are not necessarily representative of the 180 affiliated institutions of the Council for Christian Colleges & Universities, let alone the 1000+ religiously-affiliated institutions in the United States. Targeted research into specific theological traditions might reveal considerable variation even within theological subsets of the CCCU. However, the roles of organizational culture and "institutional fit" as related to attracting and retaining high-potential women, particularly in relation to leadership roles, merit continued research attention.

3.5. Theoretical Contributions and Implications for Practice

The literature that develops the theoretical foundation to explain the leadership journeys of women has been expanding in recent years, yet additional research is merited. The present study builds on a theory and model developed by Dahlvig and Longman (2014), titled "Contributors to Women's Leadership Development in Christian Higher Education"; this model identified cultural context as an influence in women's leadership development. Examining the ways in which aspects of culture influenced participants' leadership aspirations and development can contribute to understanding the relationship between institutional culture and the opportunities afforded to women for advancement to and successful longevity in leadership. Further, the findings here offer insight into possible reasons that faith-based higher education continues to operate with so few women in senior leadership.

In spite of this study's narrow scope, the findings offer implications for individuals and postsecondary institutions, centering on the themes of organizational fit, the power of choice, and personal confidence. Specifically, the concept of organizational fit seemed to be a key factor in job satisfaction for the participants in the present study. Those who were closely aligned with the organization's mission and culture self-reported greater satisfaction with the gender climate and opportunities for advancement. Conversely, increasing the points of disconnect with the institution often signaled greater potential for an upcoming departure, either voluntarily or forced. Understanding whether an individual's sense of purpose and mission is congruent with that of the organization (27) can help job seekers to identify a workplace where they are most likely to find fulfillment in their work and opportunities for advancement. Similarly, theological alignment to at least some degree obviously needs to be a matter of conversation in job searches and the hiring process. Women who sense a duty or calling to remain in the institution as a change agent may want to brainstorm ways to be a "tempered radical" (36) to influence change. Women who assume positions of broader responsibility and influence within an institution can help to increase campus-wide awareness of the value of diverse viewpoints, which is well-documented in the literature (13; 45; 46).

Finally, the contributions of female leaders have been affirmed by the findings of numerous studies (e.g., 5; 21; 25; 32; 43) and argue for organizations to proactively pursue the participation of women in organizational leadership. Similarly, women who persist as change agents may be re-energized and reassured of their professional value by reviewing the research literature regarding the value that women bring to organizations.

Beyond the noted implications for individual consideration, the findings of this study offer implications for those who hold organizational leadership responsibilities. First, the clarity of organizational leaders regarding identity, mission, values, and culture, particularly regarding women in leadership, is essential in order for job candidates to assess their congruence with the organization; it is also important for search committees to be transparent and consistent in conveying institutional realities. In addition, leaders responsible for developing internal talent may influence the institution's respect for women's ways of leading by shaping gender-specific programming (17; 29) and executive coaching that includes discussions of the value of diverse perspectives.

Finally, when gender issues are discussed, encouraging open dialogue regarding aspects of the institutional culture would represent a step toward honoring the choices of women to invest their lives in venues that align with their personal convictions and passions. Although mission-related issues may increase tension in the short term, the findings of the present study suggest that an institution's practices and views related to priorities and convictions should be clearly communicated from the outset.

Author Contributions: The authors contributed equally to this work.

Conflicts of Interest: The founding sponsors had no role in the design of the study; in the collection, analyses or interpretation of data; in the writing of the manuscript; nor in the decision to publish the results.

References

1. Ayman, Roya, and Karen Korabik. 2010. Leadership: Why gender and culture matter. *American Psychologist* 65: 157. [CrossRef] [PubMed]

2. Bergquist, William H., and Kenneth Pawlak. 2008. *Engaging the Six Cultures of the Academy: Revised and Expanded Edition of the Four Cultures of the Academy*, 2nd ed. San Francisco: Jossey-Bass.

3. Billing, Yvonne Due. 2011. Are women in management victims of the phantom of the male norm? *Gender, Work and Organization* 18: 298–317. [CrossRef]

4. Bronfenbrenner, Urie. 2009. *The Ecology of Human Development: Experiments by Nature and Design*. Cambridge: Harvard University Press.

5. Catalyst. 2013. Why Diversity Matters. Available online: http://www.catalyst.org/knowledge/why-diversity-matters (accessed on 17 March 2018).

6. CCCU (Council for Christian Colleges & Universities). 2017. About Our Work and Mission. Available online: http://www.cccu.org/about (accessed on 17 March 2018).

7. Charmaz, Kathy. 2006. *Constructing Grounded Theory*. Thousand Oaks: Sage Publications.

8. Colorado Women's College. 2013. *Benchmarking Women's Leadership in the United States*. Denver: University of Denver.

9. Creswell, John W. 2007. *Qualitative Inquiry and Research Design: Choosing among the Five Traditions*. Thousand Oaks: Sage Publications.

10. Dahlvig, Jolyn, and Karen A. Longman. 2014. Contributions to women's leadership development in Christian higher education: A model and emerging theory. *Journal of Research on Christian Education* 23: 5–28. [CrossRef]

11. Dahlvig, Jolyn, and Karen A. Longman. 2016. Influences of an evangelical Christian worldview on women's leadership development. *Advances in Developing Human Resources* 18: 243–59. [CrossRef]

12. Diehl, Amy B., and Leanne M. Dzubinski. 2016. Making the invisible visible: A cross-sector analysis of gender-based leadership barriers. *Human Resource Development Quarterly* 27: 181–206. [CrossRef]

13. Eagly, Alice H., and Jean Lau Chin. 2010. Diversity and leadership in a changing world. *American Psychologist* 65: 216–24. [CrossRef] [PubMed]

14. Eagly, Alice H., and Steven J. Karau. 2002. Role congruity theory of prejudice toward female leaders. *Psychological Bulletin* 109: 573–98. [CrossRef]

15. Egan, Chrys, S. Lynn Shollen, Constance Campbell, Karen A. Longman, Kelly Fisher, Wendy Fox-Kirk, and Brionne G. Neilson. 2017. Capacious model of leadership identities construction. In *Theorizing Women and Leadership: New Insights and Contributions from Multiple Perspectives*. Edited by J. Storberg-Walker and P. Haber-Curran. Charlotte: Information Age Publishing, pp. 121–40.

16. Ely, Robin J., and Deborah L. Rhode. 2010. Women and leadership: Defining the challenges. In *Handbook of Leadership Theory and Practice*. Edited by Nitin Nohria and Rakesh Khurana. Boston: Harvard Business Publishing, pp. 377–410.

17. Ely, Robin J., Herminia Ibarra, and Deborah M. Kolb. 2011. Taking gender into account: Theory and design for women's leadership development programs. *Academy of Management Learning & Education* 10: 474–93. [CrossRef]

18. Gagliardi, Jonathan S., Lorelle L. Espinosa, Jonathan M. Turk, and Morgan Taylor. 2017. American College President Study 2017. American Council on Education. Available online: http://therivardreport.com/wp-content/uploads/2017/07/ACPS-Report-FINAL-web.pdf (accessed on 22 March 2018).

19. Gallagher, Sally K. 2004. The marginalization of evangelical feminism. *Sociology of Religion* 65: 215–37. [CrossRef]

20. Gangone, Lynn M., and Tiffani Lennon. 2014. Benchmarking women's leadership in academia and beyond. In *Women and Leadership in Higher Education*. Edited by Karen A. Longman and Susan R. Madsen. Charlotte: Information Age Publishing, pp. 3–22.

21. Gerzema, John, and Michael D'Antonio. 2013. *The Athena Doctrine: How Women (and the Men who Think Like Them) Will Rule the Future*. San Francisco: Jossey-Bass.

22. Glanzer, Perry L., P. Jesse Rine, and Phil Davignon. 2013. Assessing the denominational identity of American evangelical colleges and universities: Part I. Denominational patronage and institutional policy. *Christian Higher Education* 12: 1–22. [CrossRef]

23. Glaser, Barney G., and Anselm L. Strauss. 1967. *The Discovery of Grounded Theory: Strategies for Qualitative Research*. Chicago: Aldine.

24. Helgesen, Sally. 2017. Gender, communication, and the leadership gap. In *Gender, Communication, and the Leadership Gap*. Edited by Carolyn M. Cunningham, Heather M. Crandall and Alexa M. Dare. Charlotte: Information Age Publishing, pp. 3–11.

25. Helgesen, Sally, and Julie Johnson. 2010. *The Female Vision: Women's Real Power at Work*. San Francisco: Berrett-Koehler Publishers, Inc.

26. Hofstede, Geert, Gert Jan Hofstede, and Michael Minkov. 2010. *Cultures and Organizations—Software of the Mind: Intercultural Cooperation and Its Importance for Survival*. New York: McGraw-Hill.

27. Ibarra, Herminia, Robin Ely, and Deborah Kolb. 2013. Women rising: The unseen barriers. *Harvard Business Review* 91: 60–66. Available online: http://bit.ly/1bjtvEo (accessed on 17 March 2018).

28. Joeckel, Samuel, and Thomas Chesnes. 2009. The challenge of gender equity within the Council for Christian Colleges & Universities. *Christian Higher Education* 8: 115–31.

29. Kassotakis, Mary E. 2017. Women-only leadership programs: A deeper look. In *Handbook of Research on Gender and Leadership*. Edited by Susan R. Madsen. Northampton: Edward Elgar Publishing, pp. 395–408.

30. Kellerman, Barbara, and Deborah Rhode. 2014. Women at the top: The pipeline reconsidered. In *Women and Leadership in Higher Education*. Edited by Karen A. Longman and Susan R. Madsen. Charlotte: Information Age Publishing, pp. 24–39.

31. Keohane, Nannerl O. 2014. Leadership out front and behind the scenes: Young women's ambitions for leadership today. In *Women and Leadership in Higher Education*. Edited by Karen A. Longman and Susan R. Madsen. Charlotte: Information Age Publishing, pp. 24–39.

32. Kezar, Adrianna. 2014. Women's contributions to higher education leadership and the road ahead. In *Women and Leadership In Higher Education*. Edited by Karen A. Longman and Susan R. Madsen. Charlotte: Information Age Publishing, pp. 117–34.

33. Koenig, Anne M., Alice H. Eagly, Abigail A. Mitchell, and Tiina Ristikari. 2011. Are leader stereotypes masculine? A meta-analysis of three research paradigms. *Psychological Bulletin* 137: 616–42. [CrossRef] [PubMed]

34. Lindholm, Jennifer A. 2003. Perceived organizational fit: Nurturing the minds, hearts, and personal ambitions of university faculty. *The Review of Higher Education* 27: 125–49.

35. McMurtrie, Beth. 2016. Evangelical colleges' diversity problem. *The Chronicle of Higher Education*, January 31. Available online: https://www.chronicle.com/article/Evangelical-Colleges-/235112 (accessed on 17 March 2018).

36. Meyerson, Debra. 2001. *Tempered Radicals*. Boston: Harvard Business Review.

37. Moreton, April L., and Ron W. Newsom. 2004. Personal and academic backgrounds of female chief academic officers in evangelical Christian colleges and universities: Part I. *Christian Higher Education* 3: 79–95.

38. O'Neil, Deborah A., Margaret M. Hopkins, and Diana Bilimoria. 2008. Women's careers at the start of the 21st century: Patterns and paradoxes. *Journal of Business Ethics* 80: 727–43. [CrossRef]

39. Padilla, Arthur. 2005. *Portraits in Leadership: Six Extraordinary University Presidents*. Westport: Praeger.

40. Reynolds, A. 2014. Gender dynamics in evangelical institutions: Women and men leading in higher education and the nonprofit sector. In *Report for the Women in Leadership National Study*. Wenham: Gordon College.

41. Schein, Edgar H. 2010. *Organizational Culture and Leadership*, 4th ed. San Francisco: Jossey-Bass.

42. Teague, Leah J., and Kim Bobby. 2014. American Council on Education's IDEALS for Women Leaders. In *Women and Leadership in Higher Education*. Edited by Karen A. Longman and Susan R. Madsen. Charlotte: Information Age Publishing, pp. 59–76.

43. Turner, Caroline. 2012. *Difference Works: Improving Retention, Productivity, and Profitability through Inclusion*. Austin: Live Oak Book Company.

44. Watkins, Michael D. 2013. What is organizational culture? And why should we care? *Harvard Business Review*, May 15. Available online: https://hbr.org/2013/05/what-is-organizational-culture (accessed on 17 March 2018).

45. Williams, Damon A. 2013. *Strategic Diversity Leadership: Activating Change and Transformation in Higher Education*. Sterling: Stylus Publishing.
46. Woolley, Anita Williams, Christopher F. Chabris, Alex Pentland, Nada Hashmi, and Thomas W. Malone. 2010. Evidence for a collective intelligence factor in the performance of human groups. *Science* 330: 686–87. [CrossRef] [PubMed]

administrative
sciences

MDPI

Article

Ascending: An Exploration of Women's Leadership Advancement in the Role of Board of Trustee Chair

Heather Inez Ricks Scott

Department of Leadership and Integrative Studies, Kennesaw State University, Kennesaw, GA 30144, USA; hscott18@kennesaw.edu

Received: 20 December 2017; Accepted: 9 March 2018; Published: 14 March 2018

Abstract: While women have made strides in leadership in the higher education sector there continues to be dismal representation of women in executive level roles of governance at colleges and universities. This article presents findings from a study that explored skills that women have identified as being useful in their ascent to the role of trustee board chair. The ascension patterns of the participants are explored through a qualitative process to provide a path to success for other women to follow. The article concludes with suggestions for increasing the number of women serving in the capacity of board chair.

Keywords: women and higher education; leadership; governing boards

1. Introduction

The trustee board plays a critical role in the stability, growth, and financial strength of colleges and universities (Baldridge et al. 1977). The board of trustees, along with the president, set the tone for the vision of an institution. The board chair plays a vital part in developing the culture of the board. The knowledge and experience these individuals contribute to the institution have a tremendous impact on the leadership effectiveness of the institution. Board positions are powerful policy making positions and the individuals who hold the chair role are extremely influential. In addition to the policy influence associated with the board chair position, the board chair position is also instrumental in creating a representation of the institution's governance at its highest level (Bowen 2008).

This work presents information from a study on collegiate governing board chairs. The study was conducted to determine the career paths taken, obstacles overcome along those paths, and assistance received along the way in an effort to develop a paradigm of ascension patterns for women trustee board chairpersons. Exploring the path of women to leadership service in the role of board chair adds to the body of knowledge regarding leadership and gender at the policy-making level of collegiate institutions. A portion of the findings from a larger study are presented here with particular focus on pathways to the role of board chair, and specific attention to the participant's own assessments of how their contributions as board members led to their accession to their chair positions.

With continued low numbers of women represented in leadership roles on the governing boards of both public and private higher learning institutions in the United States, it is important to identify the contributing factors that impact women's ascension to the role of board chair (Bontrager 2008; Glazer-Raymo 1999; Kaufman 2002; Schwartz and Akins 2004). Research assists in providing more insight into the role of women as leaders in higher education and the pathways that women take to their respective leadership roles.

The role of women in higher education has seen numerous evolutions throughout the history of academe. Much progress has been made in the education of women since Colonial times when it was considered unfeminine and anti-family for females to seek academic pursuits (Wood 2009). While American higher education dates back to the founding of Harvard College (1636), women were not allowed college entry until the 19th Century when Oberlin College allowed women to be admitted (Wood 2009). Despite National Center for Education Statistics data that shows women continually outpacing men in degree attainment, there is still not parallel representation of women in collegiate leadership roles in comparison to their male peers. The 2016 Digest of Education of Statistics reports that in 2014–2015 women earned 1,082,265 bachelor's degrees in comparison to men earning 812,669. Degree earning differences are seen at graduate levels of study as well with women earning 452,118 master's degrees, and men earning 306,590 master's degrees, and in the awarding of doctor's degrees women were represented with earning 93,626 doctor's degrees and men with 84,921 doctor's degrees. Data such as this presents a clear picture that women are now represented at beyond equivalent numbers in the academy as students, so why are women not represented in equal numbers in higher education leadership? The study presented in this article seeks to examine this phenomenon as it relates to the dearth of women trustee board chairpersons at the helm of private colleges and universities. To answer the question of why this discrepancy persists is difficult; however, the answer is worth seeking. A starting point in the examination of this dilemma is determining the leadership philosophies and roles, in particular that of the board of trustee chair, to further illuminate the issue. Literature and research in the areas of women, leadership, and governance is plentiful; however, research in the area of governing board composition and gender is inadequate. To that end, this work presents a snapshot of findings from a study that examines some of the issues regarding women and leadership, and their pathways to the position of board chair at independent institutions.

Former Secretary of Education, Margaret Spellings' Commission on the Future of Higher Education placed heavy emphasis on higher education accessibility. The Commission cited diversity as a non-academic barrier to accessibility. This provides support for the importance of diversity on college campuses. Students who see diversity represented at higher levels of administration may be encouraged to pursue opportunities for furthering their education; alternately, students who do not see individuals like themselves reflected in the governing boards of our nation's institutions may feel yet another barrier to their inclusion in the academy (United States Department of Education 2006).

The 2010 Association of Governing Boards of Universities and Colleges (AGB) survey on board composition reflected the inequity in the number of women represented in the board of trustee chair role. The board composition survey conducted by AGB showed that women comprise less than one third of governing board membership at independent and public institutions of higher learning. The study also showed a slight decline in representation of women on public governing boards from the previous two board composition surveys conducted by AGB with women making up 28.4 percent of the membership compared to a previous percentage of 29. In contrast, there was a slight increase on independent governing boards with women being represented at 30.2 percent, up from 28.4 percent in 2004. While this data shows an increase in women serving as trustees at independent institutions, men continue to hold a greater share of board chair positions at independent institutions at 81 percent, and hold 82.6 percent of board chair positions at public institutions (Schwartz 2010). These numbers reflect a history of inequity regarding women's attainment of higher level leadership roles in academe.

Based on the aforementioned issues, the purpose of this study was to determine the career paths, obstacles, and facilitators of women trustee board chairpersons in order to develop a paradigm of ascension patterns. Exploring the executive level experiences of women in the role of board chair will add to the body of knowledge regarding leadership and gender at the policy-making level. The plethora of definitions regarding leadership and leadership styles contributes to the challenges of investigating this issue. Researchers have sought to identify issues regarding gender and leadership from various perspectives, ranging in viewpoints from feminist ideology to business models, and studies, both qualitative and quantitative in nature have sought answers to the questions surrounding women and leadership roles.

Research and litigation related to parity and equality demand that as the population of participants in higher education becomes more diverse, leadership should reflect this diversity range as well (Cottrol et al. 2003). Historical precedent related to the powerful role of external influences on student success was established when Kenneth Clark's psychological research became critical to the landmark Brown decision (Brown v. Board of Education, 1954). It is important that the leadership at colleges and universities reflect the students that are being served. While educational leaders instill in students the belief that education can serve as a gateway to opportunity, students may doubt the veracity of the assertion if they do not see themselves reflected in the school's cadre of leadership (Hurtado et al. 1999).

As the previous generation of higher education leaders make preparations for retirement, it will become increasingly important to maintain a healthy pool of quality leaders from all backgrounds. As the "old guard" of academe leave their posts, the importance of having qualified and competent leaders to assume the roles left vacant will be significant. Additionally, 15.6% of institutions report a mandatory age retirement policy, with an average age of 72 (Schwartz and Akins 2004). With the increasing age of trustees, many institution's governing boards may soon find themselves in positions to rebuild their boards with new members. With the increase in women as students and graduates, the alumni pool from which trustees are selected will grow increasingly diverse. It is essential that leadership opportunities are in existence for one of the largest segments of the population. A diverse pool of leaders can lead to diversity amongst ideas regarding leadership. This diversity may be capable of creating insight into how to best approach the issues of the future that will impact higher education.

The findings of this study are significant to those concerned about gender inequality in higher education administration leadership. Additionally, findings from studies such as this one can provide insight into leadership practices in higher education and assist with the development of governing board leadership programs as it pertains to governing board composition, training, and selection process.

The findings presented in this article stem from a study set in a southeastern State in the United States. Two main factors contributed to the selection of this State. In recent history, southeastern States have had the largest gender gap in college enrollment, with an average enrollment ratio of 1.4 males to 1.0 females (United States Department of Education 2006). Additionally, this southeastern State was identified by the author as having the second largest population of female board chairs at independent institutions in the Southern Association of Colleges and Schools (SACS) eleven state accrediting region.

The study was qualitative in nature and utilized a phenomenological analysis. This methodology describes the meaning of the lived experiences for several individuals about a concept or phenomenon (Creswell 2007). The researcher identified independent institutions in a southeastern State with a female governing board chair. Individuals from these institutions were selected for participation in the study. The researcher identified the institutions in the southeastern State with past and present female board chairs though a search of the web sites of each institution. The researcher then contacted the institutions via telephone to confirm the identity of the board chair. Each female chairperson was contacted via email to gauge their interest and availability to participate in the study. The researcher confirmed participation from the respondents via telephone and mailed letters of intent and details regarding the study to the participants. The participants and researcher then confirmed dates, times, and locations for the in depth interviews to take place. An initial interview was conducted with each participant. An interview guide was used to assist the interview process. The interviews were conversational in nature, allowing for the experience of the participant to emerge. Notes regarding participant non-verbal responses were taken during the audio recorded interviews. The interviews were transcribed following each interview session. The researcher sent the resulting transcripts to the participants for review, and follow-up interviews were conducted when necessary to confirm and clarify responses. The researcher coded the transcript to identify themes which were used to address the four research questions.

The study was guided by the following research questions that were designed to gather information based on the "voices" of women who served in the positon of chair.

1. What themes will emerge when the female governing board chairs describe their experiences?
2. Will the female board chairs identify any barriers or obstacles to their success? If so, what are they?

3.   What themes will emerge in relation to overcoming any identified barriers/obstacles?

4.   What factors are identified as contributors to the attainment of the board chair role?

These questions represent core inquiries that will evolve into additional questions that emanate naturally from the "voices" of the target population. Some of those interview questions included the following: Is there a particular experience that you would like to share with me that you would describe as pivotal in your journey to board chair? Can you share with me personal experiences or individuals who have influenced your attainment of the board chair role? Are there key individuals that contributed to your successful attainment of the board chair role? Are there particular events or experiences that you would identify as contributors to your successful attainment of the board chair role?

The author utilized a phenomenological approach to explore the participant's ascension patterns and experiences in relation to achieving the board chair position. To delve into the experiences of female board chairs, the author conducted in depth face-to-face (when possible) or telephone interviews, transcribed the interviews, and employed the code-recode method to ensure reliability. Follow up interviews for additional clarification were used when necessary. These methods allowed the author to ascertain the richness of each participant's experiences. The subsequent findings provided within this article provide insight into leadership practices in higher education and are intended to assist with the development of governing board leadership programs as they pertain to governing board composition, training, and selection processes.

2. Results

2.1. Biographical Sketches of the Board Chairs

To understand the development of the skills that have equipped each respective Chair for her current successes, it is important to have an awareness of the characteristics of these individuals. All the Board Chairs at the centerpiece of this article served as female Board of Trustee Chairpersons at independent colleges and universities in a southeastern State.

The collective of Chairs includes five women. The women range in age from their early 60's to early 70's.

Chairperson One is an alumna of the institution where she serves as Board Chair. She is the third alumna to serve in the role of Chairperson in the history of the college. She has had an extensive career as a human resources executive, at the time of the interview her professional role was that of the president and principal consultant of her own human resources consulting firm. She has strong familial ties to the college and set a childhood goal at the age of five to attend the institution she now serves as Chairperson.

Chairperson Two does not have alumni or familial ties to the institution for which she serves as chairperson. She is a self-described career volunteer, and in her words has not worked "in a career to speak of". She has however, served in a variety of high level volunteer positions in the southern area of the southeastern State. She has a passion for community involvement that led her to her years of service at College Two.

Chairperson Three has a familial connection to the institution where she served as Chairperson. The institution is her mother's alma mater. Chairperson Three is an attorney by trade; her current professional role is that of co-owner along with her husband, of a prominent luxury car dealership in the southeastern State. She has an extensive background serving in a variety of leadership roles in State k-12 education and higher education.

Chairperson Four is an alumna of the institution where she served as Board Chair. She has held a variety of leadership roles at her alma mater, ranging from volunteer alumnae roles to high-level administrative roles. Chairperson Four is currently retired. She demonstrates a high level of commitment to her alma mater through a long and varied relationship with the institution.

The fifth and final chairperson is an alumna of the institution for which she served as board chair. She is an attorney by trade, and has been employed as a law school administrator for the majority of her professional career. Chairperson Five has had a longstanding relationship with the college as a Trustee and Board Chair.

These descriptive character vignettes offer a glimpse into some of the components that inspired each woman's path to the role of board chair. The impact of their respective backgrounds and the context and era in which they came of age become evident as they describe the skills that they feel have been pivotal in reaching their position as board chairpersons. These skills, which often contrast with conceived notions and stereotypes of women leaders, equipped these women with the ability to successfully obtain board of trustee chair appointments. Nuanced inquiry into these factors allows for a more informed picture of the success and hindrances to success that women face in their pursuit of executive levels of leadership.

2.2. Discussion of Findings

In analyzing the stories of these five women, two themes were identified in relation to factors identified as contributors to the attainment of the board chair role: (a) possessing skills needed to successfully fulfill the chairperson role and the use of those skills/talents as prior board members to bring about positive change to their respective boards; (b) having been identified as leaders by key individuals at their respective institutions, both when they were being considered for the board and when they were being considered for board chairperson. These themes provided the author with insight into the ascension patterns and experiences of past and present female board of trustee chairpersons at independent colleges and universities. While two overall themes were identified as contributors to the attainment of the board chair role, this article will focus on the skills that each identified as being instrumental in their ascent to the board chair role.

While there are numerous areas for exploration regarding the leadership journeys of these women, this article will focus upon the first theme, the self-identified skills that contributed to these women being named to the role of board chair. The focus on these skills may be helpful to those women who are seeking similar leadership roles. By thoroughly examining and exploring this subset of skills individuals who desire board chair roles are provided with a potential list of skill sets to develop that may assist in attaining their leadership goals.

2.2.1. Possessing Skills Needed to Successfully Fulfill the Chairperson Role

The chairpersons indicated skills that they possess that were key contributors to their respective ascensions to the chair role. Some of the women identified these skills as "skill sets". The women agreed that these skills were integral to being selected to serve as chairs and their subsequent success in the chair role as well as other leadership capacities. Additionally, the women referenced examples of how they used these skills to bring improvement to their respective boards in the capacity of board members prior to their service as chairs.

2.2.2. Skills Needed to Serve as Board Chair

Each woman came to the chairperson role in their own way, however there was a shared theme in that each individual identified specific skills they embodied and that subsequently equipped them for leadership as a board chair. The Chairpersons indicated that they worked at developing their skill sets. Chairperson One participated in leadership programs developed for trustees that were helpful to her gaining the skill set needed to serve in the capacity of trustee and chair, and she shared the following,

> I think the thing that I will say is, in preparing myself, I got involved with AGB (Association of Governing Boards). It's an organization of governing boards, so I am now on their board. So, I got involved with them. In fact, not only am I on their board, but they have me teaching in some of their programs. This intentional effort to develop this skill set was seen

as an opportunity to equip one's self with tools to strengthen the capacity to lead the board. Each chair agreed that there were leadership skills that enhanced their capability to serve as chair and to improve existing practices of their respective boards.

In speaking with Chairperson Two, her experience reiterated the fact that trustee boards seek individuals with particular leadership skills. Chairperson Two not only identified her own skills, but stated that when College Two searches for new trustees they look for individuals who possess certain skill sets as well,

> So, you can bring a love and a passion and motivated spirit to things, but you will never have the respectable skill until you work through the nominating process or the Board development process. That's one of the things we do really well now at College Two; we are intentionally and specifically targeting individuals from certain locations and with a certain skills set, so that you have a talented group of people to hold the school in trust.

She identifies among those skills, her ability to rally individuals together to utilize their passion and energy to bring about positive change in the community and civic organizations. This notion of boards intentionally seeking individuals with particular skill sets provides evidence of the importance of developing leadership skills amongst women to serve as board chairs and to do so with intention.

Many of the Chairs indicated that there were transferable skills that contributed to their success as Chair-persons and in their professional roles. Chairperson Three identifies some of the skill sets that she has refined throughout the years that have been useful to her in business and in her civic leadership roles,

> One basic skill is simply how to hold a meeting; how to set up a meeting agenda that's going to be conducive to your Board and productive. Trustees around the country don't want to spend 24/7 in a Board Meeting. So, getting to a point where you really know how to set that agenda and get other people motivated is crucial. This last meeting, our board liaison told me we had nearly 100 percent attendance, which is more than we've ever had with a large board of 30 people. So, at those meetings, you need to make sure something is happening at that Board Meeting.

One of the first things that I first did is to feature a professor or a student at every meeting. At this past meeting I featured a professor and a student, and the Board was so impressed and enthusiastic. They go back to their positions so pumped, and they know what they're working for; you work for this student.

Look how bright and sharp he/she is, and therefore we need to support this endeavor. So, that whole meeting management is one of my particular fields and how to keep people pumped and passionate about the university. Make sure you've carved out your skill of what you do well for the institution. As this Chairperson indicated she developed a skill that she already possessed. Additionally, she made herself known for that particular skill and demonstrated to the institution and the board how this skill was beneficial to the progress and success of the board.

This emphasis on bringing improvement to board functioning through implementing particular practices of leadership continued in the account of Chairperson Five's experience. Chairperson Five references how her skill set brought improvement to the board, noting,

> If you talked to the people who were on the board when I started as chair, I think they would tell you the most noticeable differences were the meetings ended on time, that they got their materials more in advance and they had better information, we moved to a consent agenda so we did not keep doing the same things over and over and we tried to move to a place where people's time was well spent and were intellectually invested when they were there. These identified skills assist in creating a catalog of skills that other individuals seeking the chair role can develop in their quest towards leading boards.

2.3. Networking and Networks

Wolff and Moser (2010) indicate that networking has been shown to be positively related to promotion. They further state that networking also provides an outlet for information sharing which can assist with establishing alliances and becoming more visible in an organization. The relationships formed through acts of networking may in some instances provide opportunities for added access. The experiences of the women in this study supported this perspective.

While several of the women recounted their stories of "accidental ascension" their accounts often circled back to professional relationships and opportunities to develop connections with their respective institutions through networking and networks. Chairperson One, an alumna of the college where she serves as Chair, spoke of her membership in a number of community organizations prior to joining the Board of Trustees. She indicated that she became known as a leader amongst her network in the community and when opportunities such as the one to serve as a trustee arose, Chairperson One was often at the top of the list of candidates. Chairperson Four, also an alumna Chair, became known in her networks and interactions with others as an individual who could come into an organization to right wrongs and turn things around. While the women described their respective ascensions to the role of chair as unintentional, it is evident that their reputations for successful leadership amongst their networks were instrumental in their rise to the chair position. This ability to network provides opportunities for women to develop and express their agency in organizations. By developing a network of women who are skilled leaders a number of women benefit. These networks enable the opportunity for adding women to the legions of leaders through providing a "pool" of leadership candidates. This is critical in succession planning and in advocating to bring more women to the table.

3. Skill Development

3.1. Familial Influence on the Development of Leadership Skills

The Chairpersons recognized that the development of their respective skill sets began in girl hood and they recount with ease the impact of their own families in their attainment of leadership roles. In the development of self-identified skill sets, the women noted the significant impact of their upbringing. One of the key themes that was identified in regards to contributors to the attainment of the board chair role was that of the influence of family and influential family members were referenced in many instances. In regards to the socio-economic background of their childhood family, many of the Chairpersons indicated that due to the "way" they grew up, success and education were expected. Expectations for success were established early and reinforced often by a variety of family member. This expectation for success and achievement served as a life-long influencers to affect change through leadership. Chairperson One was particularly influenced by an aunt, who not only inspired her to attend college, but became an inspiring force in her becoming a trustee and ultimately chair of the board,

> So, I was born in a family of three girls. I have an identical twin sister, born and raised in Los Angeles and my mother was a school teacher in Watts. We lived in Watts in Los Angeles, and my father was the local criminal lawyer in the area. I always knew that I was going to college. I come from . . . on my mother's side in particular, were well educated people. So, I always knew that I was going to college, and I always knew that I would be successful, and so, I was in a family that was focused on education as most middle class black families were in those days.

Chairperson One had this to say about her aunt who influenced her to give back to her college by serving as a trustee and chair,

> And so, what got me to College One, was I had an aunt, and this particular aunt had gone to College One, and I just knew because of her, when I was four or five years old that I wanted to go to college. I remember just being blown away by her as a person and she

became, obviously, an impactful person in my life. And, when I was four or five years old, she took the train from Atlanta to Los Angeles, and I remember her getting off the train and thinking I want to be just like her.

When asked the question of who influenced her to become involved with College One as a trustee, Chairperson One replied with the following:

So clearly my aunt was very influential on that. She was very involved, and she could see the leadership that I was doing, with these corporations that I was working for and she's saying, "You've arrived at all these big-time jobs, and why can't you give College One some of that knowledge?" So, she helped me to think about that. This encouragement from a trusted family source provoked Chairperson One to see herself in a new light, as an individual who could have an impact and make a difference.

Chairperson Two recalls her childhood family situation as being influential to her development as a leader early on,

I have found myself in leadership positions in a number of different venues. And, as I ponder and go back . . . as the older of two children, my father died when I was 13, and my mother was not a real strong person emotionally, and so, I became a decision maker sort of early in life. In high school, I laughingly say, that even in groups of teenage girls they would say, "Now what are you going to say Mother Smith" (my maiden name) and they would look to me to keep them from getting into too much trouble and smoking too many cigarettes behind the barn door.

The lived childhood experiences of Chairperson Two illustrate how these experiences were impactful in her leadership development. As she recounts stepping in to serve as a leader in her family upon her father's death, later in her life she displays the same skill of stepping in and assuming leadership when various organizations that she is involved with have a need for leadership to arise.

Chairperson Three attributes her involvement with college three directly to her mother, a graduate of the institution. She recalls a similar upbringing to Chairperson One, growing up with an educator mother and attorney father, "My father was a lawyer, and my mother was a school teacher, an educator who went to College Three here in this southeastern state." Referencing her grandparents,

I often times think that these seemingly different environments with my grandfather being a physician, my father being a lawyer, but with the farm experience (maternal grandparents) where there was no running water, wood stove and seemingly opposite experiences really converged on me and my other siblings. So, the business leanings came from both sides of the family, because my grandfather was a physician as well as a pharmacist before, so he ran a business. He ran a pharmacy and also his medical practice. Those two seemingly divergent paths really converged as I grew up, and I really believe in earnest served as a foundation for who I was to become, a business owner and operator, an entrepreneur, a community activist (if you will), and for love of my mother's institution, from which she graduated in 1938. So, all that background, sort of, came and had an impact on my life as to who I became.

She continues the conversation by sharing her reason for the strong connection to College Three, she had the following to say regarding her commitment to College Three, "I am passionate about it, my mother went there, and I saw that that's the foundation for who I am today."

Chairperson Three's experiences echoes the sentiment shared by her fellow chairpersons. It is the love and encouragement from family that inspired the same love and commitment to servant leadership at their respective institutions. The interactions with and encouragement from family proved to be a vital factor in the development of each individual's leadership skills.

3.2. Establishing One's Self as A Leader

The study identified that the chairpersons did not intentionally seek the chairperson role, in most instances they were asked by key individuals (such as the president or former board chairs) at the institutions that they serve. The chairpersons were able to identify individuals who had identified their talent to serve, be it at their institution or elsewhere. This identification of talent was integral to the trustee being appointed to their chair role.

Chairperson One identified her fellow board members as being pivotal in noticing her skill as a leader,

> It became obvious to board members that I was a natural leader. I asked all the right questions, I put in the time, and I did my homework. I worked at the things that needed to be worked at; in this case I was Chair of the Board of Affairs Committee. And then I chaired the Search Committee for the President.

Chairperson Two has the longest standing relationship with the institution that she serves as chair. She indicates that she was identified as a leader who's service would be beneficial to the college through her numerous volunteer efforts with other organizations. She speaks of her many years of service to College Two, "As for the college, I was asked at some time nearly thirty years ago to join the Board, and have stayed on the Board. I have been the Chair now for about ten years."

Chairperson Three reveals in her interview that she was asked by two individuals to serve at college three in different capacities, once by a former fellow board of regents trustee to serve as a College Three trustee and by another colleague to serve on an advisory board at the institution. Chairperson Three shared the following about her being identified to serve as a leader at College Three,

> So, I started out serving on that Advisory Board Council, which is something that may not be as typical that you start out on the advisory council for a particular school instead of communications or whatever, but I did start out on the Business Advisory Council. The school president said that this Business Advisory Council was stronger than the Board, and wanted to get us on his Board. And he asked me to serve on the Board, and I did ...

After many years as an alumnae volunteer and a past employee of College Four, Chairperson Four was identified by the college president as a leader to serve the college in the capacity of trustee and ultimately she became the chairperson, "And in 2003, the president of the college asked me to join the Board, and I did that and enjoyed it very much. I became Board Chair in May of '08."

In addition to being identified to serve the institution initially as a trustee, Chairperson Four was also recognized by her peers when the time to appoint a chair arrived,

> The board elects the chair. The Board had selected me to serve, but the President certainly influenced that and asked me to take the position, but there is a committee of trustees that nominate the officers of the Board. That committee includes the president and the current board chair ...

Chairperson Five indicates that she was identified to serve initially as a trustee by a chair, and ultimately as a chair by an outgoing chair and her fellow trustees. Chairperson Five shares her experience of being asked to serve as a trustee through connecting with the board chair at a cocktail party,

> In parallel to that ... my husband is in a big law firm, senior partner in which is the chair of the board at College Five, and so he and I are at a cocktail party and I say to ... you know I am really irritated at the college because they have refused to give tenure to a Jewish woman, and he said that is not quite right, and I said well what is quite right and so he starts explaining to me kind of what's going on and the inability to have a community that can span beyond this very limited concept, Christian entitlement just really irritates me

and the next thing I know he says to me, this is probably a year later he says to me how would you like to be on the board to see if you can make it better and I say ok . . . because I can do anything . . .

These examples of recognized leadership offer additional reinforcement of the importance of not only developing one's leadership skills but the opportunity to practice those leadership skills. In having the capability to make an impact and a difference on their individual boards these chairpersons further establish themselves as leaders in the field.

4. Future Implications

4.1. Impact of Skills on the Advancement of Women as Chairs

As illustrated by the diverse collective of women who participated in this study the impact of leadership skills that are possessed and utilized while guiding a board are critical to the advancement of women as chairs. It is this identified array of leadership skills that have proven pivotal in these chairpersons ascending to the role of chair from the group of their peers. Their ability to develop, capitalize upon and utilize their respective skills sets them apart from the crowd. While the chairs may not have felt that their pursuit of leadership was intentional it is clearly illustrated through their experiences that they exhibited their leadership prowess in such a way that ascension to the chair role was inevitable.

4.2. Using Your Skills to Influence Positive Change

Governing Boards have a multi-faceted role and purpose. The joint statement on academic institution governing boards states the following about the role of governing boards (Duryea and Williams 2000):

> Governing boards in higher education institutions operate as the final institutional authority. Governing boards have a special obligation to assure that the history of the institution serves as a prelude and inspiration to the future. Additionally, the board helps to relate the institution to its primary stakeholders. The governing board of an institution, while maintaining a general overview, entrusts the conduct of administration to the administrative officers, the president and the deans, and the conduct of teaching and research to the faculty. This statement reiterates the importance of the board and the weight of responsibility that comes with board leadership. As indicated by the chairpersons it was one thing to possess strong leadership skills but another thing to utilize those skills to affect positive change.

Information garnered from this study provides insight for women aspiring to the role of board chair as well as boards that seek to appoint more women as chairs to their institutions' trustee boards. The respective board chairs resoundingly supported an institution's attention to appropriate training for those who were being considered for the role of chair. This training ranged from one on one mentoring and shadowing with an institution's president to time spent at retreats and national training meetings focused on the role of the trustee and collegiate governance. The chairpersons collectively offered the advice that women seeking the leadership role of chair focus on developing skill sets centered around fiscal knowledge, team building, and organization. In all instances the chairpersons agreed that institutions must be intentional about succession planning and identifying and preparing individuals to serve in the role of chair. This intentionality coupled with passionate and prepared individuals provide the key for successful boards and leaders.

5. Conclusions

(1) Due to the critical role that boards play in establishing policy and maintaining fiscal accountability, it is essential that the trustees and chairs possesses certain skills. The chairpersons in this study

each referenced possessing certain skills or skill sets that assisted them in their ascension to the chair role. These skills ranged from the ability to set appropriate meeting agendas to having the business skills and knowledge to turn around a financially struggling institution. One chairperson referenced how her skill to effectively plan meetings had substantially increased the board meeting attendance and engagement at the meetings. Another chair indicated her knowledge of diversity issues and her ability to bring individuals together in spite of their differences. Her skill and passion in this area led to the development of a non-discrimination policy for the college.

(2) Possessing certain skills was deemed critical by all of the chairpersons for a successful ascension to the chair role. As each of the chairs referenced the skills that they brought to their role, they also emphasized that possessing these skills and skill sets was critical in their succession planning. As chairs depart from their roles and seek new trustees each of the chairs indicated that they look for individuals who possess these skills when inviting new trustees.

(3) All of the female chairs share the common threads of being held in high esteem by their peers, and having served in a variety of leadership positions during their lifetimes. These characteristics have equipped them to assume the mantle of leadership at the executive level. All of the women have ingrained in them the tenants of servant leadership, serving not only the institutions that made them who they are today, but also serving institutions that they will never directly benefit from.

(4) While women continue to be underrepresented in the role of chairperson in comparison to their male counterparts, these women have successfully attained the role of chairperson. The experiences of these women vary, yet commonalities can be found amongst their experiences. These experiences provide insight into the journey of the women to the chair role and present a paradigm of ascension patterns for others to follow.

Conflicts of Interest: The author declares no conflict of interest.

References

Baldridge, J. Victor, David V. Curtis, George Ecker, and Gary L. Riley. 1977. Diversity in Higher education: Professional autonomy. *The Journal of Higher Education* 48: 367. [CrossRef]

Bontrager, Katherine Adams. 2008. A profile of trustees: Characteristics, roles, and responsibilities of trustees in Ohio's two year college system. Ph.D. Dissertation, Ohio University, Athens, OH, USA.

Bowen, William G. 2008. *The Board Book: An Insider's Guide for Directors and Trustees*. Scranton: W.W. Norton & Company.

Cottrol, Robert J., Raymond T. Diamond, and Leland B. Ware. 2003. *Brown v. Board of Education: Caste, Culture, and the Constitution*. Lawrence: University Press of Kansas.

Creswell, John W. 2007. *Qualitative Inquiry & Research Design: Choosing Among Five Approaches*. Thousand Oaks: Sage Publications.

Duryea, Edwin D., and Donald T. Williams. 2000. *The Academic Corporation: A History of College and University Governing Boards*. New York: Falmer Press.

Glazer-Raymo, Judith. 1999. *Shatttering the Myths: Women in Academe*. Baltimore: The Johns Hopkins University Press.

Hurtado, Sylvia, Jeffrey Milem, Alma Clayton-Pedersen, and Walter Allen. 1999. *Enacting Diverse Learning Environments: Improving the Climate for Racial/Ethnic Diversity in Higher Education*; ASHE-ERIC Higher Education Report; Volume 26. Available online: http://eric.ed.gov/ERICDocs/data/ericdocs2sql/content_storage_01/0000019b/80/17/92/5a.pdf (accessed on 9 March 2018).

Kaufman, Barbara. 2002. Women, Boards, and Leadership. Paper presented at the National Conference on Trusteeship, Roundtable Discussions, Association of Governing Boards, Boston, MA, USA, April 23.

Schwartz, Merrill, and Louis Akins. 2004. *Policies, Practices, and Composition of Governing Boards of Independent Colleges and Universities*. Washington, DC: Association of Governing Boards.

Schwartz, Merrill. 2010. *Policies, Practices, and Composition of Governing Boards of Independent Colleges and Universities*. Washington, DC: Association of Governing Boards.

United States Department of Education. 2006. *A test of leadership: charting the future of U.S. higher education. A report of the commission appointed by Secretary of Education Margaret Spellings*; Jesup, MD: Education Publications Center. Available online: http://www.ed.gov/about/bdscomm/list/hiedfuture/reports/final-report.pdf (accessed on 9 March 2018).

Wolff, Hans-Georg, and Klaus Moser. 2010. Do specific types of networking predict specific mobility outcomes? A two-year prospective study. *Journal of Vocational Behavior* 77: 238–45. [CrossRef]

Wood, Julia T. 2009. *Gendered Lives*. Boston: Wadsworth Publishers.

administrative sciences

MDPI

Article

Rethinking Women's Leadership Development: Voices From the Trenches

Robin Selzer [1,*], Amy Howton [2] and Felicia Wallace [3]

1   Experience-Based Learning & Career Education, University of Cincinnati, Cincinnati, OH 45220, USA
2   Design Impact, Cincinnati, OH 45202, USA; amyjhowton@gmail.com
3   Academic Excellence and Support Services, University of Cincinnati, Cincinnati, OH 45220, USA;
    Felicia.Wallace@uc.edu
*   Correspondence: Robin.Selzer@uc.edu

Academic Editors: Karen Jones, Arta Ante, Karen A. Longman and Robyn Remke
Received: 16 January 2017; Accepted: 12 May 2017; Published: 31 May 2017

Abstract: As recent graduates of a women's-only leadership development program in higher education in the United States, we used autoethnography as a research methodology to provide critical insight into effective women's leadership programming and evaluation. The potential of this methodology as both a learning process and product helped elucidate two key findings: (1) to effectively develop women leaders, work must be done at the personal, interpersonal, and organizational levels, as these levels are interrelated and interdependent; and (2) women's multiple identities must be engaged. Therefore, relationship-building should be a central learning outcome and facilitated through program curricula, pedagogical methods, and evaluation. Including autoethnography as a program evaluation methodology fills a gap in the literature on leadership development, and supports our goal of making meaning of our personal experiences in order to enhance women's leadership development.

Keywords: women's leadership; leadership program evaluation; gender equity; intersectionality; identity; higher education; career advancement

---

1. Introduction

As recent graduates of a women's-only leadership development program in the United States, we came together to make sense of our own experience, and get to know each other better. Through the process, we recognized the need to define women's leadership development, so that we had a common understanding. Ely, Ibarra, and Kolb's [1] definition of women's leadership development resonated with us—we used this as a guiding framework for our meaning making. They reference leadership development as identity work, and offer three guiding principles for successful women's leadership development programs: (1) considering topics in light of gender bias; (2) supporting women's identity work; and (3) focusing on leadership purpose. This speaks to our own needs, related to our experiences as women's leadership development program participants. Our identities as women leaders are tied to our sense of purpose, and are uniquely informed by our gender and other dimensions of our identities. We came together to explore these topics for ourselves and to figure out how to make a contribution to other women in our shoes. As we did so, we wondered how the program design we participated in provided a sense of purpose, engaged our identities, and created a space to express those things with others at the interpersonal and organizational level.

2. Cracks in the Glass Ceiling and Still Feeling the Chill at University X

In the current United States climate, discussions about women's leadership have been pervasive, with thanks in part to best-selling books on the topic, such as Sheryl Sandberg's [2] *Lean In*, which have been endorsed by famous women leaders, such as Oprah Winfrey. The topic of women's leadership has also been at the forefront of popular culture due to high profile magazines, like New York Magazine, covering stories that ask questions such as whether Marissa Mayer (CEO of Yahoo) can have it all [3]. The Atlantic [4] also published an article that went viral on social media with the same headline, entitled "Why Women Still Can't Have It All." On the one hand, women are advised to lean in [2] and on the other, lean back [5]. Now, women are being told to be disruptive [6]. Much of the literature on women's professional development focuses on the need for mentors. Yet, many women's leadership experts propose that women forget about mentoring and find a sponsor to break the glass ceiling [7,8]. Needless to say, women are receiving many mixed messages on this topic.

Despite all of the discussion on how to be a woman leader, have it all, and do it well, gender disparities in higher education remain intact. Dixon [9] asserts that a chilly climate still exists. According to Cook [10], only 26% of college Presidents in the United States are women. Outside of the United States, the equivalent leaders of a college or university are also known as Chancellors or Rectors. Fink, Lemaster, and Nelson [11] asserted that the "glass ceiling is firmly intact" (p. 59). However, some have said that women have cracked the glass ceiling. Even though we have seen an incremental rise in the number of college women Presidents, challenges based on gender bias exist. For example, Dr. Angela Franklin, the first female and African American President of Des Moines University, spoke about how women in leadership are under different scrutiny than males [12]. She speaks of women being in the double bind position [13] of damned if you do, damned if you do not, where women are either too strong or too agreeable. It is important to note that these cracks in the glass ceiling can also be viewed as even smaller splits if other demographics, such as race, class, and sexual orientation are taken into account. Only small groups of women are squeezing through, and when they do, they are still subject to very constrained ideas of what leadership looks like, and who fits that mold.

In the Guardian of Higher Education [14] article "Why Women Leave Academia and Why Universities Should be Worried," Curtis Rice points to findings from a 2011 report, "The Chemistry PhD: The Impact on Women's Retention", which speaks to gender disparity among PhD candidates wishing to continue with careers in academia. The report concludes with findings specifically related to gender: first, women are told that their gender will be a barrier to success and second, these warnings are validated by the limited representation of women in the academy, particularly in leadership roles. PhD candidates interpreted this to mean that women must make incomparable sacrifices, both personal and professional, to be an academic. The under-representation of women in senior leadership positions is not unique to the United States. For example, Louise Morley has explored this phenomenon and showed that greater gender gaps exist in the professoriate in the United Kingdom. For example, in 1994, men held 80.9% of the positions and women held 19.1%of the positions [15]. In 2013, women held still just 4415 (22.4%) of 19,745 professor positions in the UK (Higher Education Statistics Agency, 2014). In addition, Fitzgerald and Wilkinson [16] examined the absence of women in senior leadership positions across Australia and New Zealand. Similar to the United States, more women are enrolling in universities in these countries, but the gender gap exists at top levels of leadership. O'Connor and Goransson [17] examined gender in university management in Ireland and Sweden. Sweden seems to be an anomaly, with real change actually being accomplished on these issues [18]. Ireland, on the other hand, is still grappling with traditional, essentialist gender stereotypes. The heads of institutions of higher education throughout Europe are slightly below 16% [17]. Essentially, "it would seem that gender inequality in higher education is a subtle but pervasive global problem" [16]. Therefore, research into gender inequalities in higher education continues to be needed to see the full picture of inequity.

Here at our own university in the United States, these problems persist. To help assess campus climate, Status of Women Reports were conducted by the campus-based Women's Center. Ultimately, the goal of these reports was to produce recommendations focused on strategies that would, ideally, work toward creating gender equity. Data shows that the percentage of women faculty at the University

X has increased, but has yet to reach 50 percent. Women are not advancing through the ranks at the same rate as their male counterparts, particularly at the senior most ranks, such as Deans and Department Heads [19]. In comparing University of X data from 1998, 2005 and 2009, there is continued documentation of a dearth of women of color at the senior administrative and academic levels and within the faculty.

To further this benchmarking discussion, the University of X Status of Women Report [19] states that faculty women are disproportionately represented in non-tenure track positions, compared to their male counterparts. Men are also much more likely to have tenure. Approximately 63% of tenured faculty is male, while about 44% are female. These statistics parallel those nationally, which according to Catalyst.org, are at 62% and 44%, respectively. The University of X has experienced a significant decline in tenure track positions, reflecting the national trend in higher education to utilize adjunct instructors. This trend is gendered insofar as most instructors hired as contingent faculty are women [20]. Assessing the status of women staff was noted as challenging in this report, due to the lack of a centralized reporting system. Disaggregating the data according to race and gender is also challenging for similar reasons.

Beyond the creation of these reports, the University of X has addressed pervasive gender disparities in several ways. In 2005, under the leadership of its first woman president, a commitment was made to allocate resources and secure staff time to administer the Women's Initiative Network (WIN). WIN was formed in 2001 to advance gender equity at the University of X and ran a Women's Institute for Leadership Development until 2014. It is currently run out of the Provost's office. For the purpose of addressing ethical implications, the pseudonym WLP will be used as the name of this program throughout this paper. WLP was first offered in 2000, and has undergone program assessment that moved it from a multi-institutional consortium to an internal leadership program, focusing on the original program's intent to assist University of X women in advancing to senior academic and administrative positions. With new and focused institutional attention on succession planning, bringing WLP home made sense.

There is still more work to be done at the University of X and beyond. Action is needed to keep the conversation moving forward and to work towards gender equity. As Rice [14] aptly posited, "The answers here lie in leadership and in changing our current culture to build a new one for new challenges. The job is significant and it will require cutting edge, high-risk leadership teamwork to succeed" (para. 15).

3. Personal and Structural Barriers to Women's Leadership

Barriers to women's leadership fall into two categories: personal and structural. Personal barriers are related to self-efficacy, or one's beliefs about what she is capable of [21]. Vital to leadership development, Bandura [21] argues that efficacy is required as a foundation for all other methods of development to function or thrive. These types of barriers are addressed in more contemporary women's leadership literature like Sandberg's [2] *Lean In*. Another commonly cited personal barrier is "the conflicting responsibilities of home and family" [22]. This personal barrier is intricately connected to structural barriers. Ways to overcome structural barriers are policy-oriented, such as pausing the tenure clock or providing flexible work schedules. While barriers for women have become "more permeable" [23], structural barriers that are discriminatory still impede the advancement of women's career trajectories. In short, you can teach women about negotiation skills in a women's leadership development program, but if exclusionary policies and practices remain in place, concrete walls will continue to exist [23].

There are some proven support strategies for addressing barriers to women's leadership and success. For example, "mentoring has been cited as a long-term practice that typically involves a more senior-ranking professional providing guidance and support for a less-seasoned professional" [24]. However, mentors may not be enough. According to Schulte [8], the practice of sponsorship also provides a possible solution. While a mentor provides advice and coaching, a sponsor is someone with a higher authority and influence in an organization that is willing to advocate and promote the upward mobility of an individual [25]. Unfortunately, women are not sponsored enough, perhaps because they may view "networking as inauthentic and akin to using people" [1].

In addition to these specific strategies, other questions have emerged in the literature on leadership development, such as the value of women's-only programming [26], how to engage women's full and multiple identities [27], the role that women's leadership development programming plays in creating organizational and institutional change [28], and the impact of program evaluation [29]. These debates were central in our autoethnographic analysis. Therefore, they will be explored in-depth later in the Discussion and Recommendations sections.

4. Theoretical Lens: Connected Knowing

Following our WLP experiences, the three of us came together in the spirit of reflective discourse because we wanted to learn from our shared experiences in this women's-only leadership development program, and to get to know each other better. We sought to make sense of our own experience and make meaning of what a program like this meant to us, personally and to our institution. As we collected data through our personal storytelling, we wanted to allow the project to be as organic and meaningful as possible—goals that became increasingly important to us throughout the process as we strengthened relationships with each other and drew personal value out of this research process. To guide our data analysis, we drew from Belenky, Clinchy, Goldberger and Tarule's theory of Connected Knowing, which centers the notion of the value of women listening to their inner voice. In their ground-breaking book, *Women's Ways of Knowing* (1997), Belenky et al. [30] found that "women repeatedly used the metaphor of voice to depict their intellectual and ethical development; and that the development of a sense of voice, mind, and self were intricately intertwined" (p. 18). They also use the concept of voice to challenge current psychological theories of human (i.e., white, male) development and to include women's stories and experiences [31]. Connected Knowing is about finding patterns in women's voices, which was a goal of our inquiry.

Moreover, Connected Knowing gives value to women's contributions as emotive, intuitive, and personal. Belenky and Stanton's [32] words clearly resonated with us when thinking about identifying a theoretical foundation, "Women have had to struggle to make their own viewpoint heard, even to themselves." (p. 78). This approach also values that learning is relational, and explores how women gain their voices and construct knowledge. However, we also recognized that Connecting Knowing felt limiting in its essentialist assumptions about gender norms and as a result, arguably perpetuates these norms. Nevertheless, as we struggled to make meaning and evaluate our experience, we found the affirming framework to be a helpful tool of analysis in its centering and in valuing our voices. The framing process for our project was inherently collaborative, driven by deep empathy. "We call them Connected Knowers because they actually try to enter into the other person's perspective, adopting their frame of mind, trying to see the world through their eyes." [32]. Our initial attempts to evaluate through examining program survey data did not suffice because it felt superficial, not getting at real issues of identity shifts and changes in beliefs. We needed time to find our voice and process our experience in a deeper way—through Connected Knowing, our truths emerged through care and empathy. Care is the quest for understanding and you have to listen for it. The most trustworthy knowledge construction comes from personal experience. Therefore, in concert with Mezirow's [33] theory of transformative learning, we chose to reflect critically with each other to interpret our experiences and shift the focus to deeper learning for continued personal growth and development.

5. Methodology

It is important to begin by describing the WLP program in detail. As an urban, public, top-tier research institution with multiple campuses, the University of X espouses strategic efforts to develop women's leadership, such as the WLP program. The program is part of a larger system-wide change effort to support gender equity on campus. During our participation, WLP was a seven-month leadership program that aimed to prepare mid-career faculty and staff women for senior leadership in higher education, and to identity participants' readiness for higher-level positions within University of X. According to Hawthorne Calizo [24], it is one of the only campuses in the country that offers joint women's leadership development programs for faculty and staff. To this end, the WLP program curriculum includes self-assessments and research-based content focused on critical skill development. The goals of the program included increased self-awareness and competencies in the following broad leadership development components: visioning and strategic alignment, finance and operations, understanding and building culture, and negotiation, teams, and conflict.

The program is exclusive and the selection process competitive. Criteria include: completion of a Master's degree, the position of a certain rank- (faculty applicants must have associate, field service, or clinical status); staff applicants must be an Assistant Director or above, earning a certain pay grade, and three years of completed employment with the university. Since the program's inception, participation has been open to both faculty and staff thereby fostering "a new dialogue and a cross-fertilization of ideas" [11]. The application requires submission of a resume or curriculum vitae, a letter of recommendation from a supervisor, and a statement of interest that outlines how the program can support the applicant's development. If accepted into the program, applicants' home departments invest $100 of financial support.

The WLP Steering Committee, comprised of women senior leaders and WLP alumnae from across the university, reviews the applications and selects candidates. WIN publicizes the class of WLP participants each year through university news, various listservs, and on the WLP website. The model is cohort-based, and 10–20 women on average participate each year. Participants are enrolled in a Blackboard group to organize communication. We were all thrilled to be selected as participants, among the competitive pool of applicants for our respective years' cohorts.

During the time we participated in WLP (2011–2012 and 2012–2013), the program met for 3.5 h monthly and featured both a didactic speaker format and interactive methods, such as case studies and group networking. During the first meeting of 2012–2013, as group guidelines, participants agreed upon community expectations to engage, demonstrate authenticity, provide feedback, honor confidentiality, and be collegial. During that same cohort year, Strengths finder was the chosen self-assessment tool. We were asked to complete this self-assessment before the program began, and results were explored in small groups during the first meeting, but not discussed further. Each WLP session provided us the opportunity to explore topics on leadership strengths and style, authentic leadership, conflict management, budgeting practices in higher education, negotiation, and navigating the culture at the University of X. Speakers included senior level leadership at the university, such as the Provost, Vice President of Finance, Associate Provost for Diversity and Inclusion, and external consultants. Assigned readings were limited and used to supplement speakers' presentations on topics such as authentic leadership, crafting a vision, and performance-based budgeting. The sessions highlighted the specific strategies and behaviors that are critical in effective leadership. For instance, during the session on Authentic Leadership, we were able to work through exercises that helped us identify our existing and potential support networks. We looked at significant events in our past, how these events helped shape our priorities, and potential future events. Program sessions sought to promote the mindset and competencies necessary to transform ourselves from effective colleagues and bosses to successful and valuable leaders. Articulated learning outcomes for the overall program included building critical networks and partnerships, deepening members' knowledge of strategy, negotiation, communication and leadership, and maximizing influence with internal and external departmental stakeholders at the university.

A unique feature and pedagogical tool the WLP program offered in 2012–2013 was the experiential learning component, known as the "stretch assignment." The two of us that participated in this cohort collaborated with each other, organizers, and internal stakeholders to find a project that would help stretch us beyond the scope of our current professional role. The overarching goal of this assignment was to pull together the newly emerging theories and lessons about leadership from this programmatic experience and apply them in relevant and meaningful ways. Each participant's project differed by genre and academic commitments according to our personal need, but connected to professional goals, hoping to increase visibility at our university. At the end of the seven months, we were offered the opportunity to share our stretch project in an informal speed-dating type format with WLP alumnae to obtain feedback. Abstracts of stretch projects were shared with all participants. Upon completion of WLP, all participants are provided with a certificate, and an email is sent to supervisors in acknowledgement of completion. In terms of program evaluation, the WLP program collects hand-written, Likert scale and brief open-ended evaluative feedback on each session from participants, and continues to make improvements based on the findings for the following year.

6. Autoethnography

Because our research centered on our personal narratives, we employed autoethnography as our research methodology. As mentioned, we came together to make meaning of our experiences, with a desire to contribute to making the program better for other women. We were interested in exploring our individual experiences in context with others, and autoethnography facilitates that exploration. Autoethnography allows for a wider and deeper understanding of what constitutes quality women's leadership development programming. It also aligns with the theoretical lens of Connected Knowing. Ellis and Bochner [34] define autoethnography as "an autobiographical genre of writing and research that displays multiple layers of consciousness, connecting the personal to the cultural" (p. 739). At the time we were collecting data, we did not know about Collaborative Autoethnography (CAE). CAE is actually a more accurate description of process of social inquiry because it is "engaging in the study of self, collectively" [35]. Furthermore, in CAE, the group explores the social and cultural meaning of their experiences. For the purposes of this paper, we refer to autoethnography as our methodology, with the understanding that CAE is a legitimate method that could be recommended to explore the phenomenon of women's leadership development programs as well.

We initially operationalized the autoethnographic methodology by developing four guiding questions to frame our narratives. Then, we each created written responses.

(1)   Why did I apply to the program?
(2)   What were my expectations of the program?
(3)   How did I experience the group dynamics of being in a women-only space?
(4)   What was the impact?

After writing responses to the questions, we came back together as a group to analyze our findings, processing our common and disparate experiences. As Dreschler Sharp, Riera, and Jones [36] note, the process of autoethnography helped us to "seek and find meaning in the stories that was deeper and more substantial than what we would find on our own" (p. 330). In contrast to quantitative research, the purpose of autoethnography is not to collect large samples, generalize the findings, nor compare programs. It is not a finite answer to a single question, but an investigation of a lived experience. Therefore, it is appropriate that this study be locally focused, using one location to deeply examine a set of experiences. It is part of the research design.

At the same time, we understand that our research questions and findings are not in isolation. We know the personal is political. We understood this methodology as feminist, helping to make connections between the personal and the structural. We worked to place our lived experiences at the center of the research process, thereby moving our voices from margin to center. Importantly, this was a challenging process and we struggled along the way to find and share our voices, even in terms of writing. For example, we kept shifting from first to third person throughout initial drafts. Our struggle with voice speaks to the power and potential in this methodology to center voice, both theoretically and practically. Our conversations and corresponding analysis became more than our personal narratives—they began to shed light on issues of larger institutional and structural gender inequity.

True to autoethnography and our theoretical framework, our personal identities informed the entire research process. As co-researchers, we share several key, social identities: age (all in our forties); motherhood (we all have children); married to men (one now divorced); holders of doctoral degrees; of similar socio-economic class (given that we are working in the same institution in comparable positions, with comparable levels of education); and geographical location. One key dimension of difference is race: one of us is African-American; two of us are White. We are also all staff, though from different areas of the institution including academic advising, student life, and academic student support services.

Ethical Considerations

In terms of the ethical approval for the study, autoethnography as a method has interesting considerations because one is writing about self and not necessarily studying others. IRB approval isn't necessary in all cases for this very reason. However, Tolich [37] raises important points about the "rights of others weighted against the interest of the self" (p. 1599). For example, our stories have the potential to identify staff involved in the design and delivery of the WLP program, as well as the University of X. We contemplated this early on, and considered whether we would do harm to our self or others. Ultimately, we concluded that ethical issues did not exist because risk was minimized. For instance, in terms of harm to self, none of us used the autoethnographic process to heal ourselves. One author has since left her professional position, and the field of higher education as well. In terms of harm to others, we agreed that risk was minimized because several years have passed since our participation and the WLP program has changed in structure and in leadership. The program has a new name and Director. In fact, an early draft of this paper was shared with the new Director for full transparency.

As Boyle and Parry [38] remind us, the autoethnographic process is intensely reflexive in nature. We found this to be true, and that analyzing our WLP experience in this way was necessary for us to make sense of it. Our focus was also to dialogue about improving the culture of the program. The point of autoethnography is to move from the local personal analysis to the larger organizational analysis. This felt inherently feminist, whereby the personal is seen as the political, where the status quo is challenged, and marginalized voices move to the center. Still, it is important for all involved to reflect on the role of the writing process so that one voice isn't privileged over others and co-generative dialogue exists [39]. In this study, we do not use pseudonyms because we have not identified which author's words are quoted. This protects anonymity.

To be sure, there are debates about ethics and autoethnography [40]. We understand that once the study is published, we may lose this anonymity and also connect ourselves to the University of X. We understand that by sharing our voices we become vulnerable; and this poses a professional risk due to our stories evoking emotions. Yet, we see this vulnerability as strength, and know we speak only for ourselves as participants intimately engaged in the experience. Just as we have provided a critique and analysis, we know we must allow the same for our stories. These stories are important to tell to help women and women's leadership development programs. In fact, WLP has made changes in the program structure since our participation, which eliminates some of this risk.

Throughout the writing process, we discovered that we need others to help demarcate our own personal and professional paths to success. Without the WLP program experience, the three of us would not have come together in this research project, with the shared goal of helping to rethink women's leadership program development and evaluation. This process allowed us to create a safe space to both acknowledge vulnerabilities and struggle with the idea of how to have it all. It was an intellectual and emotional process. The ability to take risks to share our authentic stories while writing with other supportive women was therapeutic and instrumental in shaping how we viewed ourselves as women leaders. We created a writing space and process that helped to hold us accountable to each other from a place of caring where flexibility was valued. As we continued to meet, these guidelines were renegotiated along the way. For transparency purposes, we discussed the need to be fully committed, accountable, timely, responsive, communicative, direct, not take things personally, and not deterred by personal conversations or social media/email/text distractions during work sessions. Rather than informed consent, we practiced what Tolich [37] calls "process consent", where consent to continue participating was voluntary and negotiated along the way. Even as this paper was submitted for publication and undergone revisions, we made sure each of us still wanted to participate.

Exploring how to write together on this piece helped to develop insights on collaboration and collective productivity. For example, we found a way to honor each other's processing style. We began writing over a year ago and the prioritization of producing the piece was difficult to justify with so many competing demands. In our writing group, we found a space in which inclusion and unique ambitions for success were met with support as we strived to meet our personal and collective goals. Hearing each other's stories and being reminded of our goals and successes to date provided needed strength and support.

In terms of analysis, we discussed similarities and contradictions in our personal narratives and one of us served as a recorder to transcribe our thoughts. As we shared our stories, we used Connecting Knowing to test our assumptions and further explore each other's experiences, which led to a deeper understanding. The metaphor of voice ended up depicting our ethical development, just as Belenky et al. [30] had stated. We acknowledged that our racial differences might impact our different experiences. This sparked conversation not about the strengths of the WLP program, but what was missing but expected to be addressed. In the following section, we interrogate this idea further and key themes are addressed.

7. Results

Engaging in autoethnographic methodology led to the understanding that in order to effectively develop women leaders, work must be done at the personal, interpersonal, and organizational levels; and that these levels are all interrelated and interdependent. Within these areas of development, eight emerging themes rose to the surface. At the personal level, (1) vulnerability, (2) structured space for reflection, and (3) being seen and heard; at the interpersonal level, (4) intersectionality, (5) supportive community for vulnerability and (6) networking; and at the institutional level, (7) cultivation of authentic leadership and (8) changed culture (See Figure 1). In sum, women's leadership development starts with personal reflection, involves engaging with other in identity work, and needs structural and institutional support.

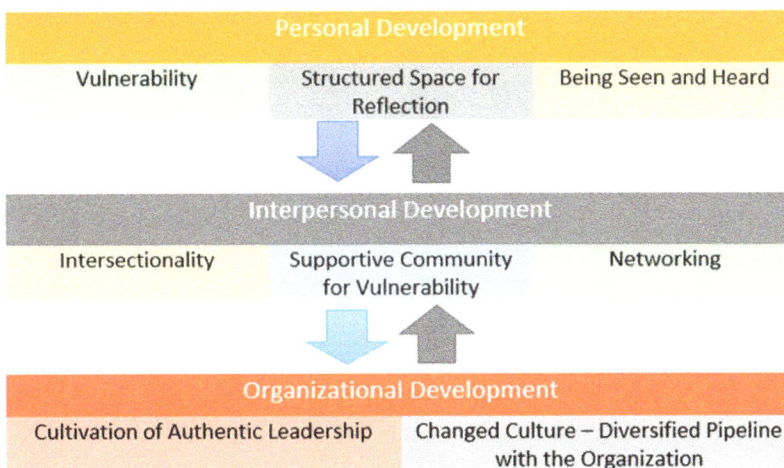

Figure 1. Women's Leadership Levels and Themes (Final Version).

Initially, our findings at these three levels were indicated by the themes in Figure 2. At the personal level, credentialing, visibility, career assessment and empowerment emerged as themes. At the interpersonal level, networking, shared experience, and support were significant. At the organizational level, cultivation for leadership and being a part of the professional pipeline were central. At that early point in our analysis, we agreed that our professional development was positively impacted by our participation in the WLP program, and that the program was successful in its goal of creating a leadership development opportunity for women at the institution. However, looking back, at this initial stage of our research process, we were in a very guarded, superficial space—both with ourselves and each other.

Figure 2. First Attempt at Defining Women's Leadership Levels and Themes.

In the next research iteration, the theoretical lens and methodology brought us to a far deeper understanding. Because we challenged ourselves to make sense of our experiences, and the data through a lens of Connected Knowing, we felt it could be an opportunity to be vulnerable with each other and ask hard questions of ourselves and each other. Common questions we would pose to ourselves in this process included: "Is that really it?" "Why do you say that?" "Help me understand." As a result, our learning evolved, moving from the initial finding of "Visibility" on the personal level, to "Being Seen and Heard." This reframing in Figure 1. elucidates the shift from the sole focus on the individual to an expectation placed on others and the organization to "recognize" and "actively support" us, thereby highlighting the need to attend to multi-level development. In addition, while Strengths quest was part of a WLP career assessment assignment, what we really needed was a structured space to reflect on our professional paths. This was reframed in Figure 1. as well. Lastly, we realized that we never felt truly empowered by our participation in WLP, and that theme was removed. This process included more generation of personal stories and accompanying introspection on identity to confront what we thought we knew about our experiences in the WLP program, and each other.

Figure 1 Themes at the Personal Development Level: Vulnerability, Structured Space for Reflection, and Being Seen and Heard.

Vulnerability involves allowing oneself to be wholly honest about one's experiences, open to emotional exposure, and risk of harm. Prevalent ideology sets up expectations that great leaders are strong and all-knowing—vulnerability is typically not understood as characteristic of a "good" leader. In Brene Brown's [41] book, *Daring Greatly*, she posits that women often feel they must hide important parts of themselves to mirror this expected type of leadership, but argues that vulnerability brings about creativity and change, allowing the leader to become stronger. In our experience, we all hoped to find a vulnerable space to explore work/life balance and integration, particularly around our motherhood identities. We needed to feel like we weren't alone in our personal experiences.

Having a structured space to reflect on our vulnerabilities as mothers allowed time that was critical, because finding time to reflect on personal and professional development is difficult to do in the context of our everyday lives. We were surprised that despite WLP being a women's-only program, structured opportunities to discuss the hot topic of work/life balance did not exist. To illustrate this point further, in our meaning-making process, we discussed "the secret." "Sometimes I would look at some of our senior administrative women, and they seemed to have it all ... kids, spouses. I thought about the stress that I felt and internal conflicts I had with responsibilities of work and home. What are they doing that I am not doing? I wanted to learn the secret. They never seemed frazzled or stressed. They had great family stories. They were respected. It was as if they had the secret I didn't know. I had hoped that I too would learn the secret."

Another author noted that she hoped for rich dialogue about the socially constructed norms around work and caregiving. Such dialogue did not exist. Building intentional space for personal reflection is critical to fostering vulnerability to be seen as a strength, and when attempting to build relationships across differences. Bell et al. [42] came to a similar conclusion in their struggle interpreting research data as Black and White women sharing a reflective space. "Coming into the room as whole people—and demystifying what we imagined about one another both within and across race lines—helped move our conversations forward" [42]. Without this structured space for reflection built into the program's curriculum, our ability to share authentically across difference was thwarted. Our writing process opened up this opportunity for us as co-authors, but we wonder how we could have unpacked our differences—particularly around race—differently with more structured space for reflection in the WLP program.

Lastly, as previously noted, we merged the ideas of credentialing and visibility in Figure 2 to "being seen and heard" in Figure 1. This theme was central to our discussion on why we applied to the program. One of the articulated learning outcomes of the WLP program included maximizing influence with departmental stakeholders at the university. Thus, "I wanted to get on a senior woman leader's radar," said one author. Becoming visible as aspiring women leaders was critical to our personal development. We wanted to be seen and noticed as competent leaders with subject matter expertise and hoped this would lead to gaining sponsors. Having this affirmation from senior women leaders was crucial to our leadership efficacy, and being accepted into WLP offered a particular credentialing of sorts. Given the increased awareness regarding the importance of gaining a sponsor to put your name forward for opportunities, we saw the connection of being seen and heard to gaining more leadership opportunities. While we were acknowledged for participating in the program with a certificate, any correspondence shared with our supervisor did not produce the desired increase in being seen and heard.

Figure 1 Themes at the Interpersonal Level: Intersectionality, Supportive Community for Vulnerability and Networking.

The two most poignant examples that exemplified the need for discussing intersectionality were based on our racial and motherhood identities. We all hoped to find both space and the support to explore the work/life balance and integration, particularly around our motherhood identities. Haynes [43] used oral history to explore identities of women accountants, embodiment, and motherhood. She discussed gendered behavior, such as how to dress and the experience of pregnancy at work. Because this is such a strong part of women's socialization, we expected to discuss these things. During the processing of our stories, one author indicated a shocking revelation. She said, "I do not even put out pictures of my kids on my desk at work because I do not want people knowing I have four children. I am afraid people would perceive me as not having enough time to do the work." This reflection supports Gatrell's [44] work on maternal bodies in management studies, where she discusses the discounting of pregnant women's capabilities based on perceptions. We all worried that people would assume we had a "low work orientation" when we prioritized our children over work [44]. Throughout our research process, we had multiple conversations about "mom guilt" for choosing career over our children at times. Gatrell [44] also speaks quite a bit about breastfeeding and disregard for the maternal body in managerial contexts. Because we were past this phase in our motherhood, we did not discuss this. However, it was noted that supportive supervisors who understood what it meant to be a working mom were critical to our overall experiences.

The message was clear to us: these struggles do not matter in organizational structures, and it is up to us as individuals to figure it out if we want to advance. While not all women are mothers or have family caregiving responsibilities, it can be a salient part of women's identities, and should at least be explored as relating to a woman's career path and in creating gender justice. It would have also been helpful to hear from women who did not have children by choice. Haynes [43] asserts "By failing to understand the impact of public and private, of professional and mothering identities, misunderstanding, reproduction of subtle forms of inequality, or even injustice may be perpetrated" [43] (p. 622). Given the prominence of this topic in popular culture and literature, it is a non-negotiable topic to include as part of the curriculum. Mothering and work identities are not separate, but entwined [43].

In terms of racial identities, the vast majority of participants in both cohorts were white women. Racial differences among the group were not acknowledged in the WLP program. However, this lack of acknowledgement does not erase the impact of race and racism on leadership development. The author who identifies as a woman of color shared an instance when a white male senior administrator commented on her hair. She said "While at commencement, I straightened my hair. When this man saw me, he said you should wear your hair like that all the time. It looks better. I felt like a lot of times I will not be accepted into higher leadership. I cannot be my authentic self. I have to burn my hair out to fit in." Her WLP cohort, with the support and structure of the WLP program, could have offered support and validation for her around this experience of racism. Additionally, as white women, we could have learned a lot about how our white privilege impacts our own leadership. Unfortunately, she didn't feel WLP offered her that safe space.

During WLP sessions, when discussing intersecting identities such as racial or ethnic identities, the conversation seemed to be redirected, as if race and racism were a distraction from the program's focus, and that these conversations were tangential. There was a particular instance in which a diverse panel of senior administrative women shared personal journeys and words of wisdom to WLP participants. Only one presenter was a woman of color; she was African American. "When she began to talk about her experiences around racism and how to deal with racism in our profession, the conversation was immediately moved to another conversation and she was cut-off. I found myself in the bathroom talking to another woman of color to discuss how we had faced this but there wasn't opportunity for us to hear how other people who had moved up had navigated this." For women of color, both racial and gender identities impact leadership development—omitting one necessarily negates the other. In fact, this holds true for all of us—we cannot explore our gendered experiences with leadership development, without simultaneously interrogating our multiple identities and how those inform and influence our leadership.

The need for a supportive community where vulnerability can be practiced is the second theme at the interpersonal development level. This theme is the catalyst for creating a culture of courage, where participants show up without the expectation of perfection. This is particularly important as strong leaders understand the role of vulnerability as connected to humility. Due to the lack of a community that was supportive of sharing vulnerabilities, one author felt "isolated", and her sense of leadership identity "more fragile", as a result of her participation. This impact translated to the interpersonal level, where relationships were kept at a superficial, surface level.

Vulnerability was not perceived as a strength in this women's-only leadership program. One author stated, "When doing an exercise on authentic leadership, I felt embarrassed to share that I was divorced and not married. I did not want to be perceived as less than perfect because I was so focused on trying to keep up with the other women leaders around me, who seemed to have it all together. But being divorced is a dominant identity among multiple identities in my lived experience." Building a strong community in which women could open up and be vulnerable about personal challenges related to leadership could support personal self-efficacy, promote strong interpersonal relationships, and begin to highlight structural inequities—thus, connecting the personal to the political.

Networking, the third theme in interpersonal development, is essential to professional life. It leads to career advice, opening up professional opportunities, and learning from others about their leadership journey. More than countless hours at the computer, leadership is the ability to connect to others, incorporate outside perspectives, and navigate groups. We hoped that through participating in WLP, we would learn how to network strategically, given the program's articulated learning outcome to build critical networks and partnerships. It is important to note that women leaders may face unique challenges when it comes to networking. For instance, one author was "uncomfortable with the idea of networking", and preferred that it was framed as "relationship-building." This was consistent with Ely, Ibarra, and Kohl's [1] thoughts on women viewing networking as inauthentic. The issue of work-life conflicts was also applicable for us in relation to networking. "I have to pick up my kids from daycare right after work and do not have the freedom to attend a networking happy hour," said one author. As a group, we were often preoccupied with caretaking duties at home, and consistently struggled to devote networking time away from family or personal interests. Again, this topic was not addressed in the WLP program.

Figure 1 Themes at the Institutional Level: Cultivation of Authentic Leadership and Changed Culture—Diversified Pipeline within the Organization.

The two themes at the institutional level were discussed as aspirations for a strong women's leadership development program. The cultivation of authentic leadership requires that we bring more of who we are to the table more often. In order to be consistently authentic, we needed to explore and accept the complex identities of each WLP participant. This is why we acknowledge that the levels are interrelated. The cultivation of authentic leadership cannot exist without structured space for personal reflection on our multiple identities and supportive community for this. How can we be confident in being seen and heard within our university without being authentic? While there was knowledge gained from an expert speaker on Authentic Leadership, the didactic format of the content delivery made personal relevance difficult because there was very little time left for group processing and interaction. If authentic leadership is truly embraced at the organizational level, it should be fully integrated throughout the women's leadership development curriculum. Only then will cultures change and bring with it a diversified pipeline of women who have made efforts to understand our multiple, intersectional identities through the practice of vulnerable sharing in a supportive community. Considering the lack of women's leadership in senior positions at University X, the WLP program attempted to resolve the problem, but did not fully respect the diversity of the women in the pipeline. The institution must change the leadership culture to authentically value this diversity, or the pipeline will remain leaky.

The WLP program offered ripe opportunity to cultivate authentic leadership and changed culture and diversify our institutional talent pipeline. Had we, as WLP participants, been able to experience at the personal and interpersonal levels what has been discussed here as emergent themes—vulnerability, critical reflection, feelings of being seen and heard, exploration of our multiple identities and intersectionality, supportive community, and networking—a critical piece of this sort of authentic leadership and changed culture would have been seeded. After all, WLP participants represent an emergent leadership, and our cohort would have had the opportunity to truly learn alongside each other, gain insight from shared personal experiences around our multiple identities, and increase empathy related to navigating leadership. With this new understanding of the barriers and opportunities women face in the workplace—and in our institution, specifically—we would be in the unique position to inform and develop relevant policies and practices to support women's leadership development at the institutional level. We would be more empowered to do that, because of our WLP experience.

Based on our own discussion that emerged through our autoethnographical work, we imagine some of these institutional policies and practices would include: strengthened stop the tenure clock policies; more flexible work schedules for staff; more convenient and available lactation rooms; equal pay practices and policies; redesign of the review for tenure process which values gendered labor equally (i.e. service and student support); diverse and inclusive hiring; strengthened sexual and gender-based harassment policies and supports; increased resources allocated to women-only programs like WLP; and creating safe spaces for other affinity groups (including women of color, LGBT women, international women, women with disabilities). WLP participants would be wonderfully positioned to advocate for and lead such institutional changes and in doing so, create a more inclusive institutional climate.

8. Discussion

Our results supported Ely, Ibarra, and Kolb's [1] definition of women's leadership development, in that our experiences in the WLP program led us to see the critical role identity work plays in this process. This insight underscores the importance of the theoretical lens used in program design and delivery. The lens that informed our research analysis, Connected Knowing [30], was effective in our own positioning as "knowers", and facilitated a fruitful critique of our experiences and institutional context. In addition, pedagogical tools that align with that lens and facilitate deeper analysis are effective in the identity work of women's leadership development programs. For example, our use of autoethnography as an evaluative method was valuable in drawing connections between the personal and political, and the individual and structural. Therefore, program curricula should be far less concerned with content covered, and more focused on program approach and process. Carefully attending to ways in which power positions participants as knowers and leaders from the outset will significantly impact the participant's personal leadership development and, ultimately, positively impact the organization. While some individual skill-development, such as budgeting and negotiating, were helpful parts of the curriculum, we were seeking a more transformative approach that gets at the root of the problem of women's leadership development—gender inequity—and flips the power. The participants themselves become the knowers and experts. This insight informs our recommendations, and is further explored in the below section.

As such, there was certain content that was overlooked in WLP that we believe all women's leadership programs must address. Gender bias, as well as other forms of discrimination based on intersectional identities, is substantive in the literature and must be covered. Structured time for reflection should be spent on addressing the personal barriers women face in leadership development, such as finding a sponsor, and sharing these stories with others. This storytelling will build empathy and understanding, as well as highlight structural barriers in place that negatively impact gender equity. Additionally, networking opportunities with other aspiring and established women leaders will support efforts to advocate for policy changes that address the structural barriers to success. Women's-only programs uniquely promote these kinds of learning experiences. Women can bind together and use their power to support one another. By incorporating the sharing of personal experiences and listening to other stories of women into women's leadership development programs, we co-construct knowledge as Connected Knowers, and learn more than we could from an experience like this, had we been on our own. Through finding and trusting our own voices, we can develop a sense of leadership purpose and truly create institutional change.

We did not complete WLP with an earned sense of purpose as women's leaders, even though we were feeling the societal pressure to "lean in" due to the popularity of Sandberg's [2] book at the time. However, we did meet the program's goal of self-awareness in the end. Throughout our participation in the program, we identified with the struggle to have it all, and turned to the WLP program to seek mentoring and sponsorship. We needed the mentoring to answer some lingering questions regarding our multiple identities, such as managing work/life balance as mothers and navigating race and racism. We needed the network for sponsoring and the visibility of being seen and heard as aspiring senior leaders, especially because we knew the climate was still chilly at the very top—and even more so for more marginalized, intersectional identities. In summary, our findings showed us that we all struggled with our own self-efficacy, because we did not have the structured space for vulnerable reflection that is needed to explore what we are capable of. It would have been especially helpful to interrogate this in a supportive community with other women leaders. We now know that we need other women to help realize our path to leadership success. Overall, our goal to make the program better for other women will come to fruition as the knowledge we have gained is applied. Next, we provide recommendations for future women's leadership development programs based on our analysis.

9. Recommendations

9.1. Recommendation 1: Practice Intersectionality in Women's-Only Leadership Development Programs

Based on our experiences in a women's-only leadership development program, we wonder about the value of a women's-only space in developing leaders. Being in our women's-only leadership development program was a critical part of our analysis. This issue is also debated in the leadership literature. Vinnicombe and Singh [26] discuss the importance of women's only leadership development programs. "Skeptics may argue that women-only programs do women a disservice", because it removes interactions with men that they will inevitably need to collaborate with [1]. A women-only space is an integral component to leadership development programs for women, as women value being seen as experts in their field, having an intrinsically interesting job, personal accomplishment, self-development, and balancing work and personal life. In contrast, men see career success in terms of climbing ladders and gaining influence, with the external trappings of success, including high salary, cars, and status [26].

Significantly, though, women-only programs should not be an add-women-and-stir approach, but should encourage women to explore how their gender, intersecting with other dimensions of their identity, influences their leadership for the quality improvement of programs [1]. For us, there was a disconnect between our hopes for what a women's only space would mean for us, and our actual experience of this gender-specific programming. For example, we expected that, participating in a women's development program, women would not be understood to be monolithic as a group. Interestingly, we learned that without complicating "women's" leadership development, we were reinforcing gender binaries. A subsequent risk of this sort of traditional practice is that women are essentialized and kept in our place. Identities are full of complexities. For example, even though all participants in the program were women-identified, some were classified as faculty and some were staff. One author was appalled at how this distinction was not engaged as a topic of conversation, especially as it relates to power dynamics. She said, "How could we sit there and pretend that there wasn't a real difference in how we were perceived in relation to women's leadership on campus, or even in that room? Why couldn't we discuss how to help each other within these clear power structures? How ironic that we were there to help women advance but didn't discuss the social inequity inherent in the program?"

We assumed a women's-only space would provide us much needed support for career and life reflection around our dominant and marginalized identities, promote authentic relationships, and empower us to create change as individuals, colleagues, and supervisors. This was not our experience. In fact, contrary to the ultimate goal of the program, in some ways we felt diminished in our growth and learning as a result of the program design. One author shared,

> "All of the sessions were completely didactic in their delivery. There was no acknowledgement that much of these uni-directional messages were coming from male guest speakers. This completely reinforced gender inequalities and dynamics related to women's leadership development."

Another commented, "Generally I'm resistant to traditional women's leadership programs because they reinforce institutional power structures, but I wanted to open myself up to the experience." Furthermore, diminished growth at the individual level extended to the interpersonal and organizational levels insofar as potential growth was stunted. Subsequently, the ability to influence or shape the organizational/institutional level was hampered. How could we create sustained, structural change that would lead to gender equity if we did not feel empowered or in authentic relationship to other women, even others who are arguably in the "pipeline" with us?

Women of color's experiences of the intersection of racism and sexism, along with other forms of identity oppression, were completely overlooked in our WLP experience. The message was clear to us: these struggles do not matter and it's up to us as individuals to figure it out if we want to advance. We recognized that which holds for white women does not necessarily hold for women of other racial backgrounds [45]. Given the data on how race impacts pay rates, tenure, and advancement, failing to attend to our racial and other identities was a significant missed opportunity to prepare us as effective change agents and leaders. As one author shared,

> "As a white woman who works actively to be an ally in racial justice work, I was so frustrated by the lack of engagement around intersecting identities, and how those intersections both inform social constructions of leadership and impact our own leadership practice. How can we be effective leaders in creating change if we cannot show up as our whole selves and see others as their whole selves, operating within complex systems? We've got to work towards a more nuanced understanding of leadership than simply 'add women and stir' if we're interested in creating transformative change. That's the only kind of change I'm interested in."

Nevertheless, through our research process, we have found value in having a women's-only space. The most significant determining factor in the identity-based programming is the theoretical framework and program design used. Merely recruiting all women to a program on leadership development risks enacting an additive/reductionist/diversity management approach to inclusion in which women's full, lived experiences are not central, and therefore women's ways of knowing and knowledge is not valued. Moreover, this approach further constrains and reinforces gender norms and therefore maintains the status quo, leaving established power structures unchallenged. To challenge gender norms and truly advance *all* women, it is critical to design a program that positions *all* women as active knowers, and engages them in the co-construction of shared knowledge with others. Women's leadership development can be significantly impacted when program conditions foster deep, transformational learning among the participants. As Ely et al. [1] argue, "Pedagogical theories, however, have failed to keep pace with practice. Practitioners and educators lack a coherent, theoretically-based and actionable framework for designing and delivering leadership programs for women" [1] (p. 6).

The question then becomes what conditions promote this sort of learning? We propose intersectionality as a theoretical framework and a key ingredient. It is worth defining what we mean by intersectionality, since this term is being increasingly used, arguably threatening its meaning and historical roots [46]. Intersectionality is defined as "the relationships among multiple dimensions of social relations" [47]. The concept of intersectionality was a major contribution from the fields of Critical Race Theory and Women's Studies, and arose out of a critique among women of color on theories of race and gender. Previous research solely focused on race or gender failed "to acknowledge lived experience at neglected points of intersection—ones that tended to reflect multiple subordinate locations as opposed to dominant locations." [47]. There is significant opportunity and need for educators to incorporate the idea of intersectionality in our scholarship, teaching, and campus work. Further, Debebe and Reinert [27] discuss how sociopolitical identities shape our actions as leaders. Consideration to the dynamic, interrelationships between and among *whole* individuals and work environments is critical in leadership development programming.

Translating a theoretical framework and concept into practice through programmatic design and implementation can be challenging. One key, practical step is to engage stakeholders in all stages of the program including development, implementation, and evaluation to ensure the program speaks to participant needs as developing leaders. Deliberate attention to multiple, intersecting identities should be evidenced in all aspects of program development, implementation, and evaluation in terms of both curriculum and pedagogy. A suggested, guiding question to help focus this attention is, "To which women is this program speaking? Who is being excluded?" For example, what is meant by "woman?" Does that include only cisgender women and/or trans women as well? If so, a first step would be to include gender inclusive language in application materials, such as the options to choose preferred gender pronouns. In sum, the longstanding intersectional approach held by feminist thinkers provides a much deeper understanding of oppressed identities, and should be used to frame women's leadership development programming, in order to result in most significant impact.

It is important to note that we did not arrive at this recommendation easily. Our selected methodology truly facilitated a challenging, critical, introspective, and enlightening process. As a result, we came to appreciate autoethnography both as fruitful research process, and also a key finding and recommendation.

9.2. Recommendation 2: Autoethnography as Methodology for Program Evaluation

Autoethnography is described in the *Handbook of Autoethnography* this way:

"Autoethnography is not simply a way of knowing about the world; it has become a way of being in the world, one that requires living consciously, emotionally, reflexively. It asks that we not only examine our lives but also consider how and why we think, act, and feel as we do. Autoethnography requires that we observe ourselves observing, that we interrogate what we think and believe and that we challenge our own assumptions, asking over and over if we have penetrated as many layers of our own defenses, fears, and insecurities as our project requires. It asks that we rethink and revise our lives, making conscious decision about who and how we want to be. And in the process, it seeks a story that is hopeful, where authors ultimately write themselves as survivors of the story they are living" [48].

Autoethnography promotes introspective self-reflexivity, in which personal narratives are considered and reconstructed to create meaning. Therefore, we argue that autoethnography holds great potential as an integrated methodological tool, in both program evaluation and in the development of women leaders through fostering transformative learning. It is important to note that the same could be said for CAE.

Program evaluation is crafted around quantitative outcomes necessary to meet the inquiries of stakeholders. Norris and Kushner [49] note that evaluation is often politicized as a tool of program funders and is viewed through a narrow, reductionist lens of accountability, used only to demonstrate 'evidence' of impact, thus missing its potential to contribute to learning [50]. Traditional measurements of program success measured by productivity or efficiency are often byproducts of capitalistic patriarchal culture. Chapman [51] asserts that ignoring unintended consequences and measuring only outcomes in program evaluation blocks learning. If the evaluation does not seek reflective, authentic feedback, responses fail to get at the underlying assumptions that frame program design, implementation. As a result, such evaluation practices maintain status quo, reinforcing these assumptions. We live in a male-dominated world where receiving reward is prioritized; and we are rewarded by saying and doing what people expect.

In addition, the design and delivery of the program evaluation itself determines both the impact of the program and the assessment findings. For example, offering limited space and time to provide feedback on program evaluation only allows for quick, superficial thinking, without appropriate time for depth of reflection. Conventional ways of thinking and conducting program evaluation are often narrow and limiting, both in terms of design and the findings subsequently yielded. By intentionally providing time and space for participants to describe and analyze personal narratives, both the process and a product of evaluating the leadership development experience are realized. For instance, Hawthorne Calizo [24] conducted an unpublished dissertation case study on the WLP program, finding that supervisors were supportive of participation, but not engaged in the participant's learning—the missed opportunity to share program evaluation findings and participant learning with stakeholders directly impacts opportunities for organizational growth.

By contrast, Burns [52] asserts that "we need to look wider than causal attribution, beyond numbers and beyond traditional qualitative material to understand the dynamics of a process, not to ask what's happening, but how and why it is happening" [52] (p. 6). Jarvis et al. [29] discuss the application of relational approaches to leadership development program evaluation, and suggest using a Complex Responsive Process theory (CRP) as a lens applied to evaluation. This suggests an approach based on relationships and trust as essential to sharing authentic accounts of experience and uncovering collective wisdom, underpinned by an approach to leadership development that values different domains of expertise and the importance of 'connecting' and peer-to-peer spaces. This resonates with our recommendation to use autoethnography.

Custer [53] found seven benefits of applying autoethnography to professional situations: 1. it changes time, 2. requires vulnerability, 3. fosters empathy, 4. embodies creativity, 5. eliminates boundaries, 6. invites and honors subjectivity, and 7. provides therapeutic benefits .We were able to utilize all of these elements to reflect on our experience from different angles and struggled with our vulnerability in particular, as we had yet to obtain a deeper understanding of our own and other other's personal story.

As we listened to each person's response to the guiding questions, put ourselves into each other's frame of reference, and allied ourselves to each other's views with empathy (not judgment), we discovered our own truths about our leadership identities. Our learning and understanding deepened, as we did not have to compromise our beliefs or leadership styles to participate. Our vulnerability allowed us to clarify our leadership purpose. Autoethnography allowed us to revisit the past, and make meaning of the impact of our experience in WLP on ourselves and our institution. Therefore, we recommend the use of autoethnography as a program strategy to develop women leaders and support relationship building. Furthermore, because it promotes authentic relationship building, connections between the personal and political are highlighted. This increased awareness and deep understanding of larger, systemic barriers and opportunities will more significantly impact organizational and institutional development, through participants' own leadership practice.

In summary, conducting reflective research (like autoethnography) is outside of the scope of traditional quantitative methodologies, and offers the inclusion of all women's voices and identities that are critical to effective implementation and evaluation of women's leadership development programs. It is worth noting, however, that the method of autoethnography has limitations. For example, it requires that participants be open and truthful about personal experiences. There are always power dynamics at play that can create resistance to this process. While we believe that this recommendation makes a methodological contribution to the literature on women's leadership development, we by no means see it as the panacea, and recognize the potential for negative outcomes, as explicated earlier when addressing ethical considerations.

10. Conclusions

As our research process reminded us, authentic leadership requires relationship building and trust in others. Employing autoethnography as a methodological tool and connected knowing as our theoretical lens allowed us the opportunity to be vulnerable with one another and share our personal stories about our participant experiences in WLP, a women's only leadership development program at University X. As a result, we moved from an initial, surface level exploration of our WLP experiences to a much deeper understanding of *how* and *why* our experiences played out as they did, granting us deeper insight and transformative learning. It is critical to note that our learning is the result of our intentional work to forge this shared reflection space ourselves, outside the parameters of the program, and in spite of the program design and previous methods of evaluation. Therefore, those who oversee women's leadership development programs should prioritize relationship building as a key strategy. The investment we made in relationship building and research methodology was fruitful, revealing a call for a multi-level approach to women's leadership development, including the personal, interpersonal, and organizational contexts. These levels are interconnected so that outcomes for each are dependent on the other, and determined by the effectiveness of relationship building. If the advancement of all women is a goal at the organizational level, practicing intersectionality from start to finish in women's leadership development programs, and including autoethnography as an evaluation method, are two suggested strategies that can effectively stop the leaky pipeline. In a program that includes these recommendations, women would be empowered to be their whole selves without restriction; there would be more visible and tangible mentoring and sponsoring of other women. We would know that women's leadership would be improved because we would see social, institutional, and cultural factors change. For example, there would be a better understanding of women leader's identities as mothers, and as having differing dominant and subordinate identities in general. Evidence of this expanded understanding, and appreciation of women's leadership, would be in the membership of the program itself with participants from different positions, and with diverse social identities. No longer would there be an artificial separation between the personal and the political. *All* women would have agency as leaders. Their voices would be lifted from the trenches.

Author Contributions: Robin Selzer designed the research study and identified the theoretical lens. All authors contributed equally to conducting the research, analyzing the data, and writing the paper. All authors read and approved the final manuscript.

Conflicts of Interest: The authors declare no conflict of interest.

Appendix A

Appendix for American University Terms:

Adjunct instructors are hired by colleges and universities on a contractual, part-time basis.
Tenure can be defined as a permanent professorial appointment.
Provosts are senior administrative officers in a college or university.
Faculty perform teaching, research, and service functions and staff perform administrative and support functions.

References

1. Ely, R.J.; Ibarra, H.; Kolb, D. Taking gender into account: Theory and design for women's leadership development programs. *Acad. Manag. Learn. Educ.* **2011**, *10*, 474–493. [CrossRef]
2. Sandberg, S. *Lean In: Women, Work, and the Will to Lead*; Random House: New York, NY, USA, 2013.
3. Miller, L. Can Marissa Mayer Really Have It All? Available online: http://nymag.com/thecut/2012/10/marissa-mayer-yahoo-ceo.html (accessed on 8 May 2017).
4. Slaughter, A. Why Women Still Can't Have It All. Available online: https://www.theatlantic.com/magazine/archive/2012/07/why-women-still-cant-have-it-all/309020/ (accessed on 8 May 2017).
5. Alcorn, K. *Maxed Out: American Moms on the Brink*; Seal Press: Berkeley, CA, USA, 2013.
6. Johnson, W.; Mohr, T. Women Need to Realize Work Isn't School. Available online: http://blogs.hbr.org/2013/01/women-need-to-realize-work-isnt-schol/ (accessed on 8 May 2017).
7. Hewlitt, S.A. *Forget a Mentor, Find Sponsor: The New Way to Fast Track Your Career*; Harvard Business School Publishing: Boston, MA, USA, 2013.
8. Schulte, B. Major National Companies Try Sponsorship as a New Hammer to break the Glass Ceiling. Available online: https://www.washingtonpost.com/local/major-national-companies-try-sponsorship-as-new-hammer-to-break-glass-ceiling/2013/11/13/6f7663c0-3ba8-11e3-b7ba-503fb5822c3e_story.html?utm_term=.2a3b6e69b025 (accessed on 8 May 2017).

9.   Dixon, K.M. In Her Own Words: How to Warm the Chilly Climate, Woman-to-Woman. Available online: http://www.wihe.com/displayNews.jsp?id=43631 (accessed on 8 May 2017).

10.   Cook, B. The American College President Study: Key Findings and Takeaways. Available online: http://www.acenet.edu/the-presidency/columns-and-features/Pages/The-American-College-President-Study.aspx (accessed on 8 May 2017).

11.   Fink, C.B.; Lemaster, B.; Nelson, K. The Women's Leadership Program: A Case Study. Available online: http://www.aacu.org/liberaleducation/le-wi03/le-wi03Perspective.cfm (accessed on 8 May 2017).

12.   Lynch, M. Diverse Conversations: Being the First. Available online: http://diverseeducation.com/article/55686/ (accessed on 8 May 2017).

13.   Catalyst. The Double-Bind Dilemma for Women in Leadership: Damned If You Do, Doomed If You Don't. 2007. Available online: http://www.catalyst.org/knowledge/double-bind (accessed on 8 May 2017).

14.   Rice, C. Why Women Leave Academia and Why Universities Should Be Worried. Available online: https://www.theguardian.com/higher-education-network/blog/2012/may/24/why-women-leave-academia (accessed on 8 May 2017).

15.   Morley, L. Glass ceiling or iron cage: Women in UK academia. *Gender Work Organ.* **1994**, *1*, 194–204. [CrossRef]

16.   Fitzgerald, T.; Wilkinson, J. *Travelling Towards a Mirage? Gender, Leadership and Higher Education*; Post Pressed: Mt. Gravatt, Australia, 2010.

17.   O'Connor, P.; Goransson, A. Constructing or rejecting the notion of the other in university management: The cases of Ireland and Sweden. *Educ. Manag. Adm. Leadersh.* **2015**, *43*, 323–340. [CrossRef]

18.   Morley, L. Women and Higher Education Leadership: Absences and Aspirations. Available online: http://www2.hull.ac.uk/pdf/LFHE_%20Morley_SP_v3.pdf (accessed on 8 May 2017).

19.   University of X. Report on the Status of Women. Available online: http://www.uc.edu/content/dam/uc/win/docs/StatusOfWomenRpt2006.pdf (accessed on 8 May 2017).

20.   Bahn, K. Rise of the Lady Adjuncts. Available online: https://chroniclevitae.com/news/206-the-rise-of-the-lady-adjuncts (accessed on 8 May 2017).

21.   Bandura, A. *Self-Efficacy: The Exercise of Control*; Freeman: New York, NY, USA, 1997.

22.   Keohane, N.O. Leadership out front and behind the scenes: Young women's ambitions for leadership today. In *Women and Leadership in Higher Education*; Longman, K., Madsen, S., Eds.; Information Age Publishing: Charlotte, NC, USA, 2014.

23.   Eagly, A.H.; Carli, L.L. *Through the Labyrinth: The Truth About How Women Become Leaders*; Harvard Business School Press: Boston, MA, USA, 2007.

24.   Hawthorne Calizo, L.S. A Case Analysis of a Model Program for the Leadership Development of Women Faculty and Staff Seeking to Advance Their Careers in Higher Education. Ph.D. Thesis, University of Maryland, College Park, MD, USA, 2011.

25.   Davis, D.R.; Maldonado, C. Shattering the glass ceiling: The leadership development of African American women in higher education. *Adv. Women Leadersh.* **2015**, *35*, 48–64.

26.   Vinnicombe, S.; Singh, V. Women-only management programs: An essential part of women's leadership development. *J. Chang. Manag.* **2003**, *3*, 294–306. [CrossRef]

27.   Debebe, G.; Reinert, K.A. Leading with our whole selves: A multiple identity approach to leadership development. In *Handbook on Race-Ethnicity and Gender in Psychology*; Miville, M., Ferguson, A., Eds.; Springer: New York, NY, USA, 2014; pp. 271–293.

28.   Ely, R.J.; Meyerson, D.E. Theories of gender in organization: A new approach to organizational analysis and change. *Res. Organ. Behav.* **2000**, *22*, 103–151. [CrossRef]

29.   Jarvis, C.; Gulati, A.; McCririck, V.; Simpson, P. Leadership matters: Tensions in evaluating leadership development. *Adv. Dev. Hum. Resour.* **2013**, *15*, 27. [CrossRef]

30.   Belenky, M.F.; Clinchy, B.M.; Goldberger, N.R.; Tarule, J.M. *Women's Ways of Knowing: The Development of Self, Voice, and Mind*; Basic Books: New York, NY, USA, 1997.

31.   Simpson, R.; Lewis, P. An investigation of silence and a scrutiny of transparency: Re-examining gender in organization literature through the concepts of voice and visibility. *Hum. Relat.* **2005**, *58*, 1253–1275. [CrossRef]

32.   Belenky, M.F.; Stanton, A.V. Inequality, development, and connected knowing. In *Learning as Transformation*; Mezirow, J., Ed.; Jossey-Bass: San Francisco, CA, USA, 2000; pp. 3–34.

33. Mezirow, J. *Transformative Dimensions of Adult Learning*; Jossey Bass: San Francisco, CA, USA, 1991.
34. Ellis, C.S.; Bochner, A. Autoethnography, personal narrative, reflexivity: Researcher as subject. In *The Handbook of Qualitative Research*; Denzin, N., Lincoln, Y., Eds.; Sage: Thousand Oaks, CA, USA, 2000; pp. 733–768.
35. Chang, H.; Ngunjiri, F.W.; Hernandez, K.C. *Collaborative Authoethnography*; Left Coast Press Inc.: Walnut Creek, CA, USA, 2013.
36. Drechsler, S.M.; Riera, J.L.; Jones, S.R. Telling our stories: Using autoethnography to construct identities at the intersections. *J. Stud. Aff. Res. Pract.* **2012**, *49*, 315–332. [CrossRef]
37. Tolich, M.A. Critique of current practice: Ten foundational guidelines for autoethnographers. *Qual. Health Res.* **2010**, *20*, 1599–1610. [CrossRef] [PubMed]
38. Boyle, M.; Parry, K. Telling the Whole Story: The Case for Organizational Autoethnography. *Culture Organ.* **2007**, *13*, 185–190. [CrossRef]
39. Roth, W.M. Autoethnography and the question of ethics. *Forum Qual. Soc. Res.* **2009**, *10*, 38.
40. Learmonth, M.; Humphreys, M. Autoethnography and academic identity: Glimpsing business school doppelgängers. *Organization* **2010**, *19*, 99–117. [CrossRef]
41. Brown, B. *Daring Greatly: How the Courage to be Vulnerable Transforms the Way We Live, Love, Parent, and Lead*; Gotham: New York, NY, USA, 2012.
42. Bell, E.L.; Meyerson, D.; Nkomo, S.; Scully, M. Interpreting silence and voice in the workplace: A conversation about tempered radicalism among black and white women researchers. *J. Appl. Behav. Sci.* **2003**, *39*, 381–414. [CrossRef]
43. Haynes, K. (Re)figuring accounting and maternal bodies: The gendered embodiment of accounting professionals. *Account. Organ. Soc.* **2008**, *33*, 328–348. [CrossRef]
44. Gatrell, C. Managing the maternal body, a comprehensive review and transdisciplinary analysis. *Int. J. Manag. Rev.* **2011**, *13*, 97–112. [CrossRef]
45. Kellerman, B.; Rhode, D.L. *Women and Leadership: The State of Play and Strategies for Change*; Oxford University Press: New York, NY, USA, 2007.
46. Luft, R.E.; Ward, J. Toward an intersectionality just out of reach: Confronting challenges to intersectional practice. In *Perceiving Gender Locally, Globally, and Intersectionally: Advances in Gender Research*; Demos, V., Segal, M.T., Eds.; Emerald Group Publishing Limited: Bingley, UK, 2009; pp. 9–37.
47. McCall, L. The complexity of intersectionality. *Signs J. Women Culture Soc.* **2005**, *30*, 1771–1800. [CrossRef]
48. Jones, S.H.; Adams, T.E.; Ellis, C. *Handbook of Autoethnography*; Left Coast Press, Inc.: Walnut Creek, CA, USA, 2013.
49. Norris, N.; Kushner, S. Dilemmas of engagement: Evaluation and the new public management. *Adv. Progr. Eval.* **2007**, *10*, 1–16.
50. Hayward, I.; Voller, S. How effective is leadership development? The evidence examined. *360° Ashridge J.* 2010. Available online: https://www.ashridge.org.uk/Media-Library/Ashridge/PDFs/Publications/HowEffectiveIsLeadershipDevelopment.pdf (accessed on 8 May 2017).
51. Chapman, J. *System Failure: Why Governments Must Learn To Think Differently*; Demos: London, UK, 2004.
52. Burns, D. *How Can Complexity Theory Contribute to More Effective Development and Aid Evaluation?* Dialogue at the Diana, Princess of Wales Memorial Fund, Panos: London, UK, 2011. Available online: http://panos.org.uk/wpcontent/files/2011/03/Panos_London_Complexity_and_Evaluation_dialogueCK5gVc.lpdf (accessed on 8 May 2017).
53. Custer, D. Autoethnography as a Transformative Research Method. Available online: http://www.nova.edu/ssss/QR/QR19/custer21.pdf (accessed on 8 May 2017).

administrative
sciences

MDPI

Article

The Implications of Contractual Terms of Employment for Women and Leadership: An Autoethnographic Study in UK Higher Education

Anne Vicary and Karen Jones *

Institute of Education, University of Reading, Reading, Berkshire RG1 5EX, UK; a.m.vicary@reading.ac.uk
* Correspondence: karen.jones@reading.ac.uk

Academic Editor: Dirk van Dierendonck
Received: 2 May 2017; Accepted: 8 June 2017; Published: 14 June 2017

Abstract: This article is concerned with the implications of casual, non-permanent forms of employment that have become a common cultural practice in higher education. It proposes that contractual terms of employment have important implications for women and leadership in higher education, since to pursue leadership, usually one must first gain permanency in an organization, in contractual terms. Based on an autoethnographic study by a female academic in a UK higher education institution, the article illustrates that temporary forms of employment, should they be protracted, can stifle leadership aspirations due to lack of career progression opportunities and lead to a sense of alienation from the target community of practice, and even to personal difficulties, such as feelings of isolation and poor self-esteem. The article discusses theoretical and practical implications for women's leadership arising from the findings and makes recommendations for improvements in practice in the higher education sector. The findings and recommendations from this study will also be relevant to other organizational contexts where casual or temporary, fixed term, zero-hours non-permanent forms of employment are common.

Keywords: autoethnography; higher education; women; leadership; identity; habitus; communities of practice

---

1. Introduction

This autoethnographic study reflects on the challenges which can be associated with short-term or non-permanent contracts of employment that have become an all-too common cultural practice in the world of higher education (HE). These contracts, which are often referred to in the UK as "sessional" (for a specified number of hours over a specified number of weeks), or "zero-hours" (guaranteeing no specific hours work at all) are casual, non-permanent forms of employment, which are typically renewable on a termly or yearly basis. Despite being one of the most highly skilled and prestigious professions, research suggests that currently more than half (54%) of all academic staff and 49% of teaching staff in UK universities are employed on some form of insecure, non-permanent contract, 48% of whom are women [1].

This situation is worse in some of the UK's highest ranking universities. In fact, up to 70% of teaching staff in the UK's most prestigious "Russell Group" universities are employed in this way (see Appendix A) [2]. It is not possible to determine the proportion that are women as gender-aggregated data are not publicly available. Contractual terms of employment have important implications for women and leadership in HE, since to pursue leadership, usually one must first gain permanency in contractual terms. Therefore, temporary forms of employment, should they be protracted, can lead to a lack of career progression opportunities and a sense of alienation from the target community of practice, and even to personal difficulties, such as feelings of isolation and poor self-esteem [3].

In striking contrast, there is compelling evidence that "smooth" career progression is what best facilitates the path to leadership through a temporal and processual learning process, born of social interaction and personal reflection within the context of the workplace [4]. Kempster [4] explores the details of this process by drawing on an eclectic mix of social and cognitive theories drawn from the fields of sociology and psychology. He focuses particularly on Bandura's [5] social cognitive learning theory and the socially situated theory of Lave and Wenger [6] and Bourdieu's theory of habitus [7]. Mead's theory of interactionism is also of importance [8]. This theory, later re-labelled "symbolic interactionism", explores in intricate detail the intrapersonal and interpersonal mechanism through which situated or "sociocultural" learning takes place, "sociocultural" being a term used by Aubrey and Riley [9] (p. 172), to refer to situated learning taking place within any specific context.

As Lave and Wenger [6] show though their theory of legitimate peripheral participation (LPP), learning is synonymous with gradually becoming a member of the workplace; career pathways are structured both by observation, modelling [5] and gradual participation in normalized workplace activities [6]. Employees' habitus is also of importance in this process; that is, their "schemes of perception, thought and action" [7] (p. 14), which have been naturally absorbed through a person's upbringing and educational experience. An employee's "familiar world" [7] (p. 18) therefore forms their baseline when entering a new workplace; it influences behavior patterns which are under constant negotiation and adaptation in line with their developing perspective of the new social space. Put simply, perspectives of the social space are subject to change depending on the positioning of the employee: "points of view are grasped as such and related to the positions they occupy in the structure of agents under consideration" [7] (p. 15). As employees participate from their peripheral outposts, gradually moving towards the center of the community of practice, they begin to interact with, absorb and embody the prevailing culture at a deeper level, reinforcing and reproducing its social structures as they go along [7]. To those who are less fortunate, an alternative construction of reality may apply.

It seems logical therefore that if the required sociocultural affordances are not in place, career development opportunities will not naturally occur. This is especially the case in HE institutions due to the precarious contractual terms through which many academics are employed. The discriminatory legacy of prolonged periods of poor contractual conditions can negatively impact on an affected individual's access to leadership roles. Such a situation can also ultimately lead to a desire to dis-identify with the target community of practice, willfully rejecting, in fact, a sociocultural infrastructure which is of crucial importance for generating career opportunities.

This paper explores the lived experience of one female academic at a UK HE institution through autoethnography. Autoethnographers, by drawing on 'the "lived realities" of their own organizations' offer insights into 'what "really" goes on in organizations' [10] (pp. 167–168). In this way, an insider can articulate her own personal and lived experiences, analyzing them in the light of their perceived social and theoretical context both to make greater sense of herself and to add value to the theoretical understanding of the social world under investigation [11]. Burnier [12] (p. 414) argues that "autoethnographic writing is both personal and scholarly, both evocative and analytical, and it is both descriptive and theoretical when it is done well". This paper will bring to life the consequences of losing an expected career trajectory because of repeated, long-term non-permanent (sessional) contracts and the gradual process of learning to lead in a context where permanency, stability and belonging seem like a distant dream. The paper seeks to contribute to a small but growing body of literature on women and leadership in HE by highlighting the implications of poor contractual terms of employment. Its secondary aim is to reach out to women and men for whom this situation may resonate and help them to make sense of their own lived experience. It is also hoped that this will contribute in some way to an awakening of HE decision-makers to the implications of current contractual practices.

The theoretical framework for the paper is drawn from Kempster's [4] theories of leadership learning as situated practice, which is underpinned by Lave and Wenger's [6] theories of peripheral and legitimate participation in communities of practice and Bourdieu's [7] theories of habitus, field, and symbolic power. The linkages between these theories and how they inform us of leadership learning is discussed in the literature review that follows. Next, we expand on the autoethnographic approach, before sharing that narration, then we discuss further insights that have arisen through sharing this autoethnography with a senior manager of the autoethnographer. This is followed by a discussion and conclusions concerning the theoretical and practice implications of the article.

2. Theoretical Framework

Kempster's [4] view of how employees learn to lead is represented in outline form in Figure 1 above. The following discussion explores in greater detail the three prominent theories (briefly outlined previously), that interlink and underpin this model of leadership learning. First, Lave and Wenger's [6] theory of legitimate peripheral participation posits that as newcomers on the periphery of a community are encouraged to participate in work-place activities, they undergo an ontological transformation; a person gradually develops work identities through a process of "becoming", synonymous with moving to a place of full participation within the community [13] (p. 154). This "smooth" transformation can only take place if there is no persistent disconnect between what the employee does and how she perceives herself to be located in relation to others within her community [3] (p. 273). This means that successful career progression within an organization relies on "feelings of belongingness" which promote opportunities for personal success and growth in self-confidence. Such successful participation increases levels of leadership salience and self-efficacy, which are both prerequisites for a successful "sense-making" and "sense-giving" leader [4] (p. 30).

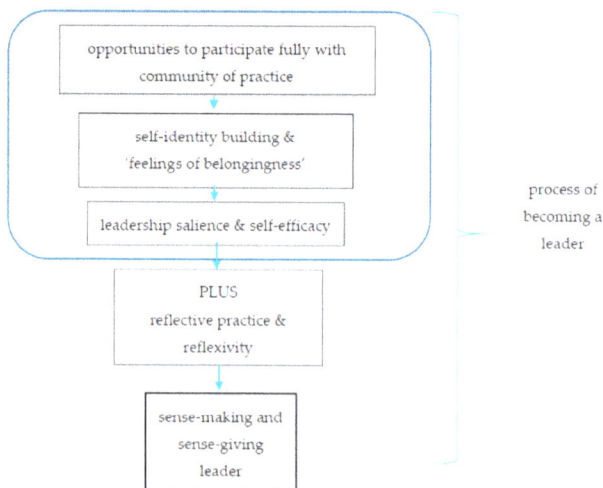

Figure 1. Process of becoming a leader (adapted from Kempster [4]).

2.1. Learning Through the Workplace Context

Second, Kempster's [4] promotion of Bandura's [5] social learning theory—that employees learn through leadership experiences via the modelling process must also be viewed within the context of LPP. Lave and Wenger [6] (p. 95) point out that 'LPP provides [learners] with more than just an "observational" lookout post: it crucially involves participation as a way of learning'. Through the process of participation, actors observe the behavior of salient others within the social context and imitate this behavior as desired and as the opportunity presents itself. This process is promoted through the opportunity to observe a variety of notable people, and through having a career-structured pathway which enables the enactment of different behavior patterns and the receiving of feedback.

Third, there is Bourdieu's [7] (p. 17) notion of habitus as "a structuring structure, which organizes practices and the perception of practices". Although this undoubtedly helps an individual to form a sense of self, it may also imply a certain level of situational determinism, which Bandura [5] rejects. He believes that "people possess the capacity to manage their own thought processes . . . people can regulate what they think, they can influence how they feel and behave." [5] (p. 145). His theory therefore bears similarities with symbolic interactionism: a person can view her "self" as an object, as if through the eyes of others, and make decisions about how to react to others' actions on the basis of the interpretation given to them [14] (p. 79). In this way, the actor has the power to exert cognitive control over the process of social learning. She has the freedom to make decisions stemming from her modelling practice according to her own self-identity. Such self-identity can be explained as a combination of self-concept and social identity [15]; "self-concept" being a "fairly stable picture we have of ourselves" [14] (p. 82), and "social identity" referring to the afore-mentioned ability to judge our positionality through the eyes of others within a particular social context [14] (p. 82).

Through this account of learning to lead through the workplace context, it can be intuitively understood that if participatory opportunities are perceived as permanently presenting themselves only in a haphazard way, leading to a view of role-modelling as a sterile practice, employees (typically female on non-permanent contracts) may begin to distrust workplace culture, and forge an independent track in order to build their identity in another way. Another possible outcome is that of persistence in building an identity which submits, at least publicly, to the norms of the workplace culture, until such time as new opportunities open up later in life. Lack of opportunity to become a full member of a community of practice due to ongoing short-term contracts must be one of the crucial elements in understanding why women do not progress as they might have expected in their careers, and are indeed consistently under-represented at HE management and leadership level [16].

2.2. Understanding the Workplace Context

According to Kempster [4], an engagement with "context and social structures" lies at heart of career progression practice. Such "structures" are embedded practices of a workplace [4] (p. 189), which have been historically set up and are further developed by humans. Bourdieu [7] believes that social practice within an organization is often viewed objectively but that it can also be viewed subjectively. For example, an updated health and safety rule book can be viewed both as a social object, and as a body of work that an administrator, tacitly colluding with the socio-cultural context, has produced, thereby choosing to preserve and reinforce current practice; in other words, the habitus of the administrator publicly acknowledges that this task is appropriate for her, so she undertakes it accordingly. She knows that her ongoing membership of the community of practice relies on "ongoing engagement with the dominant traditions" [3] (p. 283). Privately, however, her sense of self may tell her that her abilities lie far beyond this particular task, and she may resent carrying this out, but her awareness of her social identity precludes any refusal. This accounts for why an employee of low social status is less likely to challenge a particular socio-cultural norm than an employee with higher social status, who in her turn is more likely to uphold the status quo due to the influence of those agents who have invested power in her [17]. An employee who persistently works on a short-term contract does not give objective voice to her subjective thoughts; complaint may risk non-renewal of such a contract. In this way, a workplace norm is embodied within the human experience; social order is maintained and cultural practice is reproduced.

2.3. The Role of Reflection

As has been shown in Section 2.1, identity development requires both tacit and self-conscious iterative reflection; everyday social objects may indeed be subconsciously accepted and morphed into routines [4,17], or they may lead to more conscious reflective behavior [4]. Bennis and Thomas [18] point out that this is more likely to occur when social objects are particularly emotional or novel, such as good and bad boss experiences. They term such memories as crucibles, which often lead to a high level of intrapersonal reflection and a renewal of self-identity. In such cases, the self is an object to "act back on" [14] (p. 93); the thinking process is carried out in a more self-conscious, reflective fashion. Such incidents may even promote periods of reflexivity—the process of deeply reviewing and reflecting on one's own deeply-engrained habitus. In this way, new and existing employees interact with the intra- and inter-personal environment to effectively decide on their position [14]. This process can prompt an individual to ask questions of themselves such as: Who am I? Why aren't I being who I want to be? How can I be happy in the working world? These uncomfortable and unsettling questions ultimately equip an individual with the personal resources that promote a sense of self-concept and self-knowledge, self-concordance (the development of goals consistent with the self-concept), and person-role merger, which promotes a sense of authenticity [19].

Women typically are more likely to interrogate the value of an identity as an HE manager or leader than men [16]. This may be because HE socio-cultural practice is currently motivated by educational capitalism; universities need to become competitive, profit-making institutions with leaders who collude with "new managerialist" principles; they need to be competitive, entrepreneurialist and aware of their self-image [20]. New managerialist approaches may also include the requirement to implement unpopular re-structuring and redundancy policies in the interests of efficiency or to monitor their employees more closely. While such new managerial posts offered are not gender-specific, Deem [16] concludes that women are more interested in roles which seek to improve the student experience and quality of staff/student interaction whereas men are more inclined to see their roles as generating income and guaranteeing research excellence. The fact that men and women tend to have "gender-differentiated criteria for success and failure" [16] (p. 255) rather suggests that women may not even regard it as desirable to operate within a managerial or leadership culture which is at variance with their own concept of self.

3. Materials and Methods

This paper is based on a qualitative study—an autoethnography written by the first author of the paper. Put simply, autoethnography involves insider research into a context in which the researcher has "natural access" and is an active participant [10] (p. 174). Autoethnography is grounded in postmodern philosophy, and it has gained prominence among researchers in recent years. Predominantly, this rise in interest in autoethnography is related to a growing debate about reflexivity and voice in social research [21]. As Burnier [12] notes, autoethnography, along with other alternative forms of ethnographic research has gained prominence in response to a critique and "crisis" of how people, places, and practices come to be "represented" in qualitative research (p. 410). Although autoethnography has been criticized for lacking rigor, theoretical and analytical quality and for being too aesthetic, emotional, and therapeutic [22,23], Alvesson [10] argues that autoethnography (or self-ethnography as he calls it), is an ambitious and legitimate alternative to solely or mainly relying on interviews with respondents. It offers researchers a flexible and fluid form of academic writing [24] and, importantly, it can be emancipatory, especially for researchers who have lesser power and/or are a minority group in their field or practice context [21]. It has proved fruitful in contributing to organizational research [25], including university settings [26].

Autoethnography can take many forms; most relevant to this study is analytic autoethnography, which is comprised of three features, according to Anderson [11]. The researcher is (1) a full member in the research group or setting, (2) visible as such a member in published texts, and (3) committed to developing theoretical understandings of broader social phenomena. This autoethnography meets that criteria since it is written in the form of a personal narrative by the first author of this article, and it seeks to make both theoretical and practical contributions. In line with more general guidelines for authoethnography, this article attempts to present a highly personalized [21], evocative, engaging piece of writing that uses both the conventions of storytelling such as character, scene, and plot development [27], as well as reflections that produce new perspectives [28,29]. The narrative also aims to capture and provide "thick descriptions" of the cultural context [30] (p. 10) and make links to existing literature [31,32].

Ellis et al. [33] provide a detailed account of autoethnography; we draw on this to describe in more detail the methods and materials in our study. In keeping with most autoethnography research our method combines the characteristics of autobiography and ethnography. The autobiographical element involved retroactively and selectively writing about past experiences. A biographical timeline was produced as an aide memoir, following an approach used by Kempster [4]. The time line was populated with significant experiences and notable people. The researcher reflected on this time line to help focus her writing on epiphanies or significant experiences that she perceived to have impacted significantly on her trajectory and life [28,34,35]. This process enabled her to produce detailed written material about aspects of her personal and work life, explored through the normally private prism of accompanying thoughts and emotions. The ethnographic element involved the study of cultural and relational practices, common values and beliefs, and shared experiences for the purpose of helping insiders (cultural members) and outsiders (or cultural strangers) gain an understanding of that culture [36]. Precisely because the researcher was, and remains, an active participant in the study context, she was able to concentrate on her own past and present experience [37] to describe the cultural setting and use her experience and knowledge for research purposes [10]. In consequence, the material for this study came from the researcher drawing on autobiography and ethnography, retrospectively and selectively, to write about epiphanies related to culture and the particular culture and cultural identity of the institutional setting [33]. The method was iterative, and involved moving back and forth between reflection, writing, and the research literature. The method, therefore, involved much more than just story-telling, as Ellis et al. [33] explains:

> Autoethnographers must not only use their methodological tools and research literature to analyze experience, but also must consider ways others may experience similar epiphanies; they must use personal experience to illustrate facets of cultural experience, and, in so doing, make characteristics of a culture familiar for insiders and outsiders [online].

3.1. Ethics

It is of note that autoethnographic writing raises unusual ethical considerations [38]. The study upon which this paper is based received full ethical approval of the HE institution. From the onset, following guidelines for autoethnographers [38], both authors of this paper considered and followed ethical guidance, paying particular attention to the vulnerability of the researcher writing the autoethnography and other people who may be implicated through association with the autoethnographer, her department and/or the HE institution, which could result in researcher self-harm. In addition, because most autoethnographers focus on themselves primarily, this may give the impression that conventional ethical issues concerning human participants are not relevant. However, we were mindful of Chang's [39] (p. 68) argument that this assumption is incorrect:

> Whichever format you may take, you still need to keep in mind that other people are always present in self-narratives, either as active participants in the story or as associates in the background.

Even though no other individuals are named in this article, we acknowledge that individuals in the HE institution could be implicated, even though the article is referring predominantly to historical events in the past, and changes in staffing, organizational practices and culture have occurred since that time. Nevertheless, we have worked on the assumption that those people could read the paper [40]; therefore, care has been taken not publish anything we would not show to people referred to in the text [41]. In addition, "process consent" [42] (p. 23) was sought from a senior manager within the department in which the first researcher (the autoethnographer) is located, and that person has read and agreed to the publication of this article.

4. The Autoethnography

4.1. Introduction

I now realize that my working life between 1996 and 2005 involved the same increasing sense of disconnect with my community of practice as has been outlined in Section 2.1 above. My ongoing poor contractual terms, over a time period of nine years, resulted in a feeling that I did not belong; as a result, my participation never felt as if it was important. I was not a member, I did not undergo any desirable ontological transformation, nor was I able to absorb and truly identify with the prevailing socio-cultural context. As Linehan and McCarthy [43] warn, an employee who finds that the access route to a community of practice is blocked often find another way to re-invent their identities; indeed, through my reading of Hodges [3], I have become aware that this was exactly what I did. Since 1996, I have become "a person [who] ... reject[ed] the identity connected with the practice and yet ... reconstruct[ed] an identification within the context of conflict and exclusion" [3] (p. 273).

In order to explore this notion of dis-identification and reconstruction, my personal story will be uncovered as it relates to salient literature in the field. I will own this process by re-examining past events from varying perspectives, learning more about a particularly challenging period in my practice and continuing to work on resolutions. These biographical snatches will be reflexive; I will query my own personal beliefs and values as a teacher and note how these have affected and been affected by their surrounding context [44]. In this way, I can explore my own educational leadership and management journey and use reflective practice to "explain, justify and make sense of [... myself] in relation to others, and to the world at large" [44] (p. 311).

4.2. Habitus

It seems clear to me that I am comfortable with my habitus, that is, the self-identity built during my years of primary and secondary socialization. Role models within my community of practice were important to me; my parents clearly both valued education and they were both totally undiscriminating towards their children in terms of gender and educational aspirations; the school staff at my girls' school were overwhelmingly female with high ambitions for their pupils. I used to adore French and hero-worshipped my French teacher. It was during these years that my conviction grew that I would be a French teacher too. I never doubted that I would go to university to study French and then have a fulfilling and "important" job as an academic or a teacher. I was determined to speak French as much as possible, so I used to organize pen-friend exchanges for myself in the holidays, and undertook a variety of voluntary work in France, Germany and Italy in order to speak those languages that I enjoyed studying. I now realize that I was finding ways to legitimately and peripherally participate in new "life-worlds" in order to improve my languages, using them as a device to trial and develop new social identities. After my first degree, I set out on my personal journey to make sense of the world through my self-identity as a languages teacher or academic, "within the structural constraints of my own internalized reality" [7] (p. 18). After further studies and much deliberation, I decided to become a modern languages teacher and gained my first job in a local secondary school.

4.3. Dis-Identification with the Identity Connected with the Practice 1996–2005

Pupil resistance to secondary school language learning through, presumably, an oppositional stance to it learned through their primary socialization [45], and a lack of effective disciplinary support measures within the school resulted in a new lifestyle choice. I chose a teaching path that would be less stressful and allow me to juggle motherhood with a new career identity. I moved into teaching modern foreign languages part-time within the adult education sector, and then in the mid-1990s, when the marketization of higher education had begun to take hold, increasing competition for student fees led to a new climate of organizational change within universities [46]. I gained a further Master's degree in Teaching English while being employed as an hourly-paid, sessional tutor on an English for Academic Purposes (EAP) program at an HE institution within in the UK. While I was delighted with this new teaching context because of the new experiential opportunities and personal flexibility it afforded, I gradually found that such a temporary and part-time contractual status seemed to consign me to the periphery of the community.

Over these years, the full-time permanent staff became the "master practitioners" of the program [6] (p. 111). Through their various committees and management meetings, to which, as a temporary employee, I was never invited, my perception grew that they were privileged to knowledge-making which set me apart, and they took the program forward, establishing their own identities as central. Condemned to my identity as a perpetual peripheral member of the community, I felt vulnerable with no permanent work contract, taking on new project opportunities that I imagined I had only obtained because others had not found them appealing, teetering between an attitude of "submissive imitation" [6] (p. 116), and naïve acceptance, hoping that my hard work would eventually encourage ever closer involvement with the community of practice. However, I always felt that as a part-time, temporary teacher, I was considered too light-weight to be taken seriously. Over the next nine years, the increasingly corporate culture began to infiltrate my professional identity, which was gradually eroded. I felt infantilized; meetings seemed to be a sounding-board for those in power; I felt that my contributions were worthless, embarrassing and wrong; I felt paralyzed to act according to my own professional judgement. When I read Gabriel's [47] account of how contemporary corporate and marketized organizations can exert insidious emotional control over their staff, I was stunned to realize that this represented an exact account of what I had lived through.

> Even if an individual has nothing to confess, the transformation of the workplace into a confessional, with the implicit acceptance that there are right and wrong attitudes, appropriate and inappropriate behaviors, measurable performances, etc., and that the individual must continuously monitor him/herself against such standards, created pliable, self-policing, self-disciplining individuals, who lack the words (or discursive resources) to oppose or shake off the invasive tyranny of power/knowledge [47] (p. 187).

Such controls did not just lower my sense of self-esteem, but they eroded my very sense of self, together with my other personal identities. My cultural life at my place at work excluded me from its heritage—symbols of inclusion passed me by [6]; for example, I was overlooked in the distribution of circulars advertising future conferences, I was ineligible for annual performance reviews, I was not considered to be at a high enough grade for a personal business card, nor was I entitled to an individual post tray in the staff room.

I remember that I often used to think when I came home from work: "how can I possibly be a responsible wife and mother when I am obviously such an incapable and hopeless individual?". On one occasion, which turned out to be a crucible moment in my decision to leave, I remember that a manager had asked me to help to clear out a book cupboard, and I just managed to stop myself from asking the banal question "how would you like me to clear the books off the shelf?"

Needless to say, I felt excluded from this community of practice, but I desperately wanted to belong. This process of marginalization finally resulted in a dis-identification with this community of practitioners; I became increasingly resentful and hostile as two unsuccessful applications for a full-time post at my HE institution came and went. I took this as a sign. I made the decision to leave the program, and indeed the institution, to take up a job abroad. If I needed any further confirmation that I was not considered part of the community of practice, the last one finally came when there was no customary "leaving party", presumably because I did not have a "proper" post to leave behind! My new post involved teaching, setting up courses, developing in-service training sessions and supporting and observing teachers. After one year, my self-esteem finally re-surfacing, I returned home to the UK, keen to find a new working context which better suited my new, more comfortable concept of self.

With hindsight, I am now able to contemplate these difficulties and try to make further sense of them. According to Bourdieu and Wacquant [48], the EAP Program had been a social field, where participants struggled either to ensure that their position in the field remained exclusive, or alternatively as an outsider, to develop an acceptable position within it. The prevailing doxa, that is the unwritten rules of the field, had been developed by a hegemony; their chosen social structures becoming "instruments of domination" [48] (p. 14). Full-time workers had economic capital due to their permanent posts, cultural capital in that they were privy to the inner workings of the program, and social capital, as their positions enabled the development of self-serving relationships, leading to ever more influential positions as they rose up through the ranks. As a result, they had high symbolic capital, which they were able to maintain through their hegemonic practice. As a constantly temporarily-working "mother", I felt that I had low economic capital in terms of my low earnings and inexistent terms and conditions, little cultural capital (being excluded from day-to-day organizational practices), low social capital as I had few legitimate participatory opportunities at the heart of the hierarchy, and probable low symbolic capital as a woman [16]. In short, the "academic staff" (as they were termed) seemed to enjoy much higher symbolic capital than myself, who was in fact in contrast constantly referred to as a "sessional". This "symbolic violence" [7] (p. 21) was exercised over me, due to my vulnerability within the field, and I succumbed to this for years, accepting my position (albeit unwillingly), through a need to earn money and an inability to change the cultural context. My self-identity was clearly too strong to accept the social identity that my colleagues were positing for me; it was at variance with my self-concept, and I had to take action. "Resistance through physical distance" became my solution [47] (p. 192). As Spitzer [49] (p. 16) points out, "a fixed mindset", (which, on reflection, I had unwittingly acquired through my habitus) "tends to be self-evaluative: I'm smart or dumb, creative or unimaginative, a success or a failure". My earlier academic success had taught me that I was special, that I deserved to succeed, and somehow this painful experience had re-defined me as a failure.

While simultaneously criticizing myself for my "fixed" mindset, rather than viewing such challenges as opportunities for growth [50], my self-destructive experience with trying to move in a centripetal direction accords with other research into the role of women as leaders in HE. Morley [51] (p. 119) shows how many women ultimately view leadership in terms of a "loss", and Kempster's [4] research shows how women's domestic identities prejudice their opportunities for career challenge, leading to a lack of confidence. Kempster [4] (p. 153) notes in his research: "Only the women made explicit the connection of the role of confidence and the activities to maintain confidence. This does not mean that men were never unconfident—simply that they did not emphasize or highlight this issue" [4] (p. 153). Might this be because men's typical career trajectories do not tend to challenge a fixed mindset, whereas women's do? Is it likely that some women are not supported in breaking through their fixed mindset, never learning that "failure [. . .] doesn't define you. It's a problem to be faced, dealt with, and learned from" [50] (p. 33)?

4.4. Reconstructing an Identity within the Context of Conflict and Exclusion (Post-2005)

On returning home, I was again offered hourly-paid work at the same institution, within a different EAP Program. The program I had left represented a need for conformity, requiring a consistent approach to course design and delivery in order to ensure the students attending all received an equal opportunity in the high stakes assessment required for them to progress to their chosen degree programs. Now appointed to a different program, which was still being established and not such high stakes for the students, there was more flexibility in course design and delivery, and indeed specificity at course level was encouraged. In these early years, all the staff were hourly paid, the socio-cultural context was welcoming, relaxed but hard-working—we jointly had opportunities to set up new courses, manage them and develop materials. In this way, power was equally distributed between us, despite our poor contractual conditions. I was struck by the respect we had for each other, conducting our own meetings without "game playing, politicking [. . .] clashing of antlers, proliferation and waffling" (Female HoD, cited in Deem [16] (p. 251)).

In 2010, our language center became subject to new HR regulations, and all those who had been working for more than three years on a sessional, temporary contract were offered permanent posts with full rights. I was offered a permanent part-time contract with certain middle-management responsibilities. I had "arrived" at the age of 55! Being finally content at work, I made a conscious decision to not aspire to any higher management positions; I rejected more senior positions as a career possibility, partly to avoid further loss of self-esteem should I be unsuccessful, and partly because I needed at all costs to create space for myself to prioritize my own values [52]. I have now realized it was my perceived lack of membership of the community which had alienated me, and that this had been due to prevailing HE cultural practice rather than to individual behavior choices; the notion of leadership as an inclusive "sense-making" process Kempster [4] (p. 30) only prevails when community participants all truly belong. I have learned to be content with being a full member of my current community of practice. I now view leadership in terms of "loss"; that is, "loss of independence, research time, health and well-being" [51] (p. 119), and as "a normative fantasy about what constitutes success" [51] (p. 125).

4.5. Working on Resolutions

In preparing this material for publication, I felt troubled by the fact that it was certainly not my intention to secretively expose the management practices of any particular persons. I currently owe a great deal to my place of work in terms of self-fulfillment: I feel passionate about my current role; I am a full member of my current community of practice. I also have the freedom to engage in scholarship to the extent that it improves and develops our current courses. My intention, in fact, is to give voice to a phenomenon that is, for understandable reasons, rarely discussed. Not wanting to appear deceitful, I therefore took the seemingly reckless step of revealing the years of private turmoil that I had lived through to a senior manager who had been present throughout those years in my workplace. After sharing a copy of the paper with them, I arranged for us to meet face to face; the resulting discussion astonished me. With full permission and encouragement, I now present their perspective on my story. I have chosen to use the plural "they" to refer to the senior manager in order to protect anonymity.

The years between 1996 and 2005 had made seminal contribution to the gradually emerging identity of the field of EAP within the HE sector. From a management perspective, raising the EAP profile within the institution to secure understanding of the value of the work for international students and the resource to develop and expand its programs had been difficult and protracted. During this period of growth and development, new staff were employed on temporary contracts. The senior manager had always ensured that my contract was re-issued annually without any breaks between contracts in order to mitigate the disadvantages associated with variable working hours and lack of permanent status. Furthermore, significant experiences discussed herein were viewed from a strikingly different perspective to mine. It transpires that I had always been viewed as a permanent, valued member of staff within my department, even though my contract had been renewable and my working hours had varied from term to term. I was told that I had not been offered a traditional leaving party at the start of my year of my absence because the senior manager had taken the view that I was happily taking a year out to enjoy an overseas opportunity and was expected to be returning to my job! She had no memory of the lack of participation in the symbols of inclusion mentioned previously, simply asking why I had not been to discuss my concerns with them at the time. My reply that I had felt too vulnerable in my position seemed to amaze them; they felt we had had a good working relationship and that I could easily have approached them. They had never considered me as "temporary"—sessional staff members were relied on to enable the department to grow and were important for developing the business to a point where permanent contracts could be offered more widely. They explained that I had not been invited to certain decision-making meetings and committees as I did not manage staff or other departmental resources, and this was viewed as a simple fact of university life—not everyone can attend higher-level meetings. Moreover, they pointed out that at such meetings consensus is rare, as individuals do not necessarily agree on management decisions; not everyone's view can be acted upon, and compromises have to be made. They pointed out that other staff in a similar position to me at that time had appeared less daunted by this situation and had pushed through with their onwards career trajectory, a point which was in fact true.

These differing accounts of the same event reveal the pertinence of Bourdieu's statement, previously discussed, but worth repeating to allow for further consideration: "points of view are grasped as such and related to the positions they occupy in the structure of agents under consideration" [7] (p. 15). The senior manager's perspective and my own view of the socio-cultural context were colored by our own positions in the structure within which we operated; through our unfortunate lack of discussion, neither of us was in fact party to the fuller picture, and both of us had objectified our own view of the world as we saw it. We jointly realized that we could draw thoughtful conclusions from our stories which may be pertinent for both employees and their managers/leaders in HE.

5. Findings

This autoethnographic study set out to reflect on the challenges of short term or non-permanent contracts of employment in HE. Although the findings are based solely on the experience of one woman, we propose, from a theoretical perspective, that the findings tentatively extend Kempster's [4] own research results. Kempster [4,53] has shown that the salience of a leadership identity and its accompanying self-efficacy typically increase through privileged access to notable people and opportunities to practice leadership within communities of practice. The findings of this paper confirm what Kempster [53] has speculated—the salience of leadership diminishes in environments that fail to provide pathways for participation in leadership.

Further, the findings exemplify that participation-in-practice is associated with "becoming" part of a social world [6]. Through the use of autoethnography, this article highlights that employees who would like permanent status but are employed on temporary contracts may feel disconnected from their community of practice [6], to the extent that an employee can become vulnerable and marginalized. As a result, their subjective, emotional reaction may preclude a measured consideration of the social structures of the workplace; their objective view of the workplace may gradually harden over the years, particularly if their mindset is fixed [50], a notion explored in this paper. Limited opportunities for participation can therefore cause an individual to dis-identify with the community of practice and over time they may adopt a workplace habitus which secretly resents the prevailing social culture. Such experiences can stifle an individual's aspirations to become a leader and their self-efficacy beliefs, resulting in the rejection of a leader identity and/or leadership positions.

6. Conclusions

It is to be hoped that the theoretical insights and reflexive approach afforded by this autoethnography and its final discussion will help both temporary employees and their managers to better understand how the context of their workplace can seem to disadvantage a temporary worker, whose workplace behavior may belie their inner concept of self. It is important to acknowledge that men, not just women, may reject managerialist values, and indeed there are many women in leadership who may even espouse them. For myself, I have discovered the truth of Wall's belief [21], previously highlighted in Section 3, that an autoethnographic approach can be emancipatory; lifting the lid on this rather frustrating period of my life has been a therapeutic process; both my own research and subsequent frank discussions have finally laid to rest a cycle of lack of confidence and low self-esteem.

Since this study is based on one woman's experience, we recognize its limitations and we hope this paper will inspire others in similar situations to analyze and tell their stories, individually or though collaborative autoethnography, both to search for personal resolutions and to help to influence future directions of HE working practices, which should be more forward-looking, creative, less wasteful of potential talent and more representative of the diverse nature of a changing society.

7. Recommendations

We propose practical recommendations based on the findings of this study:

Firstly, the level of vulnerability that I had felt over the years had for me precluded frank discussion, but the senior manager had not in fact regarded my position as vulnerable at all; in her mind, there was no doubt that I would be re-employed year on year. Managers should not therefore underestimate the "otherness" feelings that can be created by temporary contract working; such employees may not give voice to their feelings, either because they sense that no-one is really interested, or because expressing an adverse opinion may risk their job.

Second, HE organizations, which aim to be vibrant, forward-looking centers of learning, striving for positive change in the world, should carefully consider their current workplace culture, policies and practices; managers should be aware of the symbols of inclusion, however apparently small, that may serve to mark out temporary employees as different [6]. With this in mind, temporary employees should be included in performance development reviews despite their low symbolic status; they should be encouraged to routinely and confidentially discuss their career aspirations as do permanent staff; they should be able to give feedback on the performance of their line manager; someone should take responsibility for ensuring that they are always updated with relevant information and included in the variety of opportunities open to permanent staff. In addition, there should be a budget for paying temporary staff to allow them to attend in-service training sessions without the assumption that they will give their own unpaid time for the privilege of joining in. Socialization into the community of practice [6] could also be facilitated by mentoring or sponsorship schemes, particularly in terms of encouraging women to consider crossing the divide into senior managerial roles which, as discussed in Section 2.3, they may not otherwise instantly find appealing.

Third, further consideration should be given to the fact that working women who may be juggling family and work life have a valuable role to play in the HE sector, and that some may lack confidence after a career break [4]. In consequence, return-to-work support structures should be more widely available, and job shares at a higher level of responsibility should be more positively encouraged, as should the distribution of permanent part-time contracts.

Author Contributions: Karen Jones and Anne Vicary conceived and designed the study; Anne Vicary performed the autoethnography; Karen Jones devised the methods and materials section; Anne Vicary and Karen Jones wrote the remainder of the paper.

Conflicts of Interest: The authors declare no conflict of interest.

Appendix A

Russell Group universities consist of 24 research-intensive, world-class universities based in the UK. These universities are "committed to maintaining the very best research, an outstanding teaching and learning experience and unrivalled links with business and the public sector [54]."

References

1. HESA. Staff at Higher Education Providers in the United Kingdom 2015/16. Available online: https://www.hesa.ac.uk/news/19-01-2017/sfr243-staff (accessed on 30 April 2017).
2. UCU. Precarious Work in Higher Education: A Snapshot of Insecure Contracts and Institutional Attitudes. Available online: www.ucu_precariouscontract_hereport_apr16.pdf (accessed on 30 April 2017).
3. Hodges, D.C. Participation as dis-identification with/in a community of practice. *Mind Cult. Act.* **1998**, *5*, 272–290. [CrossRef]
4. Kempster, S. *How Managers Have Learnt to Lead: Exploring the Development of Leadership Practice*; Palgrave Macmillan: Basingstoke, UK, 2009.
5. Bandura, A. *Self-Efficacy: The Exercise of Control*; W.H. Freeman: New York, NY, USA, 1997.
6. Lave, J.; Wenger, E. *Situated Learning: Legitimate Peripheral Participation*; Cambridge University Press: Cambridge, UK, 1991.
7. Bourdieu, P. Social space and symbolic power. *Sociol. Theory* **1989**, *7*, 14–25. [CrossRef]
8. Mead, G.H. *Mind, Self and Society*; University of Chicago Press: Chicago, IL, USA, 1934.
9. Aubrey, K.; Riley, A. *Understanding and Using Educational Theories*; Sage: Los Angeles, CA, USA; London, UK, 2016.

10. Alvesson, M. Methodology for close up studies—Struggling with closeness and closure. *High. Educ.* **2003**, *46*, 167–193. [CrossRef]

11. Anderson, L. Analytic autoethnography. *J. Contemp. Ethnogr.* **2006**, *35*, 373–395. [CrossRef]

12. Burnier, D. Encounters with the self in social science research: A political scientist looks at autoethnography. *J. Contemp. Ethnogr.* **2006**, *35*, 410–418. [CrossRef]

13. Wenger, E. *Communities of Practice: Learning, Meaning, and Identity*; Cambridge University Press: Cambridge, UK, 1998.

14. Charon, J.M. *Symbolic Interactionism*; Prentice-Hall: Upper Saddle River, NJ, USA, 1998.

15. Ball, D. Self and identity in the context of deviance: The case of criminal abortion. In *Theoretical Perspectives on Deviance*; Scott, R.A., Douglas, J.D., Eds.; Basic Books: New York, NY, USA, 1972.

16. Deem, R. Gender, organizational cultures and the practice of manager-academics in UK universities. *Gend. Work Organ.* **2003**, *10*, 239–259. [CrossRef]

17. Prus, R.C. *Beyond the Power Mystique: Power as Intersubjective Accomplishment*; State University of New York Press: Albany, NY, USA, 1999.

18. Bennis, W.G.; Thomas, R.J. Crucibles of leadership. *Harv. Bus. Rev.* **2002**, *80*, 39–45. [PubMed]

19. Shamir, B.; Eilam, G. "What's your story?" a life-stories approach to authentic leadership development. *Leadersh. Q.* **2005**, *16*, 395–417. [CrossRef]

20. Mackinnon, A.; Brooks, A. Introduction: Globalisation, academia and change. In *Gender and the Restructured University*; Brooks, A., Mackinnon, A., Eds.; Open University Press: Buckingham, UK, 2001.

21. Wall, S. An autoethnography on learning about autoethnography. *Int. J. Qual. Methods* **2006**, *5*, 146–160. [CrossRef]

22. Ellis, C. *Revision: Autoethnographic Reflections on Life and Work*; Left Coast Press: Walnut Creek, CA, USA, 2009.

23. Keller, E.F. *Reflections on Gender and Science*; Yale University Press: New Haven, CT, USA, 1995.

24. Ellis, C. *The Ethnographic I : A Methodological Novel about Autoethnography*; AltaMira Press: Walnut Creek, CA, USA, 2004.

25. Boyle, M.; Parry, K. Telling the whole story: The case for organizational autoethnography. *Cult. Organ.* **2007**, *13*, 185–190. [CrossRef]

26. Hernández, F.; Sancho, J.M.; Creus, A.; Montané, A. Becoming university scholars: Inside professional autoethnographies. *J. Res. Pract.* **2010**, *6*, 1–15.

27. Ellis, C.; Ellingson, L. Qualitative methods. In *Encyclopedia of Sociology*; Borgatta, E., Montgomery, R., Eds.; Macmillan: New York, NY, USA, 2000; pp. 2287–2296.

28. Couser, G.T. *Recovering Bodies: Illness, Disability, and Life-Writing*; University of Wisconsin Press: Madison, WI, USA, 1997.

29. Goodall, H.L., Jr. *Writing the New Ethnography*; AltaMira Press: Lanham, MD, USA, 2000.

30. Geertz, C. *The Interpretation of Cultures*; Basic Books: New York, NY, USA, 1973.

31. Ronai, C.R. Multiple reflections of child sex abuse: An argument for a layered account. *J. Contemp. Ethnogr.* **1995**, *23*, 395–426. [CrossRef]

32. Ronai, C.R. My mother is mentally retarded. In *Composing Ethnography: Alternative Forms of Qualitative Writing*; Ellis, C., Bochner, A.P., Eds.; Alta Mira: Walnut Creek, CA, USA, 1996; pp. 109–131.

33. Ellis, C.; Adams, T.E.; Bochner, A.P. Autoethnography: An overview. *Forum Qual. Soc. Res.* **2011**, *12*, 10. Available online: http://www.qualitative-research.net/index.php/fqs/article/view/1589/3095 (accessed on 30 April 2017).

34. Bochner, A.P.; Ellis, C. *Ethnographically Speaking: Autoethnography, Literature, and Aesthetics*; AltaMira: Walnut Creek, CA, USA; Oxford, UK, 2002.

35. Denzin, N.K. *Interpretive Biography*; Sage: Newbury Park, CA, USA, 1989.

36. Maso, I. Phenomenology and ethnography. In *Handbook of Ethnography*; Atkinson, P., Coffey, A., Delamont, S., Lofland, J.L., Lofland, L., Eds.; Sage: Thousand Oaks, CA, USA, 2001; pp. 136–144.

37. Charmaz, K. The power of names. *J. Contemp. Ethnogr.* **2006**, *35*, 396–399. [CrossRef]

38. Tolich, M. A critique of current practice: Ten foundational guidelines for autoethnographers. *Qual. Health Res.* **2010**, *20*, 1599–1610. [CrossRef] [PubMed]

39. Chang, H. *Autoethnography as Method*; Left Coast Press: Walnut Creek, CA, USA, 2008.

40. Ellis, C. Emotional and ethical quagmires in returning to the field. *J. Contemp. Ethnogr.* **1995**, *24*, 68–98. [CrossRef]

41. Medford, K. Caught with a fake ID: Ethical questions about slippage in autoethnography. *Qual. Inq.* **2006**, *12*, 853–864. [CrossRef]
42. Ellis, C. Telling secrets, revealing lives: Relational ethics in research with intimate others. *Qual. Inq.* **2007**, *13*, 3–29. [CrossRef]
43. Linehan, C.; McCarthy, J. Positioning in practice: Understanding participation in the social world. *J. Theory Soc. Behav.* **2000**, *30*, 435–453. [CrossRef]
44. Maclure, M. Arguing for yourself: Identity as an organising principle in teachers' jobs and lives. *Br. Educ. Res. J.* **1993**, *19*, 311–322. [CrossRef]
45. Willis, P. *Learning to Labour: How Working Class Kids Get Working Class Jobs*; Saxon House: Farnborough, UK, 1977.
46. Brown, R. The marketisation of higher education: Issues and ironies. *New Vistas* **2015**, *1*, 4–9.
47. Gabriel, Y. Beyond happy families: A critical reevaluation of the control-resistance-identity triangle. *Hum. Relat.* **1999**, *52*, 179–203. [CrossRef]
48. Bourdieu, P.; Wacquant, L.J.D. *An Invitation to Reflexive Sociology*; Polity Press: London, UK, 1992.
49. Spitzer, R. Lighting the fire of innovation: How to foster creativity in the workplace. *J. Qual. Particip.* **2013**, *36*, 15–18.
50. Dweck, C. *Self-Theories: Their Role in Motivation, Personality and Development (Essays in Social Psychology)*; Routledge: Abingdon, UK, 2016.
51. Morley, L. Lost leaders: Women in the global academy. *High. Educ. Res. Dev.* **2014**, *33*, 114–128. [CrossRef]
52. Woods, P.; Jeffrey, B. The reconstruction of primary teachers' identities. *Br. J. Sociol. Educ.* **2002**, *23*, 89–106. [CrossRef]
53. Kempster, S. Observing the invisible. *J. Manag. Dev.* **2009**, *28*, 439–456. [CrossRef]
54. Russell Group. Our Universities. Available online: http://russellgroup.ac.uk/about/our-universities/ (accessed on 30 April 2017).

administrative
sciences

MDPI

Article

Increasing Gender Diversity in Senior Roles in HE: Who Is Afraid of Positive Action?

Simonetta Manfredi

Business School, Oxford Brookes University, Oxford OX3 0BP, UK; smanfredi@brookes.ac.uk

Academic Editors: Karen Jones, Arta Ante, Karen A. Longman and Robyn Remke
Received: 14 March 2017; Accepted: 1 June 2017; Published: 8 June 2017

Abstract: This article argues that Higher Education Institutions should adopt positive action in recruitment and promotion to tackle women's under-representation in senior leadership roles. In a tie-break situation where two candidates are "as qualified as each other", section *159 of the UK Equality Act 2010* allows employers to give preference to a candidate from an under-represented group. The use of this measure, however, is often contested on the grounds that it is a form of reverse discrimination, it is tokenistic and that it can undermine meritocracy. This article seeks to challenge these objections and suggests that, far from undermining meritocracy, the use of positive action in recruitment and promotion could prove a useful tool to tackle gender bias, unpack stereotypes and re-appraise how merit is defined and assessed.

Keywords: gender diversity; leadership; higher education; positive action

1. Introduction

Women represent over 54% of the total workforce in the Higher Education (HE) sector in the whole of the UK yet [1], only 20% of them are in Vice-Chancellor and Principal roles. Only 19% of all HE governing bodies in UK institutions are chaired by women [2]. This lack of women in leadership roles in HE is not just an issue for the UK but one shared across Europe, where only 15% of rectors (equivalent to vice-chancellor) are women [3] and indeed across the world [4]. Lack of gender diversity at the top of Higher Education Institutions (HEIs) has been publicly questioned and the 2015 grant letter from the UK government [5] stressed the need for the sector to do more to close the gender gap, highlighting that: " . . . *currently only one Vice-Chancellor in five is female, and we believe the sector should go much further to seek out and harness the diverse talent available"*. Moreover, the HEFCE 2015–2020 [6] business plan has set an aspirational target of 40% women's representation on universities' governing bodies to be achieved by 2020 and Scottish universities are aiming to achieve a similar target by 2018 [7].

In order to achieve these outcomes, HE needs to tackle the "invisible barriers" which prevent women from progressing into senior roles. These include a gendered construction of leadership [8–16], the impact of cognitive bias, which results in women being constantly judged less favourably than men [17–19] and accumulate disadvantage throughout their career [20]. Cognitive bias is further reinforced by a persistent male-dominated culture which renders universities" an endemically homosocial gentlemen's club" [21] where, by and large, men are most comfortable to work with other men [22]. These issues are compounded by a gendered division of labour in the academy with women likely to have greater teaching, administrative and pastoral responsibilities, which tend to be less valued than research [23] and by "gendered academic rules", for example about evaluation criteria and authorships conventions [24]. All these factors can lead to what has been described as a "gendered construction of academic excellence" which can "contribute, albeit inadvertently, to institutionalised sexism" [25].

In this context, it is not surprising that research about the career trajectories of men and women in senior leadership roles in HE in the UK [26] (p. 13) found that women were more likely to have experienced sex discrimination and gender bias in their careers compared to their male colleagues. Several women reported more recent and subtle examples of gender-bias relating to appointment processes as they tried to move, successfully or unsuccessfully, into more senior leadership roles. For example, some talked about *"huge gender barriers"* that still exist in HE, including colleagues and decision makers not seeing them as suited for senior roles and that the very concept of leadership in HEIs is *"too narrowly defined"*; failing to acknowledge that there are different models and styles of leadership.

Academic institutions often defend their poor record on gender diversity in senior roles by arguing that appointments are strictly made on the basis of candidates' merit. This, however, takes us to the very core of the problem about the meaning of merit as this is not a "value-neutral" concept but one that can be measured according to different parameters [27]. As seen above, the literature on women's careers in HE clearly points to a gendered construction of merit and, therefore, there is a need to re-assess merit and unpack gender stereotypes and the norms developed on men's career experiences which can influence how merit is defined. This article argues that HEIs should adopt positive action in recruitment and promotion as permitted by s. 159 of the UK Equality Act 2010 as a tool to re-assess merit and re-address the gender balance in senior leadership roles. However, positive action legislation in recruitment and promotion that, in a tie-break situation, allows employers to give preference to a candidate from an under-represented group, is poorly understood by decision makers and often considered to be a form of reverse discrimination. As such, it has been too often rejected by both decision makers and the women themselves who could benefit from it.

In what follows, this article draws from literature theorising policy approaches to equality, legal theory on equality and positive action, empirical research about employers' perceptions of positive action in recruitment and promotion and case law developed by the European Court of Justice to gain a better understanding about the content of this measure and its practical application. It then identifies five objections which are commonly raised against the use of positive action in a tie-break situation and not only seeks to challenge them but also to generate counter-arguments to justify the need for adopting positive action in recruitment and promotion. It concludes by suggesting that there is a compelling case for HEIs to start using this measure and it proposes a model for its application in practice.

2. Positive Action Provisions in the UK Equality Act 2010

The UK Equality Act 2010 contains provisions which allow employers to adopt positive action measures to achieve greater equality. Section 158 provides for general types of positive action measures such as training initiatives to encourage under-represented groups to apply for jobs or promotion. Section 159 instead permits employers to take into account a legally protected characteristic, including gender, when making decisions about recruitment or promotion where the person with the protected characteristic belongs to a disadvantaged or under-represented group. This applies to a tie-break situation in the final stages of the hiring process where remaining candidates are "as qualified as each other". In this instance, the candidate from the under-represented group may be chosen unless there are objective reasons which would tilt the balance in favour of the other candidate. This type of measure, however, is often seen as a form of reverse discrimination rather than positive action and, as such, it remains controversial.

This raises the question as to whether, in spite of being defined as positive action, s. 159 is in fact reverse discrimination. In order to shed light on this point, Johns et al. [28] have considered the nature of this provision through the lenses of the theoretical model about policy approaches to equality developed by Forbes [29]. This distinguishes three key approaches to equality: the formal approach, the liberal and the radical one. The formal approach is predicated onto the Aristotelian proposition that likes should be treated alike and promotes a symmetrical concept of equal treatment. The liberal approach recognises the existence of obstacles that can disadvantage certain groups and aims to remove them, in order to create a level playing field. It is within this liberal framework that the concept of positive action has emerged. The liberal approach that seeks to achieve equality by ensuring equal opportunities among different groups has been most influential in the UK as it sits comfortably with liberal political ideals grounded on the rights of individuals [30] and also with the free market ideology [31]. Section 158 on general positive action measures can be located within this approach. However, as highlighted by Johns et al. [28], s. 159 does not quite fit the liberal approach as this provision is designed to achieve equality of outcomes rather than equality of opportunities. Neither does it fit with the radical approach which aims to achieve equality of outcomes but through radical interventions such as reverse discrimination and the use of quotas. This makes it more difficult for employers to understand the nature of s. 159 and how to use it correctly without risking legal challenges. Although practical guidance has been produced by the UK Government Equalities Office [32], there is little empirical evidence about the use of positive action in recruitment and selection by employers. A small exploratory study undertaken by Davies [33] with 26 employers, including some in the HE sector, found that most of them did not envisage making use of this provision. A significant majority, however, expressed personal support for a more interventionist approach to remedy persistent inequalities. Other research focusing on recruitment processes at the senior level in HE [34] (p. 28) found that, in spite of concerns about women's under-representation in senior roles, most directors of human resources in universities were against the use of positive action in recruitment and selection. The most common reasons cited by this group were that, in practice, there is always a clear winner or that it overlooks the complexities of choosing a candidate. This is in contrast to the views expressed by a number of Chairs of Universities Councils with experience of working in other sectors, who appeared to be much more open to the idea of using this provision with a few of them having actually used it in the private sector. These findings, although based on small samples of participants and, therefore, not generalisible, nonetheless suggest that senior decision makers have mixed views about the application of this provision and that it may be dismissed by some because it is poorly understood.

Noon [27] has identified a number of objections which are frequently raised against preferential treatment of under-represented groups in recruitment and selection. This article builds on Noon's arguments which contest these objections and extends them to develop a compelling argument in favour of this provision.

Five key objections are identified (including those previously highlighted by Noon) which often feature in debates relating to the use of interventions such as that provided by s. 159. These are:

- Objection one: That it is trying to remedy to women's under-representation by using reverse discrimination against men, but "two wrongs" do not make a right;
- Objection two: That it undermines meritocracy as decisions about recruitment and promotions have to be made strictly in favour of the best candidate;
- Objection three: That the application of positive action in selection and recruitment in practice would be difficult and it could make institutions vulnerable to legal challenges;
- Objection four: Women or other under-represented groups want to be appointed to a job because of their merits and not because of positive action
- Objection five: That changing the numbers by increasing women's representation does not guarantee a change in the organisational culture.

These objections will be challenged in turn but prior to this, in order to gain a better understanding of positive action in recruitment and promotion, it is essential to consider the principles that underpin s. 159.

3. Legal Boundaries around the Application of Positive Action in Recruitment and Promotion

Section 159 was introduced to bring UK law in line with European legal developments in relation to the use of positive action measures [35]. At present, the legal boundaries that define the use of positive action in recruitment and promotion in the UK reflect the parameters developed through the jurisprudence of the European Court of Justice. Although the UK has chosen to exit the European

Union, it is still worth considering these parameters, not only because for the time being they still apply, but also because they are well embedded into national legislation. Once the UK has exited the EU and is no longer bound by European law, it could choose to adopt a more radical US style approach to positive action than that currently permitted under European Law. This, however, is an unlikely scenario as it would sit uncomfortably with the UK liberal legal tradition, as discussed earlier. Of course, any UK government could, as with any other legislation, decide to abolish this provision altogether at any time, but this would not be related to the exit from the EU since this provision does not stem from a European Directive. Therefore, there is still merit in discussing the European roots of s. 159.

European Member States are not required to adopt positive action measures but they are allowed to use them to address inequalities if they wish, as stated by Article 157(4) of the Treaty on the Functioning of the European Union (TFEU) which provides that:

"With a view to ensuring full equality in practice between men and women in working life, the principle of equal treatment shall not prevent any Member States from maintaining or adopting measures providing for specific advantages in order to make it easier for the under-represented sex to pursue a vocational activity or to prevent or compensate for disadvantages in professional careers".

This recognises the limits of anti-discrimination legislation, based on the principle of equal treatment especially in tackling structural forms of discrimination [36–39]. This may not be sufficient to tackle what has been described as the second generation of discrimination which, unlike overt discrimination, is caused by cognitive bias, patterns of interaction among different groups in the workplace and power relations which result in more subtle forms of discrimination [40]. Thus, positive action measures in this respect can be seen as complementary legislative tools to tackle subtle forms of discrimination and to help identify practices which, although on the face it appears to be neutral, in practice can disproportionally disadvantage certain groups and result in indirect discrimination.

In practice, the boundaries of such measures, which represent a derogation from the principle of equal treatment which is enshrined in EU law, have been defined through a series of cases brought before the Court of Justice of the European Union (CJEU). In these judgments, the Court has established a set of key principles which govern the use of positive action.

The first principle, established in the case of *Kalanke v Freie Hansestadt Bremen* [41], is that the application of an automatic and unconditional measure in recruitment or promotion, which would give preference to a candidate from the under-represented sex in a tie-break situation, would contravene the principle of equal treatment and, therefore, it would not be permitted. In the subsequent case of *Marschall v Land NordrheinWestfalen* [42], however, the Court ruled that it would not be incompatible with the principle of equal treatment to afford preference to a candidate from the under-represented sex in a tie-break situation, provided that both candidates are equally qualified and that all candidates are subject to an individual assessment which would take into account specific circumstances that may tilt the balance in favour of the male candidate.

Two further key principles can be identified from the decision in the case of *Marschall*: First, while it reinforces the principle already established in *Kalanke*, that a candidate could not be given preference simply because it belongs to the under-represented sex, it also establishes that if the candidates are equally qualified in relation to the requirements of the job in question, the candidate from the under-represented sex may be given preference. Second it stresses that there must be an individual assessment of both candidates to respect the principle for individual merit. Consequently, preference may not be given to the candidate from the under-represented sex if there are circumstances which tilt the balance in favour of the candidate of the opposite sex. Prima facia these two principles seem to contradict one another, as it could be argued that if two candidates, a man and a woman, appear to be as qualified as each other but there are actual circumstances which tilt the balance in favour of the male candidate, then we would no longer have a tie-break situation, as one candidate would have proven to be more meritorious than the other. This apparent contradiction, however, reflects a tension between, on the one hand, the need to recognise the limits of the principle of equal treatment in achieving gender equality and, on the other hand, the need to preserve the principle of individual merit.

In an attempt to overcome this tension, the CJEU case law has highlighted the need in the application of positive action measures for striking a balance between the aim of achieving greater gender equality and the need to have a process that allows for recognition of individual merit. A key element for this balancing act is the principle of proportionality. This means that a positive action measure should be applied only when this is appropriate and necessary in order to achieve greater representation of people from the under-represented sex, but also that it should be implemented in a way that minimises the disadvantage which would result to people of the opposite sex. For example, in the case *Abrahamsson and Anderson v Fogelqvist* [43], the Swedish government, in order to remedy to women's under-representation in professorial posts within universities, introduced a rule that gave preference to female candidates. This rule provided that female candidates who had sufficient qualifications for the post would be given preference, even if they were less well qualified compared to candidates of the opposite sex, provided that the difference was not so great that it would compromise objectivity in the making of these appointments. The CJEU ruled that this measure was unlawful because, although increasing women's numbers in professorial posts where they were significantly under-represented was a legitimate aim, the application of the rule was nonetheless disproportionate in that it infringed the principle of individual merit as it did not provide for any room for an individual assessment of each candidate's circumstances to take place.

Having examined the legal boundaries around the use of positive action measures established by the CJEU, we now consider more closely the content of s. 159 of the UK 2010 Equality Act.

4. The 'Equal Merit' Requirement

Section 159 requires that candidates are "as qualified as each other" and it is important to emphasise that this is not the same as saying that candidates must be "equally qualified". The term "equally qualified" was expressly rejected by the legislator when this provision was being developed since it was argued that the concept of "equally qualified" would lead employers to take a narrow interpretation "by considering the provisions as being solely about the equality of qualifications per se . . . [and] as a requirement that candidates have identical qualifications" [44]. It was stressed that qualifications are only one component of any assessment of candidates and that their suitability for a particular job will depend on a combination of different factors which may include, for example, experience, skills and competences as well as candidates' performance during the actual recruitment process. Thus, the judgement as to whether two candidates are "as qualified as each other", in other words whether they are of "equal merit" in relation to the requirements of a particular post, will depend on a comprehensive and objective (as objective as human judgement can be!) assessment undertaken by recruiters. Furthermore, in line with the legal principles discussed above, s. 159 expressly states that positive action must be "a proportionate means of achieving the aim" of overcoming disadvantage or of remedying the under-representation of candidates with a protected characteristic. This requirement of proportionality reflects the need, as seen above, to allow for the assessment of individual merit. Moreover, it is not a mandatory provision and employers can choose whether to make use of it, provided that they do not have a policy which automatically treats more favourably those with a protected characteristic.

Having set out the legal framework which underpins positive action in recruitment and promotion, the next section seeks to challenge the arguments which are commonly deployed against the adoption of "positive action" in recruitment and promotion.

5. Five Reasons Why Positive Action in Recruitment and Promotion Should Be Used

As outlined earlier, five main objections can be identified which are commonly raised against the use of any form of preferential treatment to increase gender equality in leadership roles and these are discussed and challenged in turn.

Objection one: That it is trying to remedy to women's under-representation by using reverse discrimination against men, but "two wrongs" do not make a right.

This logic is based on a model of formal equality that understands "equality as sameness" which operates in a symmetrical way by treating like cases alike [45], as seen earlier. However, the shortcomings of such an approach have been recognised by several legal scholars, including the difficulty of identifying when likes are indeed alike [45,46]. Thus, the meaning and purpose of equality has been the subject of extensive debate [38,46,47] which has shifted from a formal understanding of equality to a more substantive one, that "rejects an abstract view of justice and instead insists that justice is only meaningful in its interaction with society" [48] (p. 235). It is not within the scope of this article to examine all different constructs of substantive equality. However, for the purpose of contesting this objection, it is helpful to focus on a more substantive model of equality which is underpinned by the idea of social inclusion. This model encompasses both the idea that equality should be seen as a means of breaking the cycle of disadvantage suffered by some groups, as well as the idea that all groups in society should be given opportunities to participate in various aspects of civic life, including work [45,49]. This focus on social inclusion, as highlighted by Vickers [50], provides the best theoretical underpinning for a more pro-active approach to equality and to positive action. Therefore, if s. 159 is considered from the perspective of equality and inclusion, the possibility of giving priority to a candidate from an under-represented group in a tie-break situation should be seen both as a way of breaking the cycle of disadvantage as well as a way of ensuring fair participation from different groups. Thus, it is suggested that the use of positive action, far from trying to remedy an injustice with another injustice, should be seen as a tool to correct existing injustice and to ensure that, in the interest of society as a whole, all groups are fairly represented within the different organisational layers of an institution.

Objection two: Positive action measures in recruitment and promotion would undermine meritocracy.

One of the most common objections to the use of positive action in recruitment and promotion is that it would undermine meritocracy and the key principle of appointing the best candidate, regardless of their gender or other characteristics. This kind of objection is underpinned by powerful arguments as exemplified by Pojman [51] (p. 112) who highlighted that "by giving people what they deserve as individuals rather than as members of groups, we show respect for their inherent worth" and that society can be "better off" if the best people are employed. Most people would agree with these ideas and it is the intention of this article to argue that far from undermining meritocracy the type of positive action measure in question would ensure that meritocracy is truly implemented and that people are given what they deserve and do not miss out because they are members of a disadvantaged group.

First of all, it is important to recognise that meritocracy as a concept has two meanings: a general one and a relative one. The general meaning of meritocracy is informed by the principles of justice and equity which require that everybody should be rewarded according to their talent and achievements which, as highlighted by Pojman, shows respect for an individual's inherent worth. The second meaning of meritocracy, however, is relative to a particular context and is defined by the way in which the principle that everybody should be rewarded according to their talent and achievements is applied in practice within a particular working context. These are two distinctive meanings which conceptually tend to be conflated. The principles that underpin the general concept of meritocracy are unlikely to be disputed but we ought to recognise that the persistent underrepresentation of women in senior leadership roles, in spite of being employed in large numbers in the HE sector, suggests that either women are not sufficiently talented to progress into leadership roles or that in practice the application of the principle of meritocracy is dysfunctional. The first hypothesis is clearly flawed since, if nothing else, it would run counter to the fact that talent is randomly distributed among men and women. Therefore, the second hypothesis which suggests that the construction and application of the principle of meritocracy in practice is dysfunctional, is more likely to be valid. There are several reasons that can explain such dysfunctionality and they will be examined in turn.

First of all, it is important to note that the definition of merit is not "value neutral" [27] (p. 743) since it can be measured according to different parameters such as "talent and ability" or "effort and achievements". Therefore, depending on the parameters which are used and how these relate to prevailing norms of a particular organisation, one person may appear more meritorious than another. Moreover, Thorton [52] suggests that there are two aspects to the construction of merit: an objective one and a subjective one. The objective aspect relates to verifiable factors such as qualifications, skills, work experience and so on. While the subjective one refers to the actual interpretation of these factors given by decision makers, involved in the recruitment and selection or promotion process. The difficulties with the subjective dimension relating to the interpretation of the actual criteria are well illustrated by a study about professorial promotion practices in HE [53] (p. 1473). This found that the interpretation of the criteria is "often characterised by confusion and contradiction" and that it can end up being "the perfect breeding grounds" for institutional micropolitics where "manipulation" may occur "in order to filter out or favour certain candidates". In organisations where senior leadership roles have been occupied predominantly by men, as is the case with HE, merit is likely to be constructed in masculine terms which have become the norm [13]. Therefore, notions of merit which present themselves as neutral are actually the product of masculine norms. Thus "merit" may become a new form of sexism [54] which denies that women are being discriminated in senior appointments and this ultimately, as highlighted by McNamee and Miller [55], can reinforce the status quo and "help those in power to perpetuate their privilege". Moreover, empirical research by Castilla and Benard [56] (p. 543) shows that organisational culture which promotes meritocracy paradoxically can result in greater bias in favour of men.

As seen earlier, women with experience of applying for senior leadership roles in the HE sector talked about leadership being "*too narrowly defined*" and that they felt that those responsible for recruitment or promotion would not see them in a leadership role. All this points to the risk that, perversely, the concept of meritocracy may end up being used to reward those who are members of the same group as those who are already in power rather than rewarding genuinely deserving individuals and "show respect for their inherent worth".

A further line of criticism that can be levelled against the "myth of meritocracy" is that it is based on a flawed assumption that we make fully rational decisions which seek to optimise outcomes; that, for example, in a recruitment situation those responsible for making an appointment will be guided by their rationality to optimise the process' outcomes and appoint the best possible candidate. Whilst optimising decisions and appointing the best candidate may be the intention, this may not happen in practice because our decision-making process is limited by our "bounded rationality" [57]. This theory stresses the complexity of reality which involves a multiplicity of options that go well beyond an individual's ability to process all the available information. Therefore, in order to manage this complexity in our decision-making process we use mental short-cuts (known as heuristics) which are shaped by the environment we live in and the kind of experiences we are exposed to. These short-cuts direct our brain to look for familiar patterns and this can explain why some women felt that people could not see them in senior leadership roles which are usually occupied by men. These are the kind of mental processes that can create cognitive biases [58] and are responsible for erecting *invisible barriers* against those candidates, such as women or BMEs, who do not look like the "*familiar type*" of leader. Conversely, for those candidates who, instead, look like the "*familiar type*" of leader, these kinds of mental processes can result in preferential treatment in their favour with some men being appointed not because they are the "best" but simply because they look "good enough" to fill the role. The question then is to what extent can we control and overcome these mental processes?

Many HE institutions offer or even require people who are likely to be part of senior appointment panels to undertake unconscious bias training and to become aware of heuristics and how these can influence their decisions. However, unconscious bias training, although undoubtedly helpful in raising awareness about these mental processes, is not a panacea and may not be sufficient to counter cognitive bias in practice, nor to challenge a notion of merit which has been constructed in masculine terms and is seen as the norm.

Therefore, it is argued that positive action, as permitted by s. 159, could be a useful tool to correct the bias which may occur in the construction of merit in two main ways. First of all, it would induce decision makers to undertake a more careful assessment of job applicants of different genders in order to establish whether they are "as qualified as each other". This would help them to be vigilant about their heuristics, avoid being drawn by candidates who look like the "familiar type" of leader, most likely to be men, and push the boundaries of their rationality to engage with alternative career paths and meaning of success which, although unfamiliar, may prove to be equally meritorious if not even more deserving. Thus, far from undermining the elusive concept of meritocracy, the use of positive action in recruitment and promotion could actually improve the decision-making process and genuinely lead to the appointment of the best candidate as opposed to the "good enough" one.

Another point worth considering is that tie-break situations are not unusual and when they do happen, in order to differentiate between two candidates who appear to be equally appointable, recruiters are likely to resort to the notion of "best fit" and select the candidate who presents more similarities with the existing groups and current organisational culture. Once again, regardless of individual merit, this is likely to favour those who are more likely to fit the existing organisational demographic rather than those who belong to under-represented groups. Noon [27] (p. 733) suggests that if "diversity" is a stated strategic objective, as it would be in the case of Higher Education Institutions, then in a tie-break situation it would be appropriate to adopt as an additional criterion "the organisational context and needs" to achieve greater diversity and use this criterion to make a final decision between two candidates who are equally appointable. This argument is strengthened by Lady Hale's comments, currently the only female judge in the UK Supreme Court, who believes that "diversity is an indispensable feature of democracy"that, for example, would justify the adoption of positive action measures [59] in the judiciary. Thus, from this perspective, diversity becomes an important additional criterion. In the specific case of HE, this can be a very compelling argument on at least on two counts: firstly because women represent more than half of the student population (56%) [60] as well as of the whole of the workforce (54%) [1] in the sector and, therefore, these levels of representation must be fairly reflected in senior posts; secondly, because HE plays a key role in shaping societal values and, unless the sector moves into a position where it can lead by example with regard to gender equality, it still lacks legitimacy.

Objection three: To judge whether two candidates are as qualified as each other is too difficult and who wrote the law has no experience of selection and recruitment processes.

As discussed earlier, research suggests [34] that HR directors in the sector are reticent about the use of positive action in a tie-break situation. Some feel that there is always a best candidate, that two candidates are never the same, while others do not see the measure as an easy one to implement in practice. In order to challenge this objection, it may be useful to draw a parallel with equal pay legislation. Initially, equal pay legislation only applied to men and women who were doing the same or broadly similar work. However, this broadly symmetrical approach did not help to address the systematic undervaluing of some predominantly female occupations such as care work, education and health where gender occupational segregation was left unchallenged. It was only when the principle of equal pay for work of equal value was introduced by legislation that "stereotypical classifications [of work] came under fire" [61] (p. 242). It has been highlighted that the right to claim equal pay for work of equal value had "a revolutionary potential because it asserts the right to override the determination of 'value' by the employer, and merely to undermine the male norm".

The concept of work of "equal value" was put to the test for the first time in the UK in the case of *Hayward v Cammell Laird* [62] and in the subsequent landmark case of *Enderby v Frenchay Health Authority* [63]. In this case, the work of a speech therapist employed by the NHS was deemed to be of equal value to that of hospital pharmacists, a predominantly male occupation, who received a higher rate of pay than speech therapists. As cases such as this demonstrate, the concept of "equal value" required employers and trade unions to re-appraise what jobs, predominantly done by women, actually entailed and "remove the inherent bias towards men in existing job evaluation systems"[61] (p. 243). Thus, it was possible to compare completely different jobs in order to ascertain whether the kind of expertise and skills required for different types of work could be comparable in terms of actual value and therefore, deserve the same amount of pay.

The notion of equal pay for work of equal value is now a well tried and tested concept which is regularly applied by HEIs as well as by other organisations through the use of job evaluation schemes, in order to ensure that male and female employees are paid fairly and to avoid or reduce the incidence of possible equal pay claims. Thus, although the assessment of "equal value" may be a complex exercise in practice, requiring the comparison of different sets of skills, qualifications and expertise to ensure that these are equitably remunerated, it is in fact a well-established practice among human resource practitioners. Therefore, there is no reason why HEIs which have dedicated human resource (HR) management departments should not draw on the expertise of their own HR practitioners to develop criteria to help assess when candidates can be deemed to be "as qualified as each other". This, for example, could become part of the training for staff involved in recruitment and selection.

Moreover, there are already examples relating to selection and recruitment practices where the assessment of applicants' skills, qualification and expertise are made on the basis of a more substantive evaluation, rather than on a formal one. For example, it is not uncommon for job specifications relating to administrative jobs in HE to require certain qualifications such as a degree or an "equivalent". The proviso of "an equivalent" is intended to avoid overlooking potential applicants, who may be perfectly capable of doing the job, but do not hold certain types of qualifications. The proviso ensures that such candidates are not excluded from the selection process due to their lack of formal qualifications. This is particularly important given that some people belonging to older generations, when fewer people attended university, may not have a university degree but this fact is compensated by their work experience. Similarly, it is not uncommon for some people to join academia later in life, having worked in a professional capacity in sectors like Education, Law or Health. People with a professional background are less likely to hold a doctorate, which would be normally required for an academic role yet they bring equally valuable practical expertise to an academic role. In both of these examples, the lack of formal qualifications would be compensated by experience and expertise acquired in practice. Thus, in these examples the proviso for an "equivalent" to a particular qualification prevents some job applicants from being indirectly disadvantaged either because of their age group or their professional background and ensures that talented people are not overlooked. It can be seen how provisions designed to encourage the adoption of a more substantive and less formal approach to assess job applicants can lead to a fairer selection process, can overcome structural barriers and ensure better outcomes for employers.

Therefore, it is argued that useful lessons can be learned from the equal pay legislation and, in particular, from the application of the concept of work of "equal value" to counter the objection that having to assess whether two candidates are "as qualified as each other" would be too complicated. It would certainly be of some complexity as the experience around the equal pay legislation indicates, but equally, as that experience shows, it could help recruiters to unpack gender stereotypes and challenge the "male norm" which, as discussed earlier, often underpins the way in which the very concept of leadership is constructed. Having to consider whether two candidates are "as qualified as each other" and thus of equal merit, would start a process of evaluation that would make institutions have to re-appraise what is valued in leadership roles and how merit is assessed. This process could have a "revolutionary potential" in helping to override a gendered construction of merit.

Objection four: Women or other under-represented groups want to be appointed to a job because of their merits and not because of positive action.

Concerns by women and other disadvantaged groups about the possibility of being appointed to a job as a result of some form of preferential treatment rather than for their abilities is well documented [64,65]. However, such concerns would be understandable if they were given an automatic preference simply because of their gender. As we have seen earlier, the use of positive action in a tie-break situation presupposes that applicants have the appropriate qualifications and experience to be included in the recruitment and selection process in the first place. Therefore, if a female candidate is given preference on the basis that she is deemed to be of equal merit to a male candidate, she would have to be a serious contender and have demonstrated through the process that she is appointable to the role. The CJEU has clearly highlighted, as discussed above, the need for ensuring that when positive action measures are applied, the process allows for an individual assessment of the merit of all the candidates involved. Thus, women candidates would need to demonstrate their ability to do the job and decision makers would need to have carefully considered all the candidates on their own individual merits, regardless of their gender.

Objection five: That changing the numbers by increasing women's representation does not guarantee a change in the organisational culture.

In the case of *Kalanke*, referred to earlier, the Advocate General Tesuaro commented that: "Formal numerical equality is an objective which may salve some consciences but it will remain illusionary ... " (p. 665). The fact that changing the numbers is not enough to achieve substantial change in organisations is often used as an argument against the use of interventions to increase gender diversity. However, although creating a critical mass of women in senior posts may not be sufficient to achieve wholescale change, it is nonetheless a necessary starting point to achieve change. Some may argue that a greater presence of women in leadership roles does not guarantee that these women will articulate the interests of other women and pro-actively promote greater gender equality. However, even if we accept that this may be the case, greater women's presence in these roles is still likely to be beneficial as it will bring different perspectives in the decision-making process and "cast light on assumptions that the dominant group perceive as universal and, enhance the store of 'social knowledge'" [48] (p. 266). This can help to avoid the pitfalls of group thinking and improve the quality of the decision-making process within organisations. Critical mass is also necessary to overcome tokenism and to establish a "self-correcting mechanism" [48] (p. 268). These arguments relate to the internal dynamics of organisations and how these may be changed by having a critical mass of women. An additional argument relates to the importance of having role models to encourage other women to aim for leadership roles and to counter the implicit assumptions existing in society which associate men with leadership roles. Thus, although it may not be enough to increase the numbers of women in roles where they are currently under-represented, these arguments demonstrate that if progress is to be made, it is nonetheless necessary to have a critical mass of women in these roles.

6. Final Reflections and Conclusions

The arguments developed above challenge the objections which tend to be commonly raised against the use of positive action in recruitment and promotion and provide a compelling case for HEIs to seriously consider the use of s. 159 when making decisions about recruitment and promotion relating to senior roles. First of all, these arguments highlight the importance of adopting a more substantive approach to equality that can break the cycle of disadvantage and lead to greater inclusion of women in the decision-making and governing structures of HEIs. This requires overcoming a major conceptual barrier as the principle of equal treatment has taught us to ignore identity categories like gender, race, age and other personal characteristics, when making decisions about the distribution of benefits like jobs and promotions. Many institutions would demonstrate their commitment to equality by claiming to be "gender blind" but the application of positive action in a tie-break situation instead requires them to be "gender conscious", taking into account candidates' identity. It is important that decision makers understand that candidates' identity would not be taken into account per se but to achieve an outcome of substantive equality and to remedy subtle forms of second-generation discrimination which, as seen earlier, can result in indirectly discriminatory and exclusionary practices.

Positive action in recruitment and promotion should be seen as a tool to achieve greater substantive equality and tackle a gendered construction of merit which is at the core of the "invisible barriers" faced by women throughout their careers. A gendered construction of merit leads to overrepresentation of men in senior roles which, in a sector where women represent half of the workforce, clearly points to the existence of dysfunctionality in the system. Simon's theory of bounded rationality [57] discussed earlier explains the complexity of decision-making processes and how these can result in less than optimum outcomes which favour those candidates who look like the "familiar type" of leader, rather than genuinely looking for the best candidates. As suggested by Sturm [40] (p. 463), organisations need to develop the capacity through problem solving "to identify, prevent and redress second generation bias" which results, for example, from patterns of interaction, informal norms and networks. We have seen before that the introduction of the concept of work of equal value has proved to be a powerful instrument to achieve better equal pay outcomes, as it has required institutions to develop the capacity to tackle stereotypical classifications of work based on the male norm. In a similar vein, this article argues that the concept of equal merit, which underpins the use of positive action in a tie-break situation, could help to develop decision makers' capacity to unpack gender stereotypes, surface structural bias and re-appraise how merit is assessed. This could challenge "decisions which are formally fair but functionally biased in favour of the dominant group" [40] (p. 473) and "the net effect would be to neutralise unfair advantage" which is enjoyed by those who benefit from a "systematic biased approach" [39] (p. 649).

Some may argue that a focus on positive action in recruitment and promotion may not be enough to tackle structural and systemic gender issues across institutions. In response to this, a model is proposed to provide a framework for enabling institutions to use the learning from the application of positive action in recruitment and promotion for senior roles to self-reflect on their practices and how merit is constructed and assessed throughout women and men's careers. This model seeks to establish a "virtuous circle" by taking the following steps: the first step would involve setting aspirational targets to increase gender diversity in senior roles across an institution. Although increasing numbers of women in senior roles may not be enough, it is nonetheless necessary to create a critical mass for change as discussed earlier. Moreover, targets provide a benchmark and help to focus the minds of those who need to make change happen. HEIs use targets all the time, for example about the number of students that they want to recruit or the amount of funding that they want to attract and, therefore, there is no reason why they should not adopt gender targets. The second step would involve the adoption of positive action in recruitment and promotion and the development of institutional capacity to unpack gender stereotypes and assess equal merit. The learning from this process would lead to a better understanding of what it means to be successful in the fast changing environment of HE and ensure that different ways in which excellence can be demonstrated are acknowledged and properly rewarded. This, in turn, would lead to the third step which would involve the adoption of a more inclusive idea of success. This should permeate the way institutions develop careers and it would not only benefit women but other under-represented groups, moving away from a narrowly constructed notion of leadership around the male norm. Finally, this process would accomplish a "virtuous circle" which would lead to the achievement of the set targets and close the gender gap in leadership roles as illustrated by Figure 1 below.

In conclusion, this article has aimed to provide a better understanding of the use of positive action in recruitment and promotion and to articulate a set of arguments, not only to challenge the conceptual objections commonly raised against this type of measure, but also to open a debate in the HE sector about the need to use this provision to re-assess the very concept of merit. Gender awareness and not gender blindness must be at the core of the decision-making process to tackle stereotypes and structural bias and s. 159 of the 2010 Equality Act offers an instrument to help mitigate and ultimately eliminate bias in decision-making processes and institutional practices.

Figure 1. Creating a "virtuous circle" to close the gender gap.

Conflicts of Interest: The authors declare no conflict of interest.

References

1. Equality Challenge Unit. Equality in Higher Education Statistical Report Part 1: Staff. Available online: http://www.ecu.ac.uk/publications/equality-in-higher-education-statistical-report-2016/ (accessed on 22 January 2017).
2. Jarboe, N. Women Count. In *Leaders in Higher Education 2016*; Women Count: Wlaes, UK, 2016. Available online: https://womencountblog.files.wordpress.com/2016/03/women-count-2016-leaders-in-he-020316.pdf (accessed on 5 February 2016).
3. European University Association. More Women Become University Leaders–Equality Still Far Away. Available online: http://www.eua.be/activities-services/news/newsitem/2016/05/13/more-women-become-university-leaders---equality-still-far-away (accessed on 26 May 2017).
4. Morley, L. *Women and Higher Education Leadership: Absences and Aspirations*; Leadership Foundation for Higher Education: London, UK, USA, 2013.
5. Funding for Higher Education in England for 2015–2016: HEFCE Grant Letter from BIS. Available online: http://www.hefce.ac.uk/news/newsarchive/2015/Name,100772,en.html (accessed on 15 October 2016).
6. Higher Education Funding Council for England Business Plan 2015–2020. Available online: http://www.hefce.ac.uk/about/plan/ (accessed on 15 October 2016).
7. Equality Challenge Unit. *Governing Bodies, Equality and Diversity in Scottish Higher Education Institutions*; Equality Challenge Unit: London, UK, 2015.
8. Berthoin Antal, A.; Izreali, D.N. A global comparison of women in management: Women managers in their homelands and as expatriates. In *Women in Management: Trends, Issues and Challenges in Managerial Diversity*; Fagenson, E., Ed.; Sage: Newbury Park, CA, USA, 1993; pp. 52–96.
9. Alimo-Metcalfe, B. Leadership: A masculine past, but a feminist future? In *Gender and Excellence in the Making*; European Commission: Brussels, Belgium, 2004.
10. Gronn, P.; Lacey, K. Cloning their own: Aspirant principals and the school-based selection game. *Aust. J. Educ.* **2006**, *50*, 102–121. [CrossRef]
11. Doherty, L.; Manfredi, S. Improving women's representation in senior positions in universities. *Employ. Relat.* **2010**, *32*, 138–155. [CrossRef]

12. Sinclair, A. Not Just 'Adding Women in': Women Re-Making Leadership. Melbourne Business School. Available online: http://works.bepress.com/cgi/viewcontent.cgi?article=1006&context=amanda_sinclair (accessed on 2 October 2016).

13. Sinclair, A. A feminist case for leadership. In *Diversity in Leadership*; Damousi, J., Rubenstein, K., Tomsic, M., Eds.; ANU Press: Canberra, Australia, 2014; Available online: http://press.anu.edu.au/apps/bookworm/view/Diversity+in+Leadership/11321/ch01.xhtml (accessed on 2 October 2016).

14. Billing, Y.D. Are women in management victims of the phantom of the male norm? *Gend. Work Organ.* **2011**, *18*, 298–317. [CrossRef]

15. Ibarra, H.; Ely, R.J.; Kolb, D.M. Women rising: The unseen barriers. *Harv. Bus. Rev.* **2013**, *91*, 60–66.

16. Morley, L. Lost leaders: Women in the global academy. *High. Edu. Res. Dev.* **2014**, *33*, 114–128. [CrossRef]

17. Thorvaldsottir, T. *Engendered Opinions in Placement Committee Decisions*; University of Iceland: Reykjavík, Iceland, 2002.

18. Foschi, M. Blocking the use of gender-based double standards for competence. In *Gender and Excellence in the Making*; European Commission: Brussels, Belgium, 2004; pp. 51–55.

19. Moss-Racusin, C.; Dovidio, J.; Brescoll, V.; Graham, M.; Handelsman, J. Science faculty's subtle gender biases favor male students. *Proc. Nat. Acad. Sci. USA* **2012**, *109*, 16474–16479. [CrossRef] [PubMed]

20. Valian, V. *Why So Slow? The Advancement of Women*; MIT Press: Cambridge, MA, USA, 1999.

21. Fisher, V.; Kinsey, S. Behind closed doors! Homosocial desire and the academic boys club. *Gend. Manag. Int. J.* **2014**, *29*, 44–63. [CrossRef]

22. O'Conner, P. Irish Universities: Male dominated? Limits and possibilities for change? *Equal. Divers. Incl. Int. J.* **2012**, *31*, 83–96. [CrossRef]

23. Deem, R. Gender, organisational cultures and the practice of manager-academic in UK universities. *Gend. Work Organ.* **2003**, *10*, 239–259. [CrossRef]

24. Bailyn, L. Academic careers and gender equity: Lessons learned from MIT. *Gend. Work Organ.* **2003**, *10*, 137–153. [CrossRef]

25. Rees, T. Measuring excellence in scientific research: The UK research assessment exercise. In *Gender and Excellence in the Making*; European Commission: Brussels, Belgium, 2004; pp. 117–123.

26. Manfredi, S.; Grisoni, L.; Handley, K.; Nestor, R.; Cooke, F. *Gender and Higher Education Leadership: Researching the Careers of Top Management Programme Alumni*; Leadership Foundation for Higher Education: London, UK, 2014.

27. Noon, M. The shackled runner: Time to rethink positive discrimination. *Work Employ. Soc.* **2010**, *24*, 728–739. [CrossRef]

28. Johns, N.; MacBride-Stewart, S.; Powell, M.; Green, A. When is positive action not positive action? Exploring the conceptual meaning and implications of the tie-break criterion in the UK Equality Act 2010. *Equal. Divers. Incl. Int. J.* **2014**, *33*, 97–113. [CrossRef]

29. Forbes, I. Equal opportunity: Radical, liberal and conservative critiques. In *Equality, Politics and Gender*; Meehan, E., Sevenhuijsen, S., Eds.; Sage: Thousand Oaks, CA, USA, 1991.

30. Jewson, N.; Mason, D. The theory and practice of equality policies: Liberal and radical approaches. *Sociol. Rev.* **1986**, *34*, 307–334. [CrossRef]

31. Kirton, G.; Green, A.M. *The Dynamics of Managing Diversity*; Buttherworth-Heineman: Oxford, UK, 2010.

32. Equalities Office. Employers: Quick Start Guide to Positive Action in Recruitment and Promotion Government. Available online: https://www.gov.uk/government/publications/employers-quick-start-guide-to-positive-action-in-recruitment-and-promotion (accessed on 25 May 2017).

33. Davies, C.M.; Robison, M. Bridging the gap: An exploration of the use and impact of positive action in the United Kingdom. *Int. J. Discrim. Law* **2016**, *16*, 83–101. [CrossRef]

34. Manfredi, S.; Vickers, L.; Cousens, E. *Increasing the Diversity of Senior Leaders in Higher Education: The Role of Executive Search Firms*; Leadership Foundation for Higher Education: London, UK, 2017.

35. Hepple, B. *Equality the New Legal Framework*; Hart Publishing: Oxford, UK, 2011.

36. Liff, S.; Ans Wajcman, J. Sameness and difference revisited: Which way forward to equal opportunities initiatives? *J. Manag. Stud.* **1996**, *33*, 73–94. [CrossRef]

37. Rees, T. *Mainstreaming Equality in the European Union: Education, Training and Labour Market Policies*; Routledge: London, UK, 1998.

38. O'Cinneide, C. Positive action and the limitations of existing laws. *Maastricht J. Eur. Law* **2006**, *13*, 351–364. [CrossRef]

39. Barmes, L. Equality law and experimentation: The positive action challenge. *Camb. Law J.* **2009**, *68*, 623–654. [CrossRef]
40. Sturm, S. Second generation employment discrimination: A structural approach. *Columbia Law Rev.* **2001**, *101*, 458–568. [CrossRef]
41. *Kalanke v Freie Hansestadt Bremen* (1995) C-450/93.
42. *Marschall v Land Nordrhein Westfalen* (1997) C-409/95.
43. *Abrahamsson and Anderson v Fogelqvist* (2000) C-407/9.
44. Hansard HL vol 717 col 658 (9 February 2010) (Baroness Royall).
45. Fredman, S. *Discrimination Law*, 1st ed.; Oxford University Press: Oxford, UK, 2002.
46. Barnard, C.; Hepple, B. Substantive equality. *Camb. Law J.* **2000**, *59*, 562–585. [CrossRef]
47. Hepple, B. The aims of equality law. In *Current Legal Problems*; Oxford University Press: Oxford, UK, 2008.
48. Fredman, S. *Discrimination Law*, 2nd ed.; Oxford University Press: Oxford, UK, 2011.
49. Collins, H. Discrimination, equality and social inclusion. *Mod. Law Rev.* **2003**, *66*, 16–43. [CrossRef]
50. Vickers, L. The expanded public sector duty: Age, religion and sexual orientation. *Int. J. Discrim. Law* **2011**, *11*, 43–58. [CrossRef]
51. Pojman, L. The case against strong affirmative action. *Int. J. Appl. Philos.* **1998**, *12*, 97–115. [CrossRef]
52. Thorton, M. Merit in a legal frame. In *Pathways to Gender Equality in Australia. The Role of Merits and Quotas*; Rodgers-Healey, D., Ed.; Australian Centre for Leadership for Women: Sydney, Australia, 2015.
53. Van den Brink, M.; Benschop, Y.; Jansen, W. Transparency in academic recruitment: A problematic tool for gender equality? *Organ. Stud.* **2010**, *31*, 1459–1483. [CrossRef]
54. Briskin, L. Merit, Individualism and solidarity. Revisiting the democratic deficit in Union Women's Leadership. In *Gendering and Diversifying Trade Union Leadership*; Ledwith, S., Hansen, L.L., Eds.; Routledge: New York, NY, USA, 2013.
55. McNamee, S.J.; Miller, R.K.J. *The Meritocracy Myth, Rowman*; Littlefield, Lanham: Mitchellville, MD, USA, 2004.
56. Castilla, E.J.; Benard, S. The paradox of meritocracy in organisations. *Adm. Sci. Q.* **2010**, *55*, 543–572. [CrossRef]
57. Simon, H.A. Bounded rationality. In *The New Palgrave: A Dictionary of Economics*, 1st ed.; Eatwell, J., Milgate, M., Newman, P., Eds.; Palgrave Macmillan: London, UK, 1987; pp. 266–268.
58. Equality Challenge Unit. Unconscious Bias in Higher Education. Available online: http://www.ecu.ac.uk/wp-content/uploads/2014/07/unconscious-bias-and-higher-education.pdf (accessed on 22 January 2017).
59. Mallenson, K. Diversity in the judiciary: The case for positive action. *J. Law Soc.* **2009**, *36*, 376–402. [CrossRef]
60. Equality Challenge Unit. Equality in Higher Education Statistical Report Part 2: Students. Available online: http://www.ecu.ac.uk/publications/equality-in-higher-education-statistical-report-2016/ (accessed on 22 January 2017).
61. Fredman, S. *Women and the Law*; Oxford University Press: Oxford, UK, 1997.
62. *Hayward v Cammell Laird* [1988] IRLR 257 (HL).
63. *Enderby v Frenchay Health Authority* (1992) C-127/92.
64. Cockburn, C. Equality: The long and short agenda. *Ind. Relat. J.* **1989**, *20*, 213–225.
65. Cockburn, C. *The Way of Women: Men's Resistance to Sex Equality in Organisations*; Macmillan: Basingstoke, UK, 1991.

administrative
sciences

MDPI

Article

Fixing the Women or Fixing Universities: Women in HE Leadership

Paula Burkinshaw [1,*] and Kate White [2]

[1]   Leeds University Business School, The University of Leeds, Leeds LS2 9JT, UK
[2]   Faculty of Education and Arts, Federation University Australia, Mount Helen VIC 3350, Australia;
      kate.white@federation.edu.au
*   Correspondence: p.burkinshaw@leeds.ac.uk

Received: 3 July 2017; Accepted: 14 August 2017; Published: 21 August 2017

Abstract: The lack of women in leadership across higher education has been problemitised in the literature. Often contemporary discourses promote 'fixing the women' as a solution. Consequently, interventions aimed at helping women break through 'the glass ceiling' abound. This article argues that the gendered power relations at play in universities stubbornly maintain entrenched inequalities whereby, regardless of measures implemented for and by women, the problem remains. The precariousness for women of leadership careers is explored through two separate but complementary case studies (from different continents and different generations) each one illuminating gender power relations at work. The article concludes by arguing that it is universities themselves that need fixing, not the women, and that women's growing resistance, particularly of the younger generation, reflects their dissatisfaction with higher education leadership communities of practice of masculinities.

Keywords: women in higher education; gender and leadership; gendered power relations

1. Introduction

This paper examines two generations of women leaders using two different case studies—the first, Vice-Chancellors (VCs) in the UK and the second, younger women at a newer Australian university who were in middle management positions or are aspiring to management jobs—and how increasing job insecurity and continuous organizational restructuring affects gender power relations at work. The case studies each involved different methods; in the first qualitative interviews with VCs and in the second a quantitative survey, which included provision for additional comments, with mid-career women who were middle managers or aspiring to management. Thus, the study examines data from a sample of top women leaders in UK universities, and a case study of the next generation of women leaders who completed a professional leadership development program for women in an Australian university. The richness of data from these varied sites and methods helped to uncover the exclusionary structures and practices and seemingly entrenched gender power relations experienced by women at all levels of leadership in universities, and how the precariousness of women's university careers compounds these relations.

The data generated from both sites and methods was analysed through a communities of practice of masculinities lens as the theoretical framework underpinning the study. Briefly, this theoretical framework builds on the work of Paechter (2003) who applied the concept of communities of practice to the learning of gender (through communities of practice of masculinities) and this study borrows the extension of her work by Burkinshaw who argues that this also applies to higher education leadership (Burkinshaw 2015).

Adm. Sci. **2017**, *7*, 30

1.1. Literature Review

Gender pervades structures and processes in organisations. Karatas-Ozkan and Chell elucidate the notion of gendering by describing gender as: "A powerful ideological device, which is produced and reproduced in social situations as the interactional scaffolding of social structure and the social control processes that sustain it" (Karataş-Özkan and Chell 2015, p. 12). Organisational culture, Bagilhole et al. suggest, is a dynamic process that can be conceived as something an organization has, something an organization is, and something an organization does (Bagilhole et al. 2007). In relation to management the concept of organizational culture has been used to refer to a complicated fabric of management myths, values and practices that legitimize women's position at the lower levels of the hierarchy and portray managerial jobs as primarily masculine (O'Connor 2011, p. 168). However, organizational structure is not gender neutral and organizational culture reflects the wishes and needs of powerful men. Thus, the ideal worker is male: "Images of men's bodies and masculinity pervade organizational processes, marginalizing women and contributing to the maintenance of gendered segregation in organisations" (Acker 1990, p. 139).

A key impact of organizational masculinity is the emotional labour expended by women in order to succeed. We refer to this emotional labour throughout the paper because it underpins the experience of many women in leadership, an additional pressure to their workload which continues to reify masculine cultures.

The transition in organizational culture from collegial to managerial governance has been a feature of universities in the past few decades (Bolden et al. 2012). Meek (2002, p. 55) explains that "increasingly pressure has been placed on universities to institute strong managerial modes of operation". Deem (1998, p. 47) argues that 'new managerialism' is characterized by public sector organisations adopting "organisational forms, technologies, management practices and values more commonly found in the private business sector", and it is suggested that this managerialism "gnaws away at professional autonomy and control" so "the power status, and role of academics in university governance and management have declined" (Deem et al. 2008, pp. 22–27); see also (Bolden et al. 2012).

Managerial universities value research above all other academic activities and especially value and reward academics who bring external funding to the organization (Acker et al. 2010). This emphasis impacts disproportionately on women who often have less success in accessing funding (Faltholm and Abrahamsson 2010). So, has new managerialism benefitted or hindered the careers of academic women? Carvalho and Machado-Taylor assert that it is not possible to identify a single impact of new managerialism on gender dominant notions or on the impact it may have on gender power relations (Carvalho and Machado-Taylor 2009). Rather, there are a myriad of non-convergent directions in the way it influences gender in organisations. However, Parsons and Priola argue that managerial universities reinforce rather than reduce gender inequalities (Parsons and Priola 2010), while Lynch et al. maintain that senior management positions in managerial universities are gendered as they are assumed to be care-free; "those appointed are assumed to be available to participate in a long-hours work environment that precludes having responsibility for primary care work" (Lynch et al. 2012, p. 200).

A great deal of literature focuses on gendered career paths in higher education. The gendering of particularly academic careerscan often be established for some women during PhD candidature through lack of support and mentoring and sponsorship particularly in relation to advice about career paths and in the early career phase (Van den Brink 2009), and can then persist throughout the careers of women in universities (see, for example, (Etzkowitz and Kemelger 2001)). Early career academics often juggle career and family. Ward and Wolf-Wendel argue that both motherhood and academic work are 'greedy institutions,' demanding total commitment and dedication (Ward and Wolf-Wendel 2012). Academic mothers must negotiate both institutions without sufficient time, support, and resources in either.

Academic women are therefore often building their careers later than their male colleagues, and are less likely to have a traditional trajectory starting as a lecturer and then progressing through the ranks to senior lecturer, associate professor and full professor (Bagilhole and White 2011). Women in administrative roles are more likely than male colleagues to have interrupted careers and to work part-time. Consequently, women in universities face increasingly precarious career paths due to lack of job security, the impact of managerialism and heavy workloads (Bagilhole and White 2013; White et al. 2011; O'Connor 2014). And although the representation of women in leadership roles has increased, it is mostly in administrative areas (Burkinshaw 2015). While Sandberg (2013) argues that women in leadership roles can improve working conditions for all women in organisations, one of her critics asserts that "Relying on one woman at the top, or even a handful, to understand what all women below them need and to act on that is simply naïve" (Covert 2013).

Hence, the focus is often on women's deficits in HE leadership rather than the "organisational culture as the problem and take[ing] a systemic approach to re-visioning work cultures" (De Vries and Webb 2005). Such explanations, O'Connor asserts: "implicitly or explicitly define women as 'the problem' and so obviate the need to look at intra-organisational culture and procedures in explaining these patterns" (O'Connor 2011, p. 179). Whereas, successful leaders in organisations question work cultures by carefully interpreting uncertainty for colleagues across the institution and frame the current situation in ways that collaboratively connect with others, so this helps to reposition organisational work cultures as problematic rather than (women) leaders (Fairhurst 2011). Fundamentally higher education leadership cultures are manifest through communities of practice as the prerequisites are well satisfied: domain of knowledge; community of people; and shared practice (Wenger 1998). Through participation in the leadership community its members establish norms and build collaborative relationships. Their interactions as members create a shared understanding of what brings them together, their joint enterprise. As part of its practice, leadership communities produce communal resources, their shared repertoire. Communities of practice provide a context for people to learn: learning skills, knowledge, behaviours and attitudes; in other words, learning leadership. Members of (leadership) communities of practice hold certain status—apprentice, legitimate peripheral participation, and full member—with some remaining as outsiders (other) who never fully belong. The *other* is an outlier, on the margins and sometimes not even tolerated. *Othering* is barely acceptable even when mainstream behaviours are absent such that leaders practicing their gender through femininities are familiar with feelings of *othering*. This positioning transfers into the workplace where *othering* is reinforced and reproduced by (leadership) communities of practice of masculinities (Paechter 2003). As the literature on communities of practice shapes the theoretical framework for this study it is explored further in the methodology section below. Furthermore, the framework used to analyse data from the two case studies was communities of practice of masculinities and femininities which Burkinshaw found help us to learn about leadership in higher education (Burkinshaw 2015). Fundamentally leadership is a community performance which historically learned masculinities.

While much has been written about women not measuring up to the demands of the modern managerial university (Bagilhole and White 2011; O'Connor 2014), women themselves assert that they have been marginalized in the gendered research economy (Lynch et al. 2012; Morley 2014) which perpetuates their continued under-representation. Although managerialism in higher education can provide opportunities for women to develop their careers, in reality it perpetuates and even intensifies the gendered organizational culture (Acker 1990). Thus, women report being more affected by heavy workloads (Barrett and Barrett 2011) often due to the precariousness of their contracts, combined with their wish to 'do a good job' (Kandiko Howson et al. 2015).

Thus 'the problem is women' appears to shift the responsibility towards programs and measures aimed at 'fixing the women' and away from the organisation reflecting on a culture that is not generally encouraging to women. This emphasis on fixing the women helps to rationalise why women are not progressing in their careers (Ely and Meyerson 2000). Such a 'deficit model' focuses on why women do not measure up to HE leadership roles and does not inspire confidence in building career paths or in their institution, adding yet again to the precariousness of their leadership careers. Not surprisingly some women can become ambivalent about their role in the academy and disengage

(Blackmore and Sachs 2007), while others look at and dismiss HE leadership, making a conscious decision in the current organizational context not to seek leadership roles (Morley 2014).

It can therefore be asserted that the organizational culture of higher education needs fixing (Fitzgerald and Wilkinson 2010), rather than the women. This viewpoint emphasises the social justice case for women not continuing to be marginalised in HE and raises the question about whether or not "it is in society's interest to perpetuate lack of diversity in senior leadership positions" (O'Connor et al. 2015).

1.2. Methodology

The first case study was semi-structured interviews with 18 senior women professors who were leading UK higher education institutions (normally as vice-chancellor/principal/president) between 2010 and 2013. The second study was an on-line survey in March and April 2014 which was an evaluation of a professional leadership development program for women (the Women in Leadership (WiL) program) at a newer Australian university undertaken nine months after its completion. 53 per cent of the 85 participants completed the survey which is the average for reported response rates in the field (Baruch and Holtom 2008). While most of the survey questions required responses on a five point Likert scale, they also provided an opportunity for respondents to make comments. This is a mixed methods study. It merges two different data sets—the first qualitative interviews and the second a quantitative survey—and uses different methods to address the research problem (Creswell and Plano-Clark 2008). The study does not seek to directly compare these two individual cases. Thus, this research design enables the findings to be generalized to different groups (Morse 2003). The study also acknowledges the similarity in the context of higher education in Australia and the UK. Australian universities were traditionally based on the British model and universities in both countries operate within national equal opportunities legislative frameworks.

The above literature review introduced the theoretical framework which was used to analyse the data from the two case studies. This framework is higher education leadership communities of practice of masculinities (and femininities). Burkinshaw found that exploring women in leadership through the lens of communities of practice of masculinities helps to illuminate HE leadership cultures and the learning of leadership (Burkinshaw 2015). Communities of practice engender networks of full members, apprentices or those practising 'legitimate peripheral participation' (Wenger 1998), whereby membership at any level requires 'fitting in' to some extent. Membership of these networks helps create "individual and group identity" (Wenger 1998, p. 73) and "learning full participation in a community of masculinity or femininity practice is about learning one's own identity and how to enact it" (Paechter 2003). Thus gender is fluid, not a fixed state, so precarious in itself, meaning that learning leadership and power relations in higher education are also fluid and determined to some extent by membership of these communities of practice. So fundamentally leadership is a community performance which historically inevitably learned masculinities because people learn to be leaders within higher education through leadership communities of practice and these predominantly perform masculinities. Moreover, these communities define their membership by initiating emerging leaders as novices, apprentices (practicing legitimate peripheral participation) and (for some) full members. By using communities of practice of masculinities to interpret the learning of leadership we allow for the fluidity of boundaries across and between different masculinities and femininities and for local and negotiated ways of being. This recognises how resistant these communities are to change and that leadership (and leaders) can be constrained by membership of communities of practice of masculinities. Hence communities of practice of masculinities traditionally have shaped leadership practices and forged the status quo and we are therefore using leadership communities of practice as a framework to analyse our data. The interviews from the UK case study were transcribed by the interviewer, so analysis started at that point. Themes emerged both inductively from the interview data as well as having been framed by the questions which were also informed by the literature. The data analysis software Atlas Ti helped to code these themes during the analysis process. In the Australian case study, thematic analysis was undertaken in the light of themes emerging from the data in conjunction with those from the literature.

We argue that this theoretical framework underpinning our data analysis helps us to understand whether or not women are 'fitting in' to those HE networks (communities of practice) which are crucial for career enhancement. This argument is strengthened by Williams' (Williams 2012) repudiation of 'ideal worker norms' which are reinforced by lack of flexibility in working practices despite equality policies (which she describes as 'shelf paper'). These ideal worker norms (long hours' culture, prioritization of work, support from home) are reproduced by communities of practices of masculinities which deny flexibility and even create 'flexibility stigma'. Williams found that 33% of professors did not request parental leave because they feared career penalties. Similarly, our framework builds on women's experiences of homosociability in the workplace (O'Connor 2014) whereby male (and female) members of leadership networks (communities of practice of masculinities) are continually "mobilising masculinities" which exclude and disadvantage "the other" (Martin 2001, p. 589), Burkinshaw proposes that this framework of higher education leadership communities of practice can contribute to the absence of networking for women (Burkinshaw 2015), another performative practice crucial to building leadership power relations and careers.

Overall our framework reflects higher education gender power relations that involve exclusionary structures and practices which are exacerbated by precarious careers. For the women in our studies this means more pressure on the one hand on their emotional workload of 'fitting in' to get on, or on the other hand resistance to taking on more leadership communities of practice (O'Connor 2001). Fundamentally we argue that our theoretical framework helps to explain the seemingly intransigent nature of leadership cultures thus perpetuating the status quo. Nevertheless, more hopefully, we also show through both our case studies that a combination of agency and dedicated initiatives has a potential to bring about change. For example, a recent initiative in the UK is 'Sci Sisters', a scientific sisterhood with the aim of building a network that underpins deserved confidence among senior women and highlights excellence (http://www.chemicalimbalance.ed.ac.uk/scisister/).

2. Results

2.1. Case Study 1

The first case study found that even women who had succeeded to very senior roles in UK higher education still experienced precarious careers in the process. Although it might be expected that women who had reached top positions would be treated with respect by senior colleagues, their experience of leadership could often be quite confronting and be characterized by men behaving in an aggressive, loud and domineering manner, particularly in meetings with other senior managers. As one interviewee described it:

> Just them [men] being louder, talking more, dominating more, whether it's round the board table or any kind of meeting men tend to be more assertive and more confident about what they are saying and they express what they are saying in a different way as well. Women use words like, perhaps, potentially, like, might wish, but the sayings, the verbs and adjectives for men are different ones. The language they use is different.

Another interviewee made a similar observation:

> I think a lot of male leaders repeat themselves and use up air time, this is a bit tricky, and I think that there is a danger for women if they do that because women who take up air time will be seen to be taking up air time and men are not seen to be taking up air time so women can't behave like that because it's not seen the same way.

It seemed here like a case of women being dammed if they do and dammed if they don't. What is being described are acceptable ways of behaving for men in HE leadership ('repeat themselves and use up air time') which are nevertheless not acceptable for women 'so women can't behave like that because it's not seen the same way'. The double bind is that women can try hard at 'fitting in' but they cannot do so in the way that men do. However, it is not clear what *is* an acceptable mode of behaviour for senior women in HE.

Consequently, women were aware that they were operating in a highly competitive environment (Acker 1990), where it was often hard to be heard, where their performance was evaluated differently and where they were not being promoted by their peers, as the following interviewee explained:

> there's something about this rather male dominated environment that says they see these pushy bright men as having more potential. Women who are perhaps not shouting so much about what they are doing, I don't know what it is, who are actually good or sometimes better at work are not being tapped on the shoulder.

Women then were often ignored by talent spotters in favour of 'pushy bright men'. The issue here was that women needed to more loudly promote their potential.

For women to be promoted through the gendered organisational hierarchy they needed to work hard at 'fitting in' to masculine models of leadership, often denying their femininity:

> It might be a male culture but there are certain things you cannot do at work. Losing emotional control, you cannot do. It's a sort of no-no.

Again, what is being described is a narrow masculinist definition of acceptable behaviour in HE leadership usually associated with transactional leadership (Currie et al. 2002). On the one hand, senior male managers can be aggressive, loud and overbearing, but on the other women cannot express themselves in a way that leads to losing emotional control. Women as leaders often prefer a more open, expressive style described as transformational leadership; that is, to use an interactive style, share power and information, use personal power, enhance people's self-worth, and make them feel part of the organization (Rosener 1990). Lipman-Blumen (1992) similarly talks about connective leadership styles—collaborative, contributive and mentoring behaviour—in which women excel. But it is evident that HE leadership continues to reward transactional leadership.

Ultimately part of this 'fitting in' was to also understand how leadership operated within higher education and how masculinist leadership was the only acceptable form of leadership, rather than to challenge these accepted norms, as the following interviewee explained:

> I think leadership is defined by powerful leadership, it's if you look at the words you use to describe leaders they tend to be male words and sometimes they put in the odd thing about nurturing and engaging people, that's a girly thing. Things like that. They tend to be male in that sense. Actually, the way that the leadership club works tends to be like that, a club. Let's have a beer. Let's meet for breakfast. That's all the constructs about meetings. You go to meetings and you have to stand from the floor and orate. That's a very male thing, rather than sitting down and having a discussion.

This description elaborates on the aggressive domineering behaviour described above. As well as the aggression, there are strict rules of conduct for university leaders—the language they use (which is male) and ways of networking which operate like a male club with rituals such as having a beer or having breakfast together. This 'clubbiness' then translates into how HE leaders behave in more formal settings: in meetings men stand from the floor and orate—suggesting a sense of performance and needing to impress that reinforces a sense of entitlement men have as university leaders (Bagilhole and White 2013). In contrast, women might prefer to sit down and discuss an issue.

The picture painted here was of exclusionary structures and practices that reflect traditional male values, consistent with Acker's view. There seemed to be no room for experimenting with a different leadership style. A consultative style—sitting around the table—was not condoned, nor was taking a less definite position in discussions—and using words like 'perhaps, potentially, like, might wish'. Rather, HE leaders needed to be confident and assertive and did this by 'being louder, talking more, dominating more'. This robust homosociability in HE leadership, also observed by O'Connor and Lynch et al. (O'Connor 2014; Lynch et al. 2012), demonstrates strong communities of practice of masculinities and provides the context in which women build their careers.

These women Vice-Chancellors had a choice about whether or not they wished to pursue leadership ambitions, given that they fully understood the masculinist context in which university leadership operates. So, in order to be successful, they had to learn to navigate and negotiate the gendered organisational culture in order to overcome its obstacles for women, as the following interviewee explains:

> I think sometimes women think that they do have to behave in this way too. Probably I find myself occasionally doing it and recognizing it's not my natural way of behaving and I see it occasionally in other women. Whether it's the women that get into roles like that have a bit of male feistiness about them and they are prepared to put themselves in that position or when they are there they change their behaviour. It's about survival partly.

It was evident here that this woman VC had to behave differently in order to fit in, and had to suppress her preferred leadership style or even to explore what might be an alternative style with which she was comfortable ('it's not my natural way of behaving'). Such a straightjacket could be the high price women paid to become successful leaders. The note that 'It's about survival partly' suggests that once women make a decision to pursue leadership roles and ultimately reached top jobs, there was little room to move; it was merely a matter of working out strategies to survive in order to maintain their position.

For women who had reached top positions, survival in HE leadership could come in many forms as demonstrated in the following two examples. One woman discussed decisions that needed to be made about how she dressed and the impact that had on perceptions of her leadership:

> I look at my own personal growth I think personally in trying to establish how I am comfortable operating. In the early days, it was power suit dressing time and there was a lot of emulating of what men would have done. I was not immune to that. I think nurture versus nature. You are influenced by what's going on and what you are about.

She admitted to being influenced by power dressing for women and trying to emulate men. In this description, there seems to be little room to move in choosing appropriate clothes for the role or exploring what clothing might be appropriate. So even a small matter such as what to wear in the role becomes precarious for women in HE leadership, as an example of a seemingly insignificant obstacle with serious consequences. Thus, dressing is performative too, subtly reinforcing critical gender and leadership norms, again reflecting assumptions about 'the ideal worker'. Similarly, another woman VC spoke about dress and not 'frightening the horses' in the way that women leaders dressed and behaved:

> So, I think there's a group going through where there is a range of masculinity. It's not just what you wear, that you have to wear a suit. It's not that. It's, the way I see it, it's by being female and entering the room I am different. I can extenuate or reduce the differences. And that puts them at their ease.

The price women therefore needed to pay to be successful in top jobs in HE was to strictly conform to accepted male norms of what a leader looked like and how they should behave. This interviewee saw it as a woman's responsibility in a senior position 'to put them at their ease', yet the mechanism for doing so was not clear. How is a woman expected to dress and behave to achieve this outcome? Therefore, in order to 'fit in' women were continually walking a tightrope because of the exclusionary structures and practices embodied through communities of practice of masculinities that made their leadership much more precarious than was the case for male colleagues.

2.2. Case Study 2

The participants in the second case study were both academic and administrative women who were either in middle management positions or who were aspiring to management roles, and were mostly in their 30s and 40s. The survey responses indicated that the Women in Leadership program at this newer Australian university provided skills and knowledge to assist career development. Most were positive about their participation and the opportunities it presented for building careers. Several mentioned strategies gained that helped them to deal with the prevailing communities of practice of masculinities: One participant had "more confidence in [the] ability to express views and learnt new negotiation skills", and another reported: "I am not easily intimidated when trying to communicate with the wider university's internal stakeholders. I now negotiate successfully with external parties as well".

But the program was less effective in providing a better understanding of the organisation, and some participants were critical of gender discrimination in the increasingly managerial university. They were clear, as the following quotes indicate, that universities were not a level playing field for women; males dominated leadership positions and gender disparities were obvious:

> Women at this institution are so poorly represented in leadership.

> I believe that women face different challenges to men. It is difficult to break into a traditionally male domain in higher education.

> The academic environment of the university-sector is generally masculinised; strong "boys" networks are in operation; academic promotion still favours male applicants. Issues confronting women are different, as they generally have many conflicting roles to juggle because of the glaring gender inequities in the workplace.

These women perceived themselves to be outsiders in the masculinist HE culture. They saw women as underrepresented as leaders, as unable to permeate the male domain, as excluded from male networks, and as needing to try that bit harder because they were women. Communities of practice of masculinities were therefore impacting on their experience of the workplace and excluding them from full participation. In some senses, their observations of men as HE leaders were not too dissimilar from the women in the first case study. But the difference between the two case studies is that the women VCs had been conditioned by the masculinist culture and decided nevertheless to pursue careers in leadership, while women in the second case study as a younger generation with a raised consciousness of gender discrimination were mostly standing on the periphery, and not wanting to be a part of this organizational culture (O'Connor 2014). Therefore, women in the leadership pipeline still perceived universities as focusing on fixing the women rather than the structure or culture of the organization, as the following respondent so incisively remarked:

> much of the 'advice' was focused on us changing rather than us working together to fix the system that is the problem. Without real "buy in" from the university's leadership and our male colleagues nothing will change.

She saw a gender mainstreaming approach—where both women and men are involved in changing the organizational culture—as the only way to fix the system and create a culture that would be more welcoming to women. Without the university's leadership demonstrating commitment to change there could be no transformation of gender relations.

Two other respondents identified weak and inadequate leadership in the organization as the main barrier to women's career advancement:

> I felt we were being encouraged to 'play the game' to get ahead and then 'manage' people so that they do what we want regardless of the adverse effects this may have on them. While this may pass as leadership at [the case study university], it really isn't.

> ... my overall experience is one of frustration because, in isolation, such a program changes nothing—I do not see any evidence of the leadership of the university doing anything to improve things for their women employees and I do not want more 'leaders' trained in ways that emulate the poor leadership I see throughout our university.

There was a strong sense of frustration, even anger, in these comments. And the message was consistent: stop trying to fix the women and instead try to improve working conditions and career opportunities for women. At the same time, they argued that the university needed to also focus on the impact of poor (mostly male) leadership models on those they managed. Presumably the solution was to 'fix the system' by greatly improving the predominantly masculinist models of leadership throughout the university, instead of offering programs to 'fix the women' that trained leaders in the same mould as the existing leadership.

Most participants were not encouraged by the program to seek new positions or look for further opportunities within the organisation, often because of their difficult work situation. A related narrative was about the stress that the current organizational restructure was causing to some participants and the impact of heavy workloads on their health and wellbeing—characteristic associated with managerial universities (Lynch et al. 2012; Bagilhole and White 2011)—as this respondent described:

> Work is a very stressful place at times and I am at a very unstable place at present. I used to be able to cope with workplace stress but in the last two years I am less able to cope. I do not think as clearly as I used to and it is almost like I have forgotten everything I know.

This is a worrying comment. It was evident that instability in the workplace and stress were all taking their toll and negatively impacting on the ability of the woman to think straight and to remember. Another had a similar experience, saying that as a result of the program: "I realised I was not coping with work life at the university". A further participant's response, after finishing the program, was resistance to the prevailing organizational culture: "Having time to think about my career and to learn and reflect on the workings of our university has had an impact ... this has acted to convince me that I am a poor fit with this university".

The program overall did not have any significant impact on the career aspirations of participants in the medium term because many felt marginalised and were unhappy and so stressed they had little time for reflection. Therefore, it had not encouraged career planning.

These women were insightful in their analysis of the problem and argued that aspiring to HE leadership was not a priority in the current organizational climate with its exclusionary structures and practices. Unless the managerial culture of the university could be changed and what they considered poor leadership could be overhauled by introducing gender mainstreaming, they would remain on the periphery. Thus, the above narratives reinforce a resistance model evident in the experiences of these younger mid-career women. They took a social justice view that fixing the university leadership model/culture could help to address the disengagement and disempowerment of women.

3. Discussion

These two case studies of two different generations of women in or aspiring to leadership in higher education indicated that they experienced gender power relations that impacted on their careers. It is not our intention to juxtapose the two case studies or to present our findings as in opposition, an either/or scenario. Instead the rich data which emerged from our international research sites explores the lived experiences of women in higher education leadership throughout their careers and the challenges masculine cultures pose for them.

The women in the first case study headed up UK universities and had learnt throughout their careers to navigate and negotiate the gendered and gendering leadership culture, and these skills were partly responsible for their success. Only when these senior women leaders had made it to the top did they feel more secure in leadership to the extent that they could 'be themselves' to some extent, while still acknowledging the straight jacket that hegemonic masculinities created for them.

Yet this research with very senior women found that being a minority creates precariousness in itself. As Charles notes, women aspiring to senior management positions "in order to be accepted ... have to behave in ways which are appropriate to the organization and the job" (Charles 2014, p. 368). Invariably during their careers women in this study had been the 'only woman in the room' and their experience of continually adapting to this minority status was emotional hard labour. Othering oneself and being othered is a precarious existence indeed, with these women positioned as outsiders on the inside (Gherardi 1995) or what can be described in communities of practice of masculinities as not yet full members.

Referring back to the explanation of our theoretical framework in the introduction, we concur that invariably the women in both our research sites had merely achieved 'legitimate peripheral participation' in leadership communities of practice of masculinities, whereas their male counterparts achieved full membership almost by default. These communities of practice function on an organisational level (as well as individually of course) to constitute gendered understandings. For example, symbolically organisational masculinity creates reification of leadership codes. Similarly, the myth of organizational rationality whereby the way universities operate through their structures, processes, and practices reinforces masculinities (Acker 1990). So much so that leadership communities of practice of masculinities work to reinforce organizational cultures where masculine power is promulgated (and sometimes resisted) (Burkinshaw 2015). Yet ironically, the women in the first case study were top university leaders operating successfully within this masculine organizational context. However, it was only once a 'critical mass' of diversity was achieved that these women felt more secure in leadership, at whatever level. They argued that this critical mass helped to dilute their insecurity and inevitable precariousness, although any minority needs to reach beyond 30 per cent for this to occur (Erkut et al. 2008). This finding reinforces our argument regarding the entrenched organizational exclusivity of HE leadership communities of practice of masculinities, where lack of diversity in organisational leadership at all levels is both cause and effect. A major feature of communities of practice of masculinities is that they are policed from within by existing full members who generally shun difference thus perpetuating masculine organizational cultures. Nevertheless, Martin and O'Meara's study demonstrates how strategies used by women leaders can challenge and change institutional culture to advance gender inclusion (Martin and O'Meara 2017), although the experience in Austria, for example, indicates that the use of quotas to get more women into leadership positions does not necessarily impact on the organizational culture (Wroblewski 2014).

The lived experiences of these women VCs reflect how precarious women's careers are within the exclusionary culture of higher education, and this finding echoes the research of O'Connor and of Morley (O'Connor 2014; Morley 2013). Their inevitably unique stories bear many similarities across the different organizations they led, fundamentally of the gendered nature of 'doing' leadership and the precariousness of 'fitting in' to leadership communities of practice. Their career stories help illuminate the choices and challenges faced by women on their leadership journey, culminating in a level of unevenness in their careers, and extra requirements on their job specification, apparently not experienced by many of their male colleagues. Of course, this is not to deny the agency of these women leaders (at all stages of their careers but especially in their most senior roles) which enables them to infiltrate and adapt leadership communities of practice for the better, perhaps reflecting the tension between more traditional male leadership styles and the requirements of modern universities for collaborative leadership. By performing leadership differently, they are influencing higher education leadership culture, however slowly. This is hopeful for the future, despite much evidence to the contrary. Williams agrees that workplace expectations are changing albeit recalcitrantly (Williams 2012). Maybe entrenched masculinities practices will be successfully challenged by younger, more agentic leaders coming through. Strategies such as professional leadership development for women can help equip this challenge, as we observed in our Australian research.

In this second case study, the impact of managerialism on the organizational culture was clear. In managerial universities decisions are from the top down, the influence of academics is reduced, and the focus is on accountability, evaluation and economic efficiency (Goransson 2011). Managerialism positions women as outsiders in competitive, managerial regimes (Lynch et al. 2012). Thus, some participants felt excluded and were strongly critical of what they perceived as a failure of leadership during this period of uncertainty in their increasingly managerial university. They spoke of the stress that poor leadership and continuous change created in their working lives. Their views reflected Bolden et al.'s observation that managerialism leads to "diminishing opportunities for academics to self-determine their own sense of direction and in so doing undermining their commitment to the institution and the profession" (Bolden et al. 2012, p. 37).

The present research therefore found that the precarious work environment did not encourage women in the leadership pipeline to be pro-active in building their careers as they confronted communities of practice of masculinities. These women were critical of the program as an initiative of management to help women to deal with rapid organizational change. Rather, they asserted that they needed more support to deal with the current restructure and the uncertainty it created, and this finding resonates with that of Carvalho et al. (2013). And similar to Sluis' observation of younger academics (Sluis 2012), they were incisive in their analysis of how the organizational culture needed to change to enable them to have decent careers. Some of the participants had seriously looked at moving into more senior roles and, like those in Morley's study (Morley 2014), were dismissing careers in higher education leadership.

Once again, our findings illuminate the theoretical framework, because leadership communities of practice of masculinities are more visible to these enlightened mid-career women. As women in the leadership pipeline they had been observing older women at the top having to fit in to get on. But many of these emerging senior leaders were uncomfortable about negotiating homophilious network apprenticeships in this way and were unwilling to settle for 'legitimate peripheral participation' either. Hence, there was evidence of resistance to traditional career paths and ambitions (Bagilhole and White 2013; Blackmore and Sachs 2007) which highlights tensions in higher education leadership whereby the environment increasingly demands collaborative approaches which generally do not flourish within masculine models. Therefore, women's missing agency is not sufficient to explain their continuing underrepresentation in senior positions in higher education; instead "talented and ambitious women may be disadvantaged by a number of structural factors associated with the recruitment and selection process for senior posts" (Shepherd 2017, p. 5).

4. Conclusions

This comparative study of two generations of women at different levels in two different countries found marked similarities in their experience of the gendered organizational culture in British and Australian higher education. Leadership communities of practice made it difficult for them to progress in their careers. Clearly the women VCs had learnt to accommodate the prevailing organizational culture in consolidating their careers on the way up to top jobs, but few considered that even as VCs they could change this culture, possibly owing to their minority status at the top—reinforcing gender power relations and exclusionary structures and practices. Nevertheless, they had mostly learnt to 'fit in' to get on, arguably choosing to fix themselves and adapt to an entrenched masculine culture rather than fixing universities. However, the younger women in the leadership pipeline mostly questioned if the price of accommodating the organizational culture to progress their careers was worthwhile (Wroblewski 2014). The current leadership in their institution did not inspire them and they resented the pressure that continuous organizational restructure placed on their working lives. Their response was ambivalence (Bagilhole and White 2013; Blackmore and Sachs 2007) or resistance (O'Connor 2001).

It can therefore be concluded that leadership communities of practice produce and reproduce hegemonic masculinities (Karataş-Özkan and Chell 2015) shaping gendered power relations and harnessing the emotional labour of fitting in to get on. While higher education continues to focus on fixing the women rather than fixing the university culture, many women currently in top management or newly appointed to management may continue to experience precarious leadership careers and those aspiring to leadership positions may struggle to find motivation to invest in further career progression. With younger, aspirational women in the leadership pipeline resisting senior leadership, exclusionary structures and practices will prevail across and beyond higher education. We recommend further research to explore this resistance more fully and to see how leadership communities of practice might be challenged, given this resistance.

Author Contributions: Each author was responsible for conducting their case study and both authors have analysed the data and written this article.

Conflicts of Interest: The authors declare no conflicts of interest.

References

Acker, Joan. 1990. Hierarchies, jobs, bodies: A theory of gendered organisations. *Gender and Society* 4: 139–58. [CrossRef]

Acker, Sandra, Michelle Webber, and Elizabeth Smyth. 2010. Discipline and publish? Early career faculty meet accountability governance, new managerialism and (maybe) gender equity. Paper presented at the Gender, Work and Organisation Conference, Keele University, Staffordshire, UK, June 21–23.

Barbara Bagilhole, and Kate White, eds. 2011. *Gender, Power and Management: A Cross Cultural Analysis of Higher Education*. Basingstoke: Palgrave Macmillan.

Barbara Bagilhole, and Kate White, eds. 2013. *Generation and Gender in Academia*. Basingstoke: Palgrave Macmillan.

Bagilhole, Barbara, Abigail Powell, Sarah Barnard, and Andrew Dainty. 2007. *Researching Cultures in Science, Engineering and Technology: An Analysis of Current and Past Literature*. London: UKRC.

Barrett, Lucinda, and Peter Barrett. 2011. Women and academic workloads: Career slow lane or Cul-de-Sac? *Higher Education* 61: 141–55. [CrossRef]

Baruch, Yehuda, and Brooks Holtom. 2008. Survey response rate levels and trends in organisational research. *Human Relations* 6: 1139–60. [CrossRef]

Blackmore, Jill, and Judyth Sachs. 2007. *Performing and Reforming Leaders: Gender, Educational Restructuring, and Organisational Change*. Albany: State University of New York Press.

Bolden, Richard, Jonathon Gosling, Anne O'Brien, Kim Peters, Michelle Ryan, and Alex Haslam. 2012. *Academic leadership: Changing Conceptions, Identities and Experiences in UK Higher Education*. London: Leadership Foundation for Higher.

Burkinshaw, Paula. 2015. *Higher Education, Leadership and Women Vice Chancellors; Fitting into Communities of Practice of Masculinities*. Basingstoke: Palgrave.

Carvalho, Teresa, and Maria Machado-Taylor. 2009. Gender and shifts in higher education managerial regimes. Paper presented at the 6th Gender Equality in HE Conference, Stockholm, Sweden, August 5–9.

Carvalho, Teresa, Ozlem Ozkanli, Heidi Prozesky, and Helen Peterson. 2013. Careers of Early and Mid-career Academic. In *Generation and Gender in Academia*. Edited by Barbara Bagilhole and Kate White. Basingstoke: Palgrave, pp. 127–68.

Charles, Nickie. 2014. Doing Gender, Practising Politics: Workplace cultures in local and devolved government. *Gender, Work and Organisation* 21: 368–80. [CrossRef]

Covert, Bryce. 2013. Lean In, Trickle Down: The False Promise of Sheryl Sandberg's Theory of Change. *Forbes*. Available online: https://www.forbes.com/sites/brycecovert/2013/02/25/lean-in-trickle-down-the-false-promise-of-sheryl-sandbergs-theory-of-change/#44def4634256 (accessed on 10 May 2017).

Creswell, John, and Vicki Plano-Clark. 2008. *Mixed Methods Reader*, 1st ed. Thousand Oaks: Sage.

Currie, Jan, Bev Thiele, and Patricia Harris. 2002. *Gendered Universities in Globalized Economies*. Lanham: Lexington Books.

De Vries, Jen, and Claire Webb. 2005. Gender in mentoring: A focus on the mentor; evaluating 10 years of a mentoring programme for women. Paper presented at the 4th European Conference on Gender Equality in Higher Education, Oxford, UK, August 31–September 3.

Deem, Rosemary. 1998. New managerialism and higher education: The management of performance and cultures in universities in the UK. *International Studies in Sociology of Education* 8: 47–70. [CrossRef]

Deem, Rosemary, Sam Hilliard, and Michael Reed. 2008. *Knowledge, Higher Education and the New Managerialism*. Oxford: Oxford University Press.

Ely, Robin, and Debra Meyerson. 2000. The Challenge and Importance of Maintaining a Gender Narrative. *Organisation* 7: 589–608.

Erkut, Samru, Vicki W. Kramer, and Alison M. Konrad. 2008. Critical Mass: Does the Number of Women on a Corporate Board Make a Difference? In *Women on Corporate Boards of Directors: International Research and Practice*. Edited by Susan Vinnicombe, Val. Sing, Ronald J. Burke, Diana Bilimoria and Morten Huse. Cheltenham: Edward Elgar New Horizons In Management Series, pp. 222–32.

Etzkowitz, Henry, and Carol Kemelger. 2001. Gender Equality in Science: A Universal Condition? *Minerva* 39: 239–57. [CrossRef]

Fairhurst, Gail. 2011. Leadership and the Power of Framing. *Leader to Leader* 2011: 43–47. [CrossRef]

Faltholm, Ylva, and Lena Abrahamsson. 2010. I prefer not to be called a woman entrepreneur—Gendered global and local discourses of academic entrepreneurship. Paper presented at the Gender, Work and Organisation Conference, Keele University, Staffordshire, UK, June 21–23.

Fitzgerald, Tanya, and Jane Wilkinson. 2010. *Travelling towards a Mirage? Gender, Leadership & Higher Education*. Mt. Gravatt: Post Pressed.

Gherardi, Silvia. 1995. *Gender, Symbolism and Organisational Cultures*. London: Sage.

Goransson, Anita. 2011. Gender Equality and the Shift from Collegiality to Managerialism. In *Gender, Power and Management: A Cross Cultural Analysis of Higher Education*. Basingstoke: Palgrave, pp. 50–77.

Kandiko Howson, Camille B., Kelly Coate, and Tania De St Croix. 2015. Mid-Career Academic Women: Strategies, Choices And Motivatio. In *Small Development Projects, Engage*. London: Kings Learning Institute, Kings College.

Karataş-Özkan, Mine, and Elizabeth Chell. 2015. Gender Inequalities in Academic Innovation and enterprise: A Bourdieuian Analysis. *British Journal of Management* 26: 109–25. [CrossRef]

Lipman-Blumen, Jean. 1992. Connective Leadership: female leadership style in the 21st century. *Sociological Perspectives* 35: 183–203. [CrossRef]

Lynch, Kathleen, Bernie Grummell, and Dympna Devine. 2012. *New Managerialism in Education: Commercialization, Carelessness and Gender*. Basingstoke: Palgrave.

Martin, Patricia Y. 2001. Mobilising masculinities: Women's experiences of men at work. *Organisation* 8: 587–618.

Martin, Amy, and KerryAnn O'Meara. 2017. Conditions Enabling Women's Leadership in Community Colleges. In *Critical Approaches to Women and Gender in Higher Education*. Edited by Pamela Eddy, Kelly Ward and Tehmina Khwaja. New York: Palgrave Macmillan, pp. 61–86.

Meek, Lynn. 2002. On the road to mediocrity? Governance and management of Australian higher education in the market place. In *Governing Higher Education: National Perspectives on Institutional Governance*. Edited by Alberto Amaral, Glen Jones and Berit Karseth. Amsterdam: Kluwer, pp. 253–78.

Morley, Louise. 2013. The rules of the game: Women and the leaderist turn in higher education. *Gender and Education* 25: 116–31. [CrossRef]

Morley, Louise. 2014. Lost leaders: Women in the global academy. *Higher Education Research & Development* 33: 114–28.

Morse, Janice. 2003. Principles of mixed methods and multimethod research design. In *Handbook of Mixed Methods in Social and Behavioral Research*. Edited by Abbas Tashakkori and Charles Teddlie. Thousand Oaks: Sage, pp. 189–208.

O'Connor, Pat. 2001. A bird's eye view...Resistance in Academia. *Irish Journal of Sociology* 10: 86–104. [CrossRef]

O'Connor, Pat. 2011. Where do women fit in university senior management? An analytical typology of cross national organisational cultures. In *Gender, Power and Management: A Cross Cultural Analysis of Higher Education*. Edited by Barbara Bagilhole and Kate White. Basingstoke: Palgrave, pp. 168–91.

O'Connor, Pat. 2014. *Management and Gender in Higher Education*. Manchester: Manchester University Press.

O'Connor, Pat, Teresa Carvalho, Agnete Vebo, and Sonia Cardosa. 2015. Gender in higher education: A critical review. In *The Palgrave International Handbook of Higher Education Policy and Governance*. Edited by Jeroen Huisman, Harry De Boer, David Dill and Manuel Souto-Otero. Basingstoke: Palgrave, pp. 569–83.

Paechter, Carrie. 2003. Masculinities and femininities as communities of practice. *Women's Studies International Forum* 26: 69–77. [CrossRef]

Parsons, Elizabeth, and Vincenza Priola. 2010. The micro-politics of feminism in the managerial university. Paper presented at the Gender, Work and Organisation Conference, Keele University, Staffordshire, UK, June 21–23.

Rosener, Joan. 1990. Ways women lead. *Harvard Business Review* 68: 119–25. [PubMed]

Sandberg, Sheryl. 2013. *Lean In: Women, Work and the Will to Lead*. New York: Alfred A. Knopf.

Shepherd, Sue. 2017. Why are there so few female leaders in higher education? A case of structure or agency? *Managament in Education* 31: 82–87.

Sluis, Rhonda. 2012. The ambivalent academic. *Journal of Nursing Education* 51: 63–65. [CrossRef] [PubMed]

Van den Brink, Marieke. 2009. Behind the Scenes of Science: Gender Practices on the Recruitment and Selection of Professors in the Netherlands. Ph.D. Thesis, University of Nijmegen, Nijmegen, The Netherlands.

Ward, Kelly, and Lisa Wolf-Wendel. 2012. *Academic Motherhood: How Faculty Manage Work and Family.* New Brunswick: Rutgers University Press.

Wenger, Etienne. 1998. *Communities of Practice: Learning, Meaning and Identity.* Cambridge: Cambridge University.

White, Kate, Teresa Carvalho, and Sarah Riordan. 2011. Gender, Power and Managerialism in Universities. *Journal of Higher Education Policy and Management* 33: 179–86. [CrossRef]

Williams, Joan C. 2012. *Reshaping the Work Family Debate: Why Men and Class Matter.* Cambridge: Harvard University Press.

Wroblewski, Angela. 2014. Female participation in management and cultural change: Precondition or high expectation. In Proceedings of the GWO Conference, Keele University, Staffordshire, UK, June 24–26.

administrative sciences

MDPI

Article

Frank and Fearless: Supporting Academic Career Progression for Women in an Australian Program

Polly Parker [1,*], Belinda Hewitt [2], Jennifer Witheriff [1] and Amy Cooper [1]

[1] Business School, University of Queensland, St. Lucia, QLD 4067, Australia; j.witheriff@uq.edu.au (J.W.); a.cooper@uq.edu.au (A.C.)
[2] School of Social and Political Sciences, University of Melbourne, VIC 3010, Australia; belinda.hewitt@melbourne.edu.au
[*] Correspondence: p.parker@uq.edu.au

Received: 20 December 2017; Accepted: 22 February 2018; Published: 27 February 2018

Abstract: The underrepresentation of women in senior positions continues to be a major challenge in higher education and most other industries. In Australia, the career trajectory for academic women stalls at a lower level than that of their male counterparts. Concern about this situation in one Australian university led to the design and delivery of a career progression program to support women's advancement from senior lecturer to associate professor. This study details the main features of the program, designed to facilitate women's transition from being leading academics to academic leaders through a focus on leadership and career progression. We report the participants' perceptions of its value based on survey data. We conclude that leadership development is difficult work and requires a supportive environment where risk-taking is encouraged, where frank and fearless feedback is provided, and where the individual is required to examine assumptions and biases and to assume a leadership identity.

Keywords: academic careers; gender; higher education; career progression; leadership

1. Introduction

The underrepresentation of women in senior positions in universities is a systemic worldwide phenomenon (Blackmore 2014; European Commission 2012) that mirrors women's low level of representation internationally and across industries (Catalyst 2012; Elliott and Stead 2008; Equality and Human Rights Commission 2011; McKinsey & Co. 2012). The increase in female participation in higher education has not changed women's academic representation at senior levels in universities in Australia, which is similar to that in other Western countries (Aiston 2014; Gardiner et al. 2007; Morley 2013).

Barriers to women's career progression include sexism, stereotypes, unconscious bias, and work-family responsibilities (Eagly and Carli 2003; Morley 2013; O'Neil et al. 2008; Reitman and Schneer 2008; van den Brink and Benschop 2012). Women are often perceived as lacking ambition (Fels 2004; Litzky and Greenhaus 2007) or being deficient in ways that prevent them from achieving similar career outcomes to men (Shapiro et al. 2008). However, there is widespread agreement that women's commitment or abilities are not the problem (Carli and Eagly 2011; Morley 2013; O'Neil et al. 2008; Reitman and Schneer 2008). Instead, women's progression is structurally constrained by inequalities arising from factors such as culture, power dynamics, and the framing of merit (Lipton 2017). The reproduction of gender inequalities related to changes occurring within the higher education system internationally has been well researched and reported (Blackmore and Sachs 2007; Burkinshaw and White 2017; Eveline 2005; Morley 2014; White 2003).

In the neoliberal university climate, leadership has become the primary vehicle by which organizational development and transformation is to be achieved (Blackmore 2008; Morley 2013). A prevalent underpinning of neoliberalism is improving educational leadership effectiveness through a focus on "leadership standards, competency and capability frameworks" (Niesche 2013, p. 220). Thus, developing career and leadership has become synergistic with advancement in higher education, highlighting the resonance between two intertwined processes (Parker and Carroll 2009). The interrelatedness is evident in recent research and practice, which reflect a shared fundamental emphasis on learning from experience (Parker et al. 2012; Valcour et al. 2007), meaning-making for the career actors (Hall 2002; Khapova et al. 2007), holism (Parker and Carroll 2009), and leadership development (Goleman 2000; Heifetz 1994; Kram 1985; Shamir 1999). The interactive flow between leadership and career emerged from academic women's stories in an empirical study (Moore 2012). The qualities and norms of leadership expected in today's universities emphasize productivity, competitiveness, hierarchy, strategy, performativity, and an intense all-consuming commitment to paid work (Devine et al. 2011; Fitzgerald 2011). Leaders are expected to demonstrate authority, affective agency, and effective communication to achieve organizational goals and influence change (Morley 2013). This definition of leadership, however, is socially constructed, articulated, and reinforced by a social and policy agenda that is primarily shaped by men. Consequently, these qualities and expectations do not necessarily align well with women's academic careers and leadership. Despite an outward tolerance and even an expressed desire for diversity, a normative fantasy pertaining to success and leadership in higher education remains inherently male, which positions women consistently as "other" (Morley 2014).

The pipeline of women's progression into senior positions within the higher education sector is leaky, due in large part to a culture that rewards male practices and patterns of interaction that is not conducive to recognizing women's different styles and pathways. The numbers of women decrease at every stage of appointment on the academic scale (Carter and Silva 2010; Eveline 2005; van den Brink and Benschop 2012). In response, several universities have developed leadership programs to foster women's career progression to leadership roles (Dutta et al. 2011; Gardiner et al. 2007; Seritan et al. 2007; Thanacoody et al. 2006). These programs have been criticized for reinforcing inequities rather than reducing them, in that they individualize the problem and aim to modify women to better assimilate them into the dominant masculine culture (Colley 2001). Furthermore, trying to effect cultural change incurs an additional emotional burden for women as they strive to advance their academic careers with nontraditional trajectories (Burkinshaw and White 2017). In the politicized context of the neoliberal university, programs promoting women's leadership suit institutional agendas because they seemingly improve gender equity without challenging the fundamental structure and culture of an organization (Devos 2008). Nevertheless, in line with Morley (2013), we argue that such programs, if well designed, can and do add value beyond counting more women in senior ranks. Programs have the potential to be subversive, to challenge the status quo from within, pushing for change, particularly when the program is a genuine initiative by others to reach equitable outcomes for academic faculty and pursue a genuinely diverse leadership profile (White 2003). This paper contributes to the literature on leadership and women-only career progression programs by investigating the perceived benefits reported by a group of women who participated in a leadership program at a large university in Australia.

1.1. Careers in Higher Education

Internationally, women in academia are clustered at lower levels (Airini et al. 2011; Eveline 2005). The dearth of women in senior roles suggests that at some point careers peak, stall, or derail. A recent national study of Australian universities by Strachan et al. (2016) shows that the numbers of men and women are similar until they reach the top of the senior lecturer scale. In the 2011 academic workforce, 22% of women and 23.5% of men were employed at Level C (senior lecturer). The gender gap widens substantially after Level C, with more men attaining Level D (associate professor) positions than women, and the greatest gender difference is evident at the next step, with only 7% of women in academia holding Level E (full professor) positions compared to 19% of men (Strachan et al. 2016). Other cross-national studies have noted a similar disparity between numbers of midcareer academics and those in the senior ranks, indicating that this is a global trend (Morley 2014).

Promotion beyond senior lecturer into the professoriate specifically requires demonstrated leadership ability. Thus, at this point "career" and "leadership" become interrelated as markers of career progression, as expressed in promotion criteria. However, leadership is a broad concept that is often context-specific, such as in higher education, as noted above. Promotion processes are inherently political and "steeped in the discourse of neoliberalism, competition and metrics" (Sutherland-Smith 2014, p. 31). Despite the gender gap, there are marked similarities between men and women in terms of how they think about their university careers (Doherty and Manfredi 2010). The gap is therefore attributable to a range of factors, including personal (work-family interface and self-belief that affects motivation to achieve goals), professional (such as navigating masculine cultures and developing political savvy), and organizational shifts toward managerialism (Airini et al. 2011).

Women enact their careers differently from men (Powell and Mainiero 1992; Sullivan and Mainiero 2007), embedding paid work within a larger life context (O'Neil et al. 2008; Reitman and Schneer 2008). Numerous factors work in tandem. A nonlinear push-pull dynamic between family and work interrupts traditional patterns for women's careers (Cabrera 2007). The patterns are important, as they reflect times and spaces within women's careers when accumulation of human and social capital, critical for career success, is compromised (Probert 2005). Once women lose career momentum, they find it difficult to catch up, and the penalty persists throughout their careers (Reitman and Schneer 2008).

There are also differences in the ways women and men carry out leadership roles (Eagly and Johannesen-Schmidt 2007). A comprehensive meta-analysis of influential Multifactor Leadership Questionnaires (Avolio and Bass 1990) showed that women scored higher on transformational leadership measures (Eagly and Carli 2003). Transformational leaders develop and inspire their followers and consequently contribute to greater organizational success. While this measure should make women ideal candidates for leadership, other research has reported detrimental outcomes from differences that can impinge on success. Women practice a "softer" leadership style than men, which is less helpful in university settings, where the preferred style is "harder-nosed" (Doherty and Manfredi 2010). The result echoed Eagly and Johannesen-Schmidt's (2007) earlier finding that women display more democratic and participative leadership and less autocratic or directive leadership than men. Not only are these different, but also less likely to be valued or recognized. However, a double bind occurs at times when these "norms" are expected and not evident (Ely et al. 2011).

Gender stereotypes are well-documented factors that create resistance to women's influence and authority (Carli and Eagly 2011; Lipton 2017). Women's contributions are measured against male norms, particularly in research outputs in academia, which creates barriers for those with different styles and career patterns (Obers 2015). In the 1990s, gender inequality was described as tenacious because it was built into the structure of work organizations (Acker 1990). Three decades later, the situation is little different and a hidden curriculum creates cultural norms that hinder women's aspirations and careers (Morley 2014). It is one thing to understand what women do differently from men and how this may impact their career progression. Career and leadership factors interact and affect women's careers and their progression into academic leadership roles. Thus it is necessary to identify effective ways to develop women for career growth and leadership.

As indicated earlier, one response from universities has been to deliver women-only leadership development programs. University settings are strongly grounded in an ideology of meritocracy, so specific women's programs are not unanimously supported (van den Brink and Benschop 2012). They have also been criticized for encouraging women to enact their careers in ways that are more like men's, rather than valuing their unique contributions and qualities (Lipton 2017). Other key criticisms include that the programs are focused on fixing women rather than the systemic issues within the university context (Burkinshaw and White 2017; Strachan et al. 2016). Nevertheless, segregated programs, designed to provide a safe environment (Debebe 2011; Vinnicombe and Singh 2003), enable women to share their experiences authentically and help dispel the notion that they are deficient.

Research suggests that these programs, classified as soft positive action, can engage women and be of real value (Doherty and Manfredi 2010).

1.2. Career Progression for Women: Promoting Equity

This study examines a program at a large Australian university that recognizes particular challenges in relation to achieving gender equity at senior levels. Analysis of the 2009 workforce data at the university found that gender parity at the level of lecturer and senior lecturer did not translate to gender parity at more senior levels. Women represented only 19.1% of academic staff at associate professor and professor levels, compared with 48.8% of nonacademic professional staff at the highest levels.

A comprehensive university-wide externally conducted review identified the systemic and structural barriers that may influence the promotion of women to senior academic positions. Attention was paid to aspects of such positions that would make them undesirable for women or seemingly unattainable (Morley 2014). A seminal Australian study (Blackmore and Sachs 2007, p. 13) identified dual problems of perception and structure that "work together in unpromising ways for women." Others have noted that a minority representation increases the challenge of being authentic in personal style and decision-making (Morley 2013). The university review and consultation with female academics led to a range of recommendations to address the barriers, including developing a women-only career development program, facilitated by women and focused on leadership and career progression, designed to facilitate women's transition from being leading academics to academic leaders. Other critical issues identified were a general lack of understanding and negative perceptions among the female participants about the academic promotion process, a perceived lack of female role models and mentors, and associated difficulties with balancing multiple roles within the workplace and competing demands. The university has now been running the career progression program for women who are or were at Level C since 2010. The explicit aim of the program is to support women's advancement from senior lecturer to associate professor. At this career transition point, a key requirement of the university's promotion criteria is that applicants demonstrate their leadership in the domains of teaching, research, engagement, and/or clinical service. Therefore, leadership recognition and development was a core element in the program design. Furthermore, leadership was positioned as a process and differentiated from a title or level of authority. We are mindful of research that highlights the dearth of women leaders in higher education as an outcome of a corporatized academy presenting a cruel paradox (Blackmore 2014; Lipton 2017). Therefore, rather than adopting a pejorative model, the program in question encourages a broad range of evidence to support strength-based leadership. The program focuses on enabling women to provide evidence of their leadership in a broad, flexible narrative grounded in their experience and addressing promotional criteria. The pedagogy focused on accentuating strengths to enhance personal leadership rather than any underlying assumption that the women were not leaders and needed to be shaped to fit an institutional model. In sum, the program was not about changing the women to be promotable, but focused on highlighting their capabilities and developing a narrative to align with and broaden the university criteria.

The content and structure of the program were tailored to address individual development needs while capitalizing on the power of the group structure and dynamics. Since its inception, the program was developed and has been facilitated by a female academic, and from 2012, the course has been facilitated in partnership with a specialized organizational leadership trainer (also female). The number of women in the program is limited to 24, and each year it has been oversubscribed. Participants are required to write an application and, due to the large time commitment, obtain support from their head of school. Selection into the program is made on the basis of this application and commitment to attend all modules. Participants complete three modules over a 12-month period, comprising a 3-day core module followed by two 2-day modules spaced a few months apart to allow new learnings to be absorbed and practiced. Each module is grounded in learning activities based on personal experience and related to the published criteria for academic promotion, particularly those of demonstrated leadership. Sessions within modules include guided reflection through journaling (Daudelin 1996), experiential skill development, personal career planning, and academic portfolio development. Feedback is a feature of the program, with each participant undertaking a 360-degree leadership feedback assessment, as well as individual academic appraisal and review. Panels of senior university academic staff, both men and women, share their insights regarding academic career advancement and leadership though interactive group discussions. The support from female senior faculty also extends to group and individual mentoring of participants. These components are generally recognized as elements of effective career and leadership programs (Amagoh 2009; Clawson 2011; Ely et al. 2011).

In addition, the participants develop personal network maps, highlighting their diversity and breadth of support, access to information, and transmission of reputation, to emphasize the importance of developing appropriate relational and network support. The activity is reinforced with an introduction to the concept of developmental networks (Higgins and Kram 2001), peer coaching (Parker et al. 2008), and mentoring (Kram 1985; Ragins and Kram 2007). Peer coaching within and between modules enables participants to apply the coaching skills they learn to embed learning into day-to-day activities, maintain momentum, and provide ongoing support for each other (Parker et al. 2014).

Small groups of participants are assigned to senior female mentors in the organization and are expected to meet on a mutually agreed schedule for the length of the program. Generally, women receive less mentoring and grooming than men for senior management positions from top-level administrators such as vice chancellors, and instead receive support from less senior persons and from their families (Obers 2015; White et al. 2010). The value of both career and psychosocial support from mentors is long recognized to support vocational advancement and self-esteem (Kram 1985; Murphy and Kram 2014). A dearth of female role models and mentors may particularly affect the self-esteem building of female academics (Obers 2015). Implementing a mentoring program that pairs women with senior women may facilitate a positive culture with the potential to effect change and promote women and minority academics (Gibson 2006).

It should be noted that the Career Progression for Women program is one of several initiatives the university has implemented over time to create and promote a diversity agenda and, as part of that, gender equity. Initiatives such as participation in the UK's Athena Swan Awards to advance gender equality (see https://www.ecu.ac.uk/equality-charters/athena-swan/); changes in selection, recruitment, and promotion polices to be more inclusive; pay equity reviews for all academics; and unconscious bias training have been implemented as part of the overall strategy to promote equal opportunity and address the underrepresentation of women at senior academic levels. Together, these initiatives reflect an awareness of the need for fundamental cultural change in higher education to counter disadvantage and discrimination (Bagilhole and White 2011; White 2003).

2. Results

2.1. Comparing Social and Demographic Characteristics of Course Participants with Nonparticipants

In our first analysis, we compare the women in our sample who participated in the Career Progression for Women (CPW) course to those who have not attended the course on a range of social and demographic characteristics. We do this to better understand whether there are systematic differences between women who were both nominated and selected to participate in the course and those who did not participate. In Table 1 we report results of a series of cross-tabulations with chi-square tests to ascertain whether the women who attended the career progression course were systematically different from women at Level C in the broader university population.

Table 1. Women at Level C between 2010 and 2015: social and demographic characteristics of women who have not attended the career progression course and women who have attended the course.

	Have Not Participated in Course		Participated in Course		Total	
	N	Column %	N	Column %	N	Column %
Relationship Status						
Single	15	16	4	9	19	14
Cohabiting	12	13	6	13	18	13
Married	61	66	34	72	95	68
Refused	4	4	3	6	7	5
Total	92	100	47	100	139	100
Pearson chi2(3) = 1.8059 Pr = 0.614						
Number of Children						
No children	26	28	11	22	37	26
1 child	15	16	9	18	24	17
2 children	41	44	21	42	62	43
3 or more children	12	13	9	18	21	15
Total	94	100	50	100	144	100
Pearson chi2(3) = 1.1215 Pr = 0.772						
Born in Australia						
Yes	55	57	29	58	84	58
No	41	43	21	42	62	42
Total	96	100	50	100	146	100
Pearson chi2(1) = 0.0068 Pr = 0.935						
Providing Care						
Yes	16	19	3	7	19	15
No	69	81	39	93	108	85
Total	85	100	42	100	127	100
Pearson chi2(1) = 3.0146 Pr = 0.083						
Employment Interruption: Career Break						
Yes	55	61	27	56	82	59
No	35	39	21	44	56	41
Total	90	100	48	100	138	100
Pearson chi2(1) = 0.3068 Pr = 0.580						
Employment Interruption: Spouse Support						
Yes	6	7	4	8	10	7
No	84	93	44	92	128	93
Total	90	100	48	100	138	100
Pearson chi2(1) = 0.1294 Pr = 0.719						
Educational Qualification						
PhD	89	93	46	90	135	92
Professional Doctorate	2	2	1	2	3	2
Master's	1	1	3	6	4	3
Other postgrad	4	4	1	2	5	3
Total	96	100	51	100	147	100
Pearson chi2(3) = 3.3699 Pr = 0.338						

We report the number (N) and percent (%) of women we observed in each group, with the chi-square tests reported below each factor. The results for relationship status, number of children, born in Australia, educational qualification, and whether they had career breaks for caring responsibilities or to support their spouse's career indicate that the CPW women were not significantly different on these factors from women who had not participated in CPW. The sample is ethnically diverse, with around 42% of women born overseas. Overall, the majority of women in our sample were in a relationship, and most of them were married. A large proportion of women did not have children (26%), and most women with children had two children (43%). It is worth noting here that a slightly higher proportion of women who attended the CPW had three or more children (18% compared to 13%) and were also less likely to have no children at all compared to non-CPW women (22% compared to 28%). This suggests the possibility that women with children are more likely to seek support. Seven percent of CPW women had caring responsibilities compared to 15% of non-CPW women, which is marginally significant at $p < 0.08$. Relatedly, the main reason for taking an employment break was to provide care (69% of women), whereas far fewer women took an employment break to support their spouse. The majority of women in our sample had a PhD, with only 8% of women having other types of qualifications.

2.2. Women's Responses to Design Features of Program and Application of Program Learnings to Their Career

We report the women's assessment of different components of the course and how beneficial they found them in Table 2. The most positively assessed aspect of the course was the guest speakers, rated by 89% of respondents as quite or extremely beneficial. The speakers included both men and women involved in an aspect of the promotion process, senior university leaders, or past participants who spoke about how they responded to the program. Also highly rated was the portfolio review, in which the women submitted their academic portfolio to be assessed independently for promotion to Level D by senior academics in the university, with 83% of women saying it was quite or extremely beneficial. Third highest was the female-only design of the program, which was seen to be quite or extremely beneficial by around 79% of participants. The networking opportunities; the 360-degree feedback, by which women received feedback about their performance and leadership from supervisors, peers, and staff; and the three-module design over 12 months were also perceived as among the most beneficial aspects of the course. Peer coaching and mentoring had more mixed responses, with most finding them quite beneficial, but not extremely beneficial. Journaling about the process, their experience with the course modules, and activities between modules were viewed as the least beneficial aspects of the course design.

Table 2. Evaluation of course features by women who attended the Career Progression for Women (CPW) course.

Module Design	N	Column %
Not beneficial	1	2
Mildly beneficial	2	4
Unsure	10	21
Quite beneficial	18	38
Extremely beneficial	16	34
Total	47	100
360-Degree Feedback	**N**	**Column %**
Not beneficial	2	4
Mildly beneficial	5	11
Unsure	4	9
Quite beneficial	19	40
Extremely beneficial	17	36
Total	47	100

Table 2. *Cont.*

Module Design	N	Column %
Academic Portfolio Review	**N**	**Column %**
Not beneficial	1	2
Mildly beneficial	4	9
Unsure	3	7
Quite beneficial	11	24
Extremely beneficial	27	59
Total	46	100
Peer Coaching	**N**	**Column %**
Not beneficial	3	6
Mildly beneficial	8	17
Unsure	7	15
Quite beneficial	21	45
Extremely beneficial	8	17
Total	47	100
Mentoring from Senior Women	**N**	**Column %**
Not beneficial	4	9
Mildly beneficial	6	13
Unsure	11	23
Quite beneficial	17	36
Extremely beneficial	9	19
Total	47	100
Guest Speakers	**N**	**Column %**
Not beneficial	1	2
Mildly beneficial	3	7
Unsure	1	2
Quite beneficial	23	50
Extremely beneficial	18	39
Total	46	100
Keeping a Journal	**N**	**Column %**
Not beneficial	10	21
Mildly beneficial	8	17
Unsure	8	17
Quite beneficial	16	34
Extremely beneficial	5	11
Total	47	100
Networking	**N**	**Column %**
Not beneficial	0	0
Mildly beneficial	5	11
Unsure	6	13
Quite beneficial	12	26
Extremely beneficial	24	51
Total	47	100
Women Only	**N**	**Column %**
Not beneficial	3	6
Mildly beneficial	2	4
Unsure	5	11
Quite beneficial	9	19
Extremely beneficial	28	60
Total	47	100

Table 2. *Cont.*

Module Design	N	Column %
Academic Portfolio Review	N	Column %
Graduation Dinner	N	Column %
Not beneficial	5	11
Mildly beneficial	6	14
Unsure	17	39
Quite beneficial	11	25
Extremely beneficial	5	11
Total	44	100
Off-site Training	N	Column %
Not beneficial	1	2
Mildly beneficial	5	11
Unsure	4	9
Quite beneficial	15	33
Extremely beneficial	21	46
Total	46	100

Note: total numbers vary due to differences in missing values for each variable.

In Table 3 the results show women's reflections on whether they used the learnings from the program and their perceptions of whether the program contributed to their career since. First, the results show that most women felt that they had successfully applied some or all of the learnings obtained in the course to their academic career, with 56% indicating they had been very successful and 35% moderately successful at applying aspects of the course to their career. Second, an overwhelming majority (96%) reported that the program had contributed positively to their career.

Table 3. Participants' assessment of broader contributions of CPW to their career.

Overall, How Successful Have You Been at Applying This Learning to Your Career?	N	Column %
Very	27	56
Moderately	17	35
Not at all	4	8
Total	48	100
Please Indicate If You Think Undertaking CPW Contributed Positively to Your Career	N	Column %
Yes	45	94
No	3	6
Total	48	100

2.3. Open-Ended Comments: Qualitative Responses to the Program

Respondents were asked if they had other comments or feedback about the program that they wished to share. The overall results of this open-ended question are presented in Figure 1. The findings indicate that 89.66% of the women had positive assessments of their experience of the course, 3.45% were ambivalent, and 6.90% had negative assessments. Two main themes emerged from the positive comments: personal growth and development, both professional and personal, and reflections on the value of the program for other women and in the context of the broader university environment.

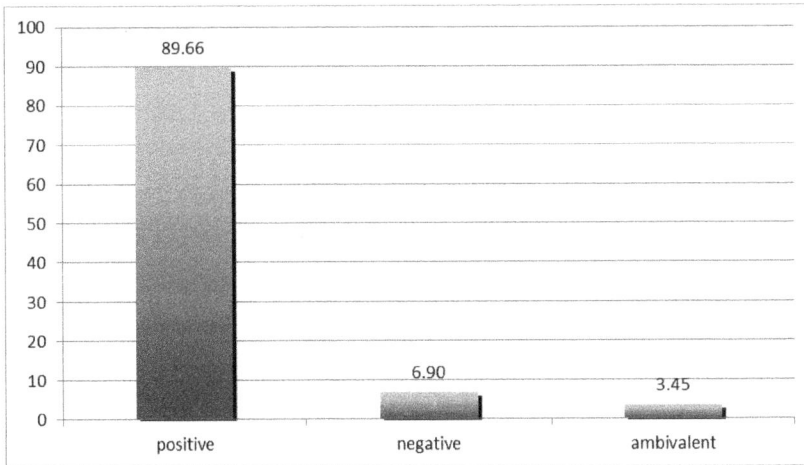

Figure 1. Summary of verbatim responses to open-ended survey question "Do you have any other comments or feedback about the CPW that you would like the opportunity to share?"

Within the first theme of personal development, approximately half of the women indicated that they had a better understanding of themselves in relation to their career and aspirations. For some, this meant reconsidering their possibilities for the future, exemplified by the following quote:

"CPW makes you think differently and really helps you in understanding who you are, your core values, what you believe in, and the change you want to bring about and your leadership skills, which will enable you to create the change you want as an academic." (#1)

Thinking differently was also reflected in women's perceptions of the dramatic changes they felt in themselves and their attitude or approach to their career; for example:

"The CPW program was a game changer for me. I think it created a dramatic change in my attitude in many aspects of my work. Extremely positive." (#4)

"It was a transformative program for me and I do not think I would have achieved my current position without it." (#25)

Some of the women reported an acceptance and better understanding of their position within the university.

"The program gave me time to reflect on my career and my choices. I am now more accepting of my current position even though I have not yet applied for promotion." (#13)

"It helped me to locate myself in the institution and work out what was important for me." (#29)

As exemplified in this series of quotes, for many women who participated, the program was transformative in a range of ways. This is indicative of the potential to change and transform how women see themselves and the value of what they contribute to the university. The second main theme concerned women's reflections on the value of the course for other women and the university more broadly:

"I frequently recommend the program to other staff members." (#8)

"This was an excellent program, which I have recommended to several colleagues." (#28)

Several of the women commented on the importance of the program and advocated for its continuation by the university:

"I think this program is incredibly valuable. I would like a 'refresher' half-day course each year or every other year, to help facilitate continued progression and development." (#15)

"Really pleasing that [university] have continued to grow and develop this program. I know a lot of women who have done the course and benefitted in a whole range of ways." (#17)

From these quotes, there is a sense that many individuals who participated in the course benefited from the program and that institutionally it signaled a commitment to improving gender equality. Nevertheless, while individuals benefited, there was no sense of an accompanying structural change. In this respect, a number of the women's responses were more ambivalent. While positive about the program, they were skeptical about any real change, particularly with regard to the university's capacity for genuine change in relation to gender.

"The culture at [university] can only change if senior women change that culture. Career progression is one thing, but collaborative, diverse, and equitable safe work places should be our ultimate aim." (#12)

"The program was really good and I enjoyed getting to know so many great [university] women. However, the main impediments to women's advancement has little to do with them. I think there is a great lack of implicit bias and gender issue awareness among those in senior positions at [university] (Heads of Schools and up)." (#18)

"To give context to the above, it is an excellent program. However, being placed in a service role with constantly changing expectations and increasing workload, I feel this has precluded possible career development." (#30)

These comments, while generally positive about the women's individual experiences, strongly echo concerns raised in the feminist literature on the real capacity for change (Devos 2008; Morley 2013). In these quotes, the women articulate the structural and cultural barriers that are the reality that female academics face in their careers, irrespective of any individual change they experience. Removing these barriers requires higher-level institutional change, which underscores the importance of running women-only programs as one component of a broader range of strategies to achieve genuine institutional diversity. Not all participants were positive; those who viewed the course in a more negative light highlighted the time commitment required as a major burden, as exemplified by the following quotes:

"The time commitment for the program was very intense and similar commitments were not required by male staff members." (#3)

"The course was way too time consuming. There was too much emphasis on finding our values. Most women already know their values." (#24)

These quotes, particularly the reference that male staff members do not have to go through the same time-intensive program as women to progress in the university, highlight the additional burden on women who are interested in institutional progression.

3. Discussion

The aim of this study was to provide an overview of the perceived benefits of a leadership program for women in a major Australian university. Prior feminist literature on the position of women in higher education has criticized this type of approach, because it does not directly undermine and challenge the misogynist structure of the neoliberal university, but rather forces women to contort themselves to fit within it (Burkinshaw and White 2017; Lipton 2017). However, our findings suggest that a well-designed course can empower and enable women to challenge the system while working within it, reinforcing a successful approach to change, as noted by Bilimoria et al. (2008). The only way to change entrenched institutional logic is to make experiences of discrimination visible (Sinclair 2000), and the career progression program is one such avenue.

The guest speakers were the most highly rated aspect of the program, with 87% of participants agreeing that they were quite or extremely beneficial. The speakers were both male and female academic leaders, who shared their insights on the promotion process and their personal experience of navigating an academic career. Their experiences challenged the assumption of a linear academic career; the concept of merit being only an objective requirement based on ability, skill, and achievement (Lipton 2017); and the notion that leadership is about position held in service or engagement roles. The guest speaker sessions were an integral aspect of the workshop design and acted as an impetus to connect presenters and participants following the presentations. Furthermore, the participants were encouraged by the facilitators to reflect on the content though peer coaching and journaling, both recognized ways of promoting relational learning (Parker et al. 2018).

A key aspect of the design was the multiple sources of developmental feedback, including portfolio review, 360-degree feedback, and peer coaching. Each of these provided developmental feedback that was necessary to identify strengths, areas for change in focus, and strategies for growth (Ely et al. 2011). Participants' feedback suggests that one of the barriers to applying for promotion is uncertainty about how one's performance compares to the university selection criteria and how it aligns with that of other academics outside of one's professional area. This is of particular concern for women whose academic career path may not be perceived as traditional or standard due to career breaks and other barriers. The program encourages and supports women to think differently and more holistically about their careers, positioning achievements relative to opportunity and valuing different approaches to leadership. By doing so, women could establish a career narrative rather than a list of publications and achievements in academic CVs recognized as neoliberal measures that epitomize traditional and linear career development markers (Lipton 2017; Niesche 2013). The survey results indicate that these features were highly valued by the participants.

Eighty-seven percent of the survey respondents identified the portfolio review process as beneficial or extremely beneficial. This feedback, while sometimes challenging to receive, facilitated a change in thinking about the how the participants "ticked the boxes" required for promotion. The feedback challenged the self-limiting assumptions that many participants had about their readiness for promotion and added to their developing a holistic view of their career. The portfolio review was a critical element in the program design, and each participant's portfolio was given to two senior academic reviewers, often heads of departments, for assessment. The reviewers were selected based on their experience in the university promotion process, including one from the participant's discipline and the other from a different discipline (which ensured that the language was readily understood without jargon). Reviewers provided written feedback, which could be anonymous. However, many reviewers not only declared themselves, but also invited the participants to meet for further coaching around improving their portfolios.

The women-only program design (in terms of both facilitation and participation) was essential to create an experience that established a safe space for learning and encouraged the women to build a community of peer support, and it was strongly supported by the participants of this program. While there is criticism that women's programs focus on "fixing women" and inherently blame them for their own inequitable outcomes (Pyke 2018) rather than focusing on the university culture (Burkinshaw and White 2017), support for women-only programs identifying the opportunity to learn and share with women validates their experiences (Debebe 2011). When women are in a majority position, in contrast to the more familiar male-dominated work context, this can provoke powerful insights (Ely et al. 2011). More women-only programs that support participants in navigating the challenges of the higher education context are required.

Another highly valued component of the course was the creation of developmental networks. The women-only program design was also essential to this experience, as it provided an avenue for sustaining relationships through an established community of peer support, building from a shared experience. Developmental networks are effective ongoing support systems (Murphy and Kram 2014). They are also critical elements of any effective leadership development program (Ely et al. 2011). The findings indicate that 77% of respondents considered networking to be quite or extremely beneficial, supporting evidence that networking is critical to the advancement of women's leadership as a means of mobilizing the work of change.

The open-ended qualitative findings from the survey suggest that women who participated in the Career Progression for Women program evaluated it highly on average, and many perceived that they obtained career benefits and advantages from participating. Most of the women found the course transformative, and this suggests that women-only programs have the potential for "tempered radicalism." The leadership development focus, incorporating technical aspects of preparing for promotion into a more strategic agenda of tailoring the program to support women's trajectory into senior academic positions, was mostly successful. However, even though the program clearly inspired and enabled women to view themselves and their positions within the university differently, the change was individual rather than structural. This dilemma was also a main theme of the open-ended responses and strongly reflects the feminist critiques of such programs being implemented as stand-alone solutions.

Objectively, the program was successful, in that 32% of participants have been promoted to Level D, and the proportion of women represented at Level D in the university has increased by 5% since the course has been running. The increase in numbers not only benefits individual women, but also contributes to significant changes in the demographic balance; women cannot be what they cannot see. More role models also gives women more options of leadership styles to emulate. Broader representation across all forms of leadership is essential to address the dearth of women at senior levels, and to improve statistics that reflect attainment levels. Dynamics subtly shift across environments in which these women work.

Nevertheless, gender equity will not be solved by merely "count[ing] more women into elite systems" (Morley 2014, p. 124). As Karen Pyke noted, a sense of safety and inclusivity means that all forms of discrimination and bias, including bullying and sexual harassment, require institution-wide structural change to align the rhetoric of diversity with the lived experience of all academics (Pyke 2018). The situation that initially promoted the program has also resulted in changes to key aspects of the university's strategic plan, which now includes a strong focus on attracting and supporting diversity among staff and students with identifiable targets. Thus, although the profile of the leadership program has increased because of the larger numbers of women being promoted, and gaining recognition collectively is creating a climate for more change, the program is not expected to effect change alone, and other initiatives are being implemented to address systemic inequities. One example is engaging more diverse promotion panels to increase understanding of the challenges women confront in achieving leadership roles. This is just one more part of the larger challenge that frames the issue of increasing the number of women in senior roles. Thus, highlighting the readiness for gender equity within the university is a major outcome of the program. It demonstrates an increasing willingness to engage with women to understand the barriers they confront in their careers and underpins the evolution of a larger cultural change taking place within the university setting. Future programs may consider including sexual harassment, as we have become more and more aware over the past couple of years of how pervasive the problem is.

4. Materials and Methods

4.1. Data and Analytic Sample

The data come from a survey of academics at an Australian university. The survey was not commissioned by the university administration to specifically examine the program, but more broadly targeted to better understand men's and women's career progression from senior lecturer (Level C) to associate professor (Level D). The sample was drawn from administrative data obtained from the Human Resources division at the university comprising all academics who were at Level C between 2010 and 2015. The initial administrative data sample frame comprised 1038 academics. After excluding those who were ineligible and those who had left the university, the final sample frame comprised 1009 people. The survey was conducted online using Survey Monkey. A pilot survey was conducted with 17 people in June 2016, with follow-up face-to-face interviews with 6 of those respondents, and the survey was modified based on their feedback. The full survey went into the field in early October 2016. All potential participants were contacted via university email addresses and participation was voluntary. To maximize response rates, two follow-up reminders were sent four weeks and eight weeks after the initial invitation. In total, 385 people responded, with 346 fully completed surveys and 39 partially completed surveys received. An overall response rate of 38% was achieved, which is comparable with other surveys using similar samples and approaches.

The analytic sample for the present study comprised 147 women who responded to the survey and provided valid responses on the variables of interest. Of the women who responded to the survey, 48 participated in the program between 2010 and 2016. This was 55% of the 88 women who participated in the program and were still employed by the university. The women who participated in the career progression course were asked a series of additional questions in the survey about their experience with the course and their opinions about whether or not the course was helpful for them. The responses of these women are the focus of this paper.

4.2. Measures

Social and Demographic Characteristics

All survey participants were asked to provide social and demographic information as well as information about their career. We use a selection of these measures in the current paper. Relationship status comprised three groups: single (not in a relationship), cohabiting (living with someone in a relationship, but not married), and legally married. Number of children was categorized into no children, one child, two children, or three or more children. We also differentiated between whether the respondent was born in Australia or overseas (1 = yes, 2 = no). Participants were asked if they were currently providing child care or elder care (1 = yes, 2 = no), and if they had taken significant career breaks to provide care or to support their spouse's career (1 = yes, 2 = no). Respondents were also asked for their highest level of academic qualification: PhD, professional doctorate, master's, or other postgraduate qualification.

4.3. Questions Asked of Course Participants

The survey respondents who indicated that they had participated in the Career Progression for Women program were asked additional questions about how beneficial they thought 11 features of the program were: the three-module design, 360-degree feedback, portfolio review, peer coaching, mentoring from senior women, guest speakers, keeping a journal, networking, women only, graduation dinner, and off-site training. Responses were on a 5-point Likert scale: 1 = not beneficial, 2 = mildly beneficial, 3 = unsure, 4 = quite beneficial, and 5 = extremely beneficial.

In addition, this group of women were asked two questions about the course's contributions to their career. The first was "Overall, how successful have you been at applying this learning to your career?" Possible responses were 1 = very, 2 = moderately, and 3 = not at all. The second was "Please indicate if you think undertaking CPW contributed positively to your career" (1 = yes, 2 = no). Course participants were also asked to respond to an open-ended question: "Do you have any other comments or feedback about the CPW that you would like the opportunity to share?"

4.4. Analytic Procedure

Analysis proceeded in four main stages. First, to examine whether the 48 women who participated in the Career Progression for Women course were different from other women at Level C, we compared the social and demographic characteristics of women who had and had not participated in the course. Group differences were assessed using chi-square tests that compared the distribution of the observed frequencies to the expected frequencies that would be present if the distributions were identical for the women who had participated and those who had not. If these differed enough, the chi-square test was significant ($p < 0.05$). Second, we undertook a descriptive analysis of women's responses to a series of questions about the design features of the Career Progression for Women course. Third, we undertook a descriptive analysis of the two questions regarding the contribution of the course to the women's careers. Fourth, we undertook a qualitative analysis of the open-ended responses to comments about the career progression course. Of the 48 participants in the course who responded to the survey, 33 provided answers to the open-ended question and 29 of the responses were relevant to the current paper. The answers to this open-ended question did not lend themselves to a full qualitative analysis, as they were mostly short sentences. Nevertheless, the information provided was sufficient to identify several themes.

5. Conclusions

For women, transitioning from being a leading academic to an academic leader requires more than a promotion to a higher organizational level. It requires changes in mindset and identity. It is difficult work and requires systemic change and personal courage in a supportive environment. The CPW program creates a learning environment where risk-taking is encouraged, where frank and fearless feedback is provided, and where academics are required to examine assumptions and biases and assume a leadership identity. Thus there are benefits in challenging the rhetoric and traditional patterns of career pathways in higher education as a means of encouraging cultural change. Until we reach a critical mass of women, we will continue to focus on both external context and internal courage.

Acknowledgments: We wish to thank the program participants. We would also like to thank the three anonymous reviewers for their constructive feedback on the paper.

Author Contributions: Polly Parker led the project including the overall conceptual design of the evaluation. She contributed to framing and writing the paper and coordinating the efforts of other authors. Belinda Hewitt contributed to the conceptual and overall development of the project and survey. She processed the data and conducted all the analysis for the current paper, including writing the methods and results sections and has edited and provided feedback on other sections of the manuscript. Jennifer Witheriff contributed to the conceptual and overall development of the project and survey. She has deep knowledge of the program and links with extant literature. Amy Cooper contributed to the overall development of the project, performed literature reviews, administered the pilot survey, subsequent interviews and built and administered the full survey.

Conflicts of Interest: The authors declare no conflict of interest. The founding sponsors had no role in the design of the study; in the collection, analyses, or interpretation of data; in the writing of the manuscript, and in the decision to publish the results.

References

Acker, Joan. 1990. Hierarchies, jobs, bodies: A theory of gendered organizations. *Gender and Society* 4: 139–58. [CrossRef]

Airini, Sunny Collings, Lindsey Conner, Kathryn McPherson, Brenda Midson, and Cheryl Wilson. 2011. Learning to be leaders in Higher Education: What helps or hinders women's advancement as leaders in universities. *Educational Management Administration and Leadership* 39: 44–62. [CrossRef]

Aiston, Sarah Jane. 2014. Leading the academy or being led? Hong Kong women academics. *Higher Education Research & Development* 33: 59–72.

Amagoh, Francis. 2009. Leadership development and leadership effectiveness. *Management Decision* 47: 989–99. [CrossRef]

Avolio, Bruce J., and Bernard M. Bass. 1990. *Transformational Leadership Development: Manual for the Multifactor Leadership Questionnaire*. Palo Alto: CA Press.

Bagilhole, Barbara, and Kate White, eds. 2011. *Gender, Power and Management: A Cross-Cultural Analysis of Higher Education*. New York: Palgrave Macmillan.

Bilimoria, Diana, Simy Joy, and Xiangfen Liang. 2008. Breaking barriers and creating inclusiveness: Lessons from organizational transformation to advance women faculty in academic science and engineering. *Human Resource Management* 47: 423–41. [CrossRef]

Blackmore, Jill. 2008. Re/positioning women in educational leadership: The changing social relations and politics of gender in Australia. In *Women Leading Education across the Continents: Sharing the Spirit, Fanning the Flame*. Edited by Jill Blackmore. Lanham: Rowman and Littlefield Education, pp. 73–83.

Blackmore, Jill. 2014. Wasting talent? Gender and hte problematics of academic disenchantment and disengagement with leadership. *Higher Education Research & Development* 33: 86–99.

Blackmore, Jill, and Judyth Sachs. 2007. *Performing and Reforming Leaders: Gender, Educational Restructuring, and Organizational Change*. Albany: State University of New York Press.

Burkinshaw, Paula, and Kate White. 2017. Fixing the women or fixing universities: Women in HE leadership. *Administrative Sciences* 7. [CrossRef]

Cabrera, Elizabeth F. 2007. Opting out and opting in: Understanding the complexities of women's career transitions. *Career Development International* 12: 218–37. [CrossRef]

Carli, Linda L., and Alice H. Eagly. 2011. Gender and leadership. In *The Sage Handbook of Leadership*. Edited by Bryman Alan, D. Collinson, K. Grint, B. Jackson and M. Uhl-Bien. London: Sage, pp. 103–17.

Carter, Nancy M., and Christine Silva. 2010. Women in management: Delusions of progress. *Harvard Business Review* 88: 19–22.

Catalyst, Census. 2012. *Catalyst Census: Fortune 500 Women Board Directors*. New York: Catalyst Census.

Clawson, James G. S. 2011. The Handbook for Teaching Leadership: Knowing, Doing & Being. *Academy of Management Learning & Education* 10: 535.

Colley, Helen. 2001. Righting rewritings of the myth of Mentor: A critical perspective on career guidance mentoring. *British Journal of Guidance and Counselling* 29: 177–97. [CrossRef]

Daudelin, Marilyn Wood. 1996. Learning from experience through reflection. *Organizational Dynamics* 24: 36–49. [CrossRef]

Debebe, Gelaye. 2011. Creating a Safe Environment for Women's Leadership Transformation. *Journal of Management Education* 35: 679–712. [CrossRef]

Devine, Dympna, Bernie Grummell, and Kathleen Lynch. 2011. Crafting the elastic self? Gender and identities in senior appointments in Irish education. *Gender, Work and Organization* 18: 631–49. [CrossRef]

Devos, Anita. 2008. Where enterprise and equity meet: The rise of mentoring for women in Australian Universities. *Discourse: Studies in the Cultural Politics of Education* 29: 195–205. [CrossRef]

Doherty, Liz, and Simonetta Manfredi. 2010. Improving women's representation in senior positions in universities. *Employee Relations* 32: 138–55. [CrossRef]

Dutta, Rina, Sarah L. Hawkes, Elizabeth Kuipers, David Guest, Nicola T. Fear, and Amy C. Iversen. 2011. One year outcomes of a mentoring scheme for female academics: A pilot study at the Institute of Psychiatry, King's College London. *BMC Medical Education* 11: 13–22. [CrossRef] [PubMed]

Eagly, Alice H., and Linda L. Carli. 2003. The female leadership advantage: An evaluation of the evidence. *Leadership Quarterly* 14: 807–34. [CrossRef]

Eagly, Alice H., and Mary C. Johannesen-Schmidt. 2007. Leadership style matters: The small, but important, style differences between male and female leaders. In *Handbook on Women in Business and Management*. Edited by D. Bilimoria and S. K. Piderit. Cheltenham: Edward Elgar.

Elliott, Carole, and Valerie Stead. 2008. Learning from leading women's experience: Towards a sociological understanding. *Leadership* 4: 159–80. [CrossRef]

Ely, Robin J., Herminia Ibarra, and Deborah M. Kolb. 2011. Taking Gender into Account: Theory and Design for Women's Leadership Development Programs. *Academy of Management Learning & Education* 10: 474–93. [CrossRef]

Equality and Human Rights Commission. 2011. *Sex and Power—Who Runs Britain?* London: Equality and Human Rights Commission.

European Commission. 2012. *Structural Change in Research Institutions: Enhancing Excellence, Gender Equality and Efficiency in Research and Innovation.* Brussels: European Commission.

Eveline, Joan. 2005. Women in the ivory tower. *Journal of Organizational Change Management* 18: 641–58. [CrossRef]

Fels, Anna. 2004. Do women lack ambition? *Harvard Business Review* 82: 50–60. [PubMed]

Fitzgerald, Tanya. 2011. Troubling leadership? Gender, leadership and higher education. Paper presented at the Australian Association for Research in Education Conference, Hobart, Australia, 27 November–1 December.

Gardiner, Maria, Marika Tiggemann, Hugh Kearns, and Kelly Marshall. 2007. Show me the money! An empirical analysis of mentoring outcomes for women in academia. *Higher Education Research and Development* 26: 425–42. [CrossRef]

Gibson, Sharon K. 2006. Mentoring of women faculty: The role of organizational politics and culture. *Innovative Higher Education* 31: 63–79. [CrossRef]

Goleman, Daniel. 2000. Leadership that gets results. *Harvard Business Review* 78: 78–90.

Hall, Douglas T. 2002. *Careers in and out of Organizations.* Thousand Oaks: Sage.

Heifetz, Ronald A. 1994. *Leadership without Easy Answers.* Cambridge: Harvard University Press.

Higgins, Monica C., and Kathy E. Kram. 2001. Reconceptualizing mentoring at work: A developmental network perspective. *Academy of Management Review* 26: 264–88.

Khapova, Svetlana, Michael B. Arthur, and Celeste P. M. Wilderom. 2007. The subjective career in the knowledge economy. In *Handbook of Career Studies.* Edited by P. Gunz Hugh and Maury Peiperl. New York: Sage, pp. 114–30.

Kram, Kathy E. 1985. *Mentoring at Work: Developmental Relationships in Organizational Life.* Glenview: Scott Foresman.

Lipton, Briony. 2017. Measures of success: Cruel optimism and the paradox of academic women's participation in Australian higher education. *Higher Education Research & Development* 36: 486–97.

Litzky, Barrie, and Jeffrey Greenhaus. 2007. The relationship between gender and aspirations to senior management. *Career Development International* 12: 637–59. [CrossRef]

McKinsey & Co. 2012. *Making the Breakthrough.* Paris: McKinsey & Co.

Moore, Anne. 2012. Looking for Flow in the Storylines of Leadership and Career in Women's Development. Master' thesis, University of Auckland, Auckland, New Zealand.

Morley, Louise. 2013. The rules of the game: Women and the leaderist turn in higher education. *Gender and Education* 25: 116–31. [CrossRef]

Morley, Louise. 2014. Lost leaders: Women in the global academy. *Higher Education Research & Development* 33: 114–28.

Murphy, Wendy, and Kathy Kram. 2014. *Strategic Relationships at Work.* New York: McGraw Hill.

Niesche, Richard. 2013. Politicizing articulation: Applying Lyotard's work to the use of standards in educational leadership. *International Journal of Leadership in Education* 16: 220–33. [CrossRef]

O'Neil, Deborah A., Margaret M. Hopkins, and Diana Bilimoria. 2008. Women's careers at the start of the 21st century: Patterns and Paradoxes. *Journal of Business Ethics* 80: 727–43. [CrossRef]

Obers, Noëlle. 2015. Influential structures: Understanding the role of the head of department in relation to women academics' research careers. *Higher Education Research & Development* 34: 1220–32.

Parker, Polly, and Brigid Carroll. 2009. Leadership development from a careers perspective. *Leadership* 5: 261–83. [CrossRef]

Parker, Polly, Douglas T. Hall, and Kathy E. Kram. 2008. Peer Coaching: A relational process for accelerating career learning. *Academy of Management Learning and Education* 7: 487–503. [CrossRef]

Parker, Polly, Kathy E. Kram, and Douglas T. Hall. 2012. Exploring Risk Factors in Peer Coaching: A Multilevel Approach. *Journal of Applied Behavioral Science* 49: 361–87. [CrossRef]

Parker, Polly, Kathy E. Kram, and Douglas T. Hall. 2014. Peer coaching: An untapped resource for development. *Organizational Dynamics* 43: 122–29. [CrossRef]

Parker, Polly, Douglas T. Hall, Kathy E. Kram, and I. Wasserman. 2018. *Peer Coaching at Work: Principles and Practices.* San Francisco: Stanford University Press.

Powell, Gary N., and Lisa A. Mainiero. 1992. Cross-currents in the river of time: Conceptualizing the complexities of women's careers. *Journal of Management* 18: 215–37. [CrossRef]

Probert, Belinda. 2005. I just couldn't fit in: Gender and unequal outcomes in academic careers. *Gender, Work and Organization* 12: 50–72. [CrossRef]

Pyke, Karen D. 2018. Insitutional betrayal: Inequity, discrimination, bullying, and retaliation in academia. *Sociological Perspectives* 61: 5–13. [CrossRef]

Ragins, B. R., and Kathy E. Kram. 2007. *The Handbook of Mentoring at Work: Research, Theory and Practice.* Los Angeles: Sage Publications.

Reitman, Frieda, and Joy A. Schneer. 2008. Enabling the new careers of the 21st century. *Organization Management Journal* 5: 17–28. [CrossRef]

Seritan, Andreea L., Robinder Bhangoo, Sylvia Garma, Jane DuBé, Ju Hui Park, and Robert Hales. 2007. Society for women in academic psychiatry: A peer mentoring approach. *Academic Psychiatry* 31: 363–66. [CrossRef] [PubMed]

Shamir, Boas. 1999. Leadership in boundaryless organizations: Disposable or indispensable? *European Journal of Work and Organizational Psychology* 8: 49–71. [CrossRef]

Shapiro, Mary, Cynthia Ingols, and Stacy Blake-Beard. 2008. Confronting career double binds: Implications for women, organizations and career practitioners. *Journal of Career Development* 34: 309–33. [CrossRef]

Sinclair, Amanda. 2000. Teaching managers about masculinities: Are you kidding? *Management Learning* 31: 83–101. [CrossRef]

Strachan, Glenda, D. Peetz, G. Whitehouse, J. Bailey, K. Broadbent, C. Troup, and M. Nesic. 2016. *Women, Careers and Universities. Where to from Here?* Nathan: Centre for Work, Organisation and Wellbeing (WOW).

Sullivan, Sherry E., and Lisa Mainiero. 2007. Women's kaleidoscope careers A new framework for examining women's stress across the lifespan. *Research in Cccupational Stress and Wellbeing* 6: 205–38.

Sutherland-Smith, Wendy. 2014. You're on the cusp but not there yet. Braving the promotion process. In *Career Moves: Mentoring for Women Advancing Their Career and Leadership in Academia.* Edited by Athena Vongalis-Macrow. Rotterdam: Sense Publishers, pp. 17–34.

Thanacoody, P. Rani, Timothy Bartram, Michelle Barker, and Kerry Jacobs. 2006. Career progression among female academics: A comparative study of Australia and Mauritius. *Women in Management Review* 21: 536–53. [CrossRef]

Valcour, Monique, Lotte Bailyn, and Maria Alejandra Quijada. 2007. Customised careers. In *Handbook of Career Studies.* Edited by P. Gunz Hugh and Maury Peiperl. London: Sage, pp. 188–210.

van den Brink, Marieke, and Yvonne Benschop. 2012. Slaying the seven-headed dragon: The quest for gender change in academia. *Gender, Work and Organization* 19: 71–92. [CrossRef]

Vinnicombe, Susan, and Val Singh. 2003. Women-only management training: An essential part of women's leadership development. *Journal of Change Management* 3: 294–306. [CrossRef]

White, Kate. 2003. Women and leadership in higher education in Australia. *Tertiary Education and Management* 9: 45–60. [CrossRef]

White, Kate, Sarah Riordan, Özlem Atay Ozkanli, and Jenny Neale. 2010. Cross culture perspective of gender and management in universities. *South African Journal of Higher Education* 24: 646–60.

administrative sciences

MDPI

Article

Towards Social Justice in Institutions of Higher Learning: Addressing Gender Inequality in Science & Technology Through Capability Approach

Kalyan Kumar Kameshwara * and Tanu Shukla *

Department of Humanities & Social Sciences, Birla Institute of Technology & Sciences, Pilani 300031, India
* Correspondence: 3k.kalyan@gmail.com (K.K.K.); tanus@pilani.bits-pilani.ac.in (T.S.)

Received: 4 May 2017; Accepted: 3 July 2017; Published: 8 July 2017

Abstract: The focus of the study is to examine and relocate gender equality in higher education using Capability Approach as the background frame. The paper discusses how gender relations are rooted in the socio-cultural matrix in India. It attempts to explore the factors prevalent in the structure which impacts woman's opportunities and functionalities in the higher education. The database includes faculty from one of the central universities of South India, the study deals with the dynamics of constructs in Science and Technology indicating socio-psychological obstructions faced by women. Based on thorough analysis, the oppressed capabilities are conceptualized thereby enabling the researchers to relocate the gender equality and the capabilities that need to be enriched for women can be contemplated which helps in reducing the existing disparity. The intention of the study is essentially not to quantify the attributes of inequality to make them measurable but to choose attributes which enable an effective comparative basis to address inequality. The empirical study reveals an existence of the element of stereotyping as a single entity and capability approach restores the uniqueness by the fractional combination of capabilities listed.

Keywords: Discrimination; science and technology; stereotypes; women; capability

---

1. Introduction

Gender stereotypes in society have led to the formation of normative beliefs about the different roles expected to be performed by men and women. The lineage of these normative dogmas may be attributed to the sexual division of labor in society. Persistence of such normative dogmas in the society is reinforced by the fact that an individual in the society irrespective of their gender practices gender stereotypes. Gender discrimination at the workplace can normally be traced back to the roots of certain segments of time and contexts of society. Modern and industrial life, just like its prior times have reshaped the social roles and these transformations also have had impacts differently on men and women. Due to the changes in the society and in the organizational structures (referred to as workplace), explicitly or implicitly, there was also an ample space carved for oppression, discrimination and inequality.

Despite several reforms by the government for inclusion of women in education, women's literacy rate has always lagged men's literacy rate in India and this trend is more pronounced in rural areas than urban. Literacy rates among women have had external benefits of reduced infant mortality, higher work participation of women and bolstering woman's agency in a society which continues to be patriarchal. In various surveys carried out by the Institute of Social Studies Trust (ISST), it has been made apparent that parental opposition for girl's education is continuously decreasing. If the right infrastructure is provided—schools and colleges located in the neighborhood, preferably with women as teachers—there is a greater chance for parents to allow their daughters to study. Hence, there is a need not only to improve the quality of education but also, to encourage participation of women as teachers.

The discrimination component is much higher in scientific and technical fields in India than among social sciences and other fields. Women have less access to resources as funding, financing, technology and education, which are required to remain actively engaged in science, technology and innovation. Kulandaiswamy (2005) analyzed that there will be a need for a massive increase in opportunities for higher education by 2020. There has been an increase in the growth of teaching staff over the last decade (from 20 thousand in 1950 to 0.93 million in 2013), still, that doesn't match with the exponential growth of colleges that have risen at a far greater rate (Deloitte 2013). This has resulted in a high student-teacher ratio, which increases the burden on teachers and overburdened teachers are unable to pursue any research or encourage their students to do so (Ministry of Human Resource Development 2013).

It has also been observed that registration and participation of women are less than that of men in science and technology. The representation of Indian women in the Sciences & engineering compared to women in all disciplines has been just 12.5 percent, though this rate is considerably high compared to other places like US, European Union, South Africa, South Korea, Indonesia and Brazil (Huyer and Halfkin 2013). Statistically, Pereira (2014) in her study found that women in science and engineering account for only 31% of the student population at the first level. This percentage increases with level, rising to 38% of women at the student PhD level and 35% at the graduate PhD level. The report demonstrates the lack of appeal for young women of science and engineering studies. India also has a low representation of women in decision-making, only 22% of legislators, senior officials & managers are women and only 26 percent of listed companies in India have a woman on their board of directors. An important reason responsible for this is private-public divide is associated with the notions of gender. Women are linked by the society within the private domain of household, whereas men are associated with authority and productive work.

Women are under-represented in management positions all over the world in all kinds of professions even though, women qualified for management jobs are increasing. Women are disadvantaged and marginalized by the men's culture and the associations that are constantly made, imagined about flexibility, rationality and efficiency at workplace. They suffer from discrimination and inequality in all societies despite there being no significant difference in productivity between men and women as managers (Donnell and Hall 1980).

Gender mainstreaming is a globally accepted strategy for promoting gender equality. It is a process rather than a goal of creating knowledge and awareness of and responsibility for gender equality among all education professionals engaged in higher education. It is not an end in itself but a strategy, an approach, a means to achieve the goal of gender equality in higher education institutions—through sensitization and educating key stakeholders that the costs of women's marginalization and gender inequalities are born by all in the education sector as a whole.

In 'She Figures' Report by European Commission (2013), it was clearly established that despite the steadily growing number of women with a scientific or technical university degree in most European countries, women are still under represented in science and technology (S&T) professions, be it in companies or universities. It further reveals that women in scientific research remain a minority (33% of researchers in the EU-27 in 2009). Their proportion is growing faster than that of men but not enough to indicate that the gender imbalance in science is self-correcting.

Jobs customarily and historically held mainly by women were often denied to men based on social stigmas. Some of the more common jobs that fell into this category were nurses, childcare providers, hospitability, management, flight attendants and secretaries etc. In countries where gender discrimination is considered an aspersion, it is also often difficult to prove. It is usually not as overtly evident as racial discrimination since the perpetrator can claim miscellaneous reasons to why an individual was denied equitable opportunities. Relocating gender equality deals with the degree of association between both men and women.

The division and discrimination in labor processes and professions on gender basis is closely linked to educational outcomes, opportunities, and disparities. Many scholars and policymakers attempted to address the problem of gender inequality through education. Amongst many others, education is viewed as a critical tool to uplift the marginalized sections, empower the subjugated; thereby contributing its share in creating a fair and just society. Education viewed as a socialization process has interesting insights to offer in the study of inequalities prevailing in the society. After poverty, gender is the most influential factor to keep people out of reach with regard to education (United Nations 2013). The gender disparity rises as one moves from primary to tertiary level, the only relief being that girl are more likely to reach the last grade in a particular level, once enrolled, than boys (United Nations 2013) and also as we towards higher enrollment rates, women at higher levels of education seem to outnumber men (United Nations 2013).

Furthermore, gender inequality follows even after the education to educational institutions as the workplace. The nature of gender relations at the higher education centers (as a workplace) is more crucial than at other organizations as it impacts the gender relations among the students who attend the colleges and institutions. At the higher education level, many efforts and studies are focused on bridging the gender gap by improving the enrollment rate of women in colleges and ensuring the fall in drop-out rates. This would ensure a quantitative gender balance, but significant qualitative differences continue to persist.

According to the Educational Statistics at a Glance (Government of India 2016), the Gender Parity Index of India is 1.03 for primary level, 1.01 for secondary level and 0.92 for a tertiary level. The emphasis needs to be shifted to higher education. After the entitlement until 14 years in India through the legislation of Right to Free & Compulsory Education, the suppression of women can be said to be further dependent on the highly unequal capabilities at the tertiary level and in the organization or workplace. The organization as an institution consisting of many interconnected individuals can identify opportunity and risks that an individual may be unable to perceive. This enhanced perception is essential because of the assumption of radical uncertainty—organizations as institutions have better capacities of orientation in these uncertain environments. Bringing diverse individuals together in an organization fills gaps in knowledge, motivation, and capability, and creates synergies. This is in line with the assumption of a distinctive distribution of knowledge, motivation and capabilities in the competence-based theory of organizations. The organizational ambiance widens the room for action in the sense of those who try to increase their opportunities by permanently looking for new goals, means, and alternatives. A single actor's possibilities are typically more restricted than several interconnected actors who combine their abilities in an organization.

The focus of this paper would try to look at both the former and later aspects. Theories such as invisible glass ceiling and dual work burden explain the lack of gender balance as we reach the apex of the organizational structure of academia but fail to gauge the inequality and discrimination even at the bottom of the pyramid. To tackle the inequality even at the lower rungs, mainstreaming gender is offered as the solution to adjust and deal with the multifaceted and various forms of discrimination and marginalization.

2. Gender and Capability Approach

Gender equality is incorporated in one of the Millennium Development Goals and now Sustainable Development Goals, where India has made a progress but not sufficient to meet the targets. South Asia lacks in witnessing an improvement in removing the disparity between men and women's enrollments at higher education level and in addressing the inequality at the workplace. The progress in nearing the SDG's for a developing nation is largely determined by the enhancement of women's capabilities (which also removes the disparity automatically). Moreover, proactive promotion of greater and equitable participation of women and men of all social and ethnic groups can have a significant downstream impact. More women both in public and private sectors, such as school teachers, health care providers, journalists, development workers, bank employees and so on, have a ripple effect—creating role models for women and girls in traditional communities where gender discrimination and sex segregation are normative (UNESCO 2010a). Similarly, Pereira (2014) explored the gender segregation and found that despite the change of the professional careers in recent years; the balance of women is still negative and progress has been uneven in science in general and in engineering in particular.

The research of 'gender' in higher education and relocating gender equality using capability approach framework relates to the third millennium development goal in two indicated ways, firstly achieving gender equality by working on the capabilities of women contributes to an increase in the effective/participation of women in academia which is an organizational structure and can be viewed as workplace. Secondly, women teaching staff has positive effects on the girls and their education (affecting their enrollment, learning, motivation, participation & dropout rates) (Kirk 2008; World Bank 2006; Ministry of Foreign Affairs, Government of Netherlands 1999) thereby contributes to the elimination of gender disparity at various levels of education, esp. higher education in this case. Pereira (2014) found in her official study that female students lack female role models to follow; they seem to be unable to find self-esteem as professional scientists and suggests that the involvement of more female engineers in professional engineering, including teaching duties, should serve as example and role models in students' education and future careers.

Sen (2005) in discussing capability approach argued that increasing women's agency can have a significant positive impact on the wellbeing of all people. In households, where women enjoy relatively more freedom, reflect in higher enrollment in higher education and access to outside employment. A relatively more amount of freedom reduces the dual work burden of being a woman thereby leaving more space for a higher education professional for spending quality time with one's work in any chosen way (Sen 1985). In the context of the capability approach, the gender discrimination can be fundamentally opposed to the equality of opportunity for women in any chosen dimension. Robeyns (2003) used capability approach to study gender inequality. The capability approach has enormous potential for addressing feminist concerns and questions related to health, voting power, political power, domestic violence, education and women's social status (Robeyns 2003; Alkire 2005). Feminist concerns and activism have played a role in expanding the capabilities of women vis-à-vis higher education (Rosenberg 1993; Stromquist 1993). Robeyns considered capabilities as real opportunities and selected a list of relevant capabilities. Gender inequality assessment was detailed after a four-step process: unconstrained brainstorming; testing draft list against literature available; engaging with other lists of capabilities; debating the list with other people. Education and knowledge were among the list of capabilities she put forth. She defined education and knowledge as "being able to be educated and to use and produce knowledge" and suggested that capability analysis of educational equality should investigate the hurdles faced by girls in educational achievements, such as sexist behavior, sexual harassment, gender differences in expectations and encouragement, a men-dominated class atmosphere, etc. (Robeyns 2003).

Through this study, the capability that needs to be enriched for women can be contemplated which helps in reducing the existing disparity. Mostly, in understanding the subjugation in the case of women, it is important to judge it using combined capability approach. Women all over the world lacked support for central human functions, and the lack of support is to some extent caused by them being women. However, in partial fulfillment of the MDG's, the potential of women to be capable of these human functions is restored to some extent, although much remains to be done (Nussbaum and Glover 1995). According to Nussbaum (2003), the unequal failure in capability is a problem of justice. In continuation, the reasons behind the deficiencies in their functionalities can also be explored under this study. In relocating the gender equality, it is essential to execute a holistic study. Firstly, in determining a set of capabilities that helps us in contemplating and contextualizing the state of women esp. in higher education. This can be done by reviewing the existing literature. Secondly, collecting and investigating the inequality, focusing on the causes, in the above-chosen domain (higher education).

The major objective of the present paper is to uncover the hidden aspects that contribute and maintain the subjugation of women at the workplace in higher education institutions. To recognize the concerns that women as an employee in academia face in India; it is, therefore, vital to explore the Indian socio-cultural matrix in which gender relations are rooted. Lastly, achieving a mere increase in the number of women or an equal proportion of men and women does not guarantee equality. Although gender parity (in quantitative figures) may be achieved but the barriers to equality (qualitative in nature) would not entirely cease to exist. Capability approach could a large extent guarantee that, as it involves both the organizational level as well as individual level barriers that restrict the progression towards parity and equality.

This paper attempts to develop the list of capabilities in the Indian higher education context which help in assessing gender inequality in academia and which act as indicators to be focused on, to proceed towards relocating gender equality. By querying the answers broadly, it is tried to enquire deeper into teacher's attitudes and their readiness to upkeep procedures and contribute in movements against gender discrimination and inequality, and to foster a gender welcoming ambiance in university. This study probes into the nature and attitudes of teaching and administrative staff to the concept of feminism and indicators that denote gender-responsive practices. We attempt to examine gender practices locating it within a conceptual framework of Capability Approach (CA).

3. Method

Pattern of access in higher education in India is itself an evidence of discrimination and the most appropriate method for unfolding would be interaction with individuals who negotiated access to higher education and those who could not. Informant Interviews were found to be the most appropriate method to be used, key informant interviews are helpful in exhaustive and qualitative information about experiences, opinions, and beliefs. The themes covered for interviews were social inclusion, opportunities, social and cultural capital and negotiation of access to higher education.

The subject matter of this research was so diverse that any number of respondents could not be sufficient. Therefore, it was appropriate to find out individuals those who had gone through a transition. So snowballing technique was used and forty respondents (25 percent men and 75 percent women) across all departments were selected but we started observing repetitive answers just after thirty respondents, still ten more were required to find out further variation in answer, yet no significant variation was found. The database includes one of the central universities from Andhra Pradesh in India. We have supplemented the obtained data through field notes and recorded interaction patterns. Faculty and staff were consulted based on convenience sampling for semi-structured in-depth interviews based on open-ended as well as close-ended questions that were settled pertaining to the functionalities that they have a reason to value as academicians and the obstructions in beings (as teacher, researcher, in satisfaction, happiness etc.) or doings (performance).

The nature of the research problem requires investigation from qualitative perspectives only. Secondary data had been collected mostly through the documents of regulatory bodies such as Ministry of Human Resource Development and various other committees and commissions on higher education. Qualitative method is found to be suitable measures for examining the personal and social perception of employees at the workplace (academia). A crucial limitation recognized through review of the literature reveals that most of the studies were frequently explored merely on the theoretical and conceptual basis. Hence, the present study attempts to view the factor of marginalization in a more understandable way by field inquisition.

4. Results and Discussion

The discourses on gender dimensions have been one of the important focuses of research over the past years. This has provided new insights into empirical underpinnings by recognizing gender as a critical analytical category. Gender as a category of analysis suggests that each gender must be examined in relationship to other to get the entire account. Gender as the analytical category is vital as it confers to the idea of subjugation and power relations. Literature asserts that gender issues are enclosed in a dissimilar way depending on theoretical and political perspectives. Largely the understanding of gender issues is grounded in feminist perspectives. The responses in our study exemplify that some teachers, especially men are in absolute refutation of the gender inequality and uneven power relations. Collaborating one's understanding of various social process and structures about gender were argued to be exaggerations and not realistic. This is not unusual but insightful of societal opinions about women's pursuit for gender parity. Yet gender inequality is recognized and challenged by most of the female faculty. One of the respondents from sciences obscures the gender processes using arguments related to merit and thus explains scholarship as an alien entity thus delinking the human participation in constructing or discovering knowledge:

> "There is no denial that inconsistencies and irregularities are a part of any system ... , but the higher education and research ought to be only in pursuit of scholarship and promoting merit. Hence, for the production of knowledge, merit should realign the standing of actors and their relationships, it should not happen that actors and their roles reshape and determine the way scholarship can be produced; this might have grieved impacts and compromise on the production of knowledge itself in academia ... The role of women should be looked into and perhaps reformed but cannot become a determining base or a code book in an institutional framework as the output would justify the nature of relations and power equations that persist."

Though, the portals of education have opened up for women, the extent of their integration and progress in science and technology (S&T) is still governed by patriarchal and old-fashioned mores in the Indian context. This determines the position of women in the society/workplace and, colors perceptions of young girls about science as a career (Datta 2010). Women complained about the hard attitude towards them, especially in traditionally men-dominated disciplines (S&T). Women opined that colleges and universities can attract more women in science and engineering if they improve the departmental ambiance to promote the integration of women as faculty and researchers (Evetts 1994). This would serve as a motivational factor for future generations and will help to combat stereotypes like women don't perform well in S&T.

Faculties in Sciences and Technology cited the problem that institutes lack faculty mentors and has overwhelming work requirements. Women faculties also expressed concern about spousal employment and child care. Many private colleges do not provide appropriate benefits to women like paid maternity leaves and child care facilities which is a great concern for women. Men should be equally involved in raising their children which demands paternity leave and child care facilities which will help in advancing equal rights for both men and women. Few women agreed that due to the societal pressure they took breaks in their careers for child bearing and rearing and re-entry was quite difficult for them. Even with equal qualifications and achievements to that of their counterparts, women are perceived less favorable in terms of their ability and accomplishments. This stereotyping tends to be reflected in evaluations and promotions and places women at a disadvantage for advancement (Eagly and Karau 2002).

Explanations have been offered as to why gender differences exist within the institution. Most of them have considered gender differences as an outcome of socio-cultural and historical/psychological conditions. Liberal feminism upholds individual competition in a hierarchical society arguing that one's sex should be irrelevant to one's chances for mobility, choices and personal fulfillment. Radical feminism argues that gender is the most fundamental social category and celebrates the biological capacities and cultural creations of women. Socialist feminism regards to gender and social class as fundamental categories and analyses how women's status is a function of patriarchy, capitalism, and racism. Recently feminists have entered the poststructuralist debate as post-structuralism assumes that there is no fixed set of meanings that depend on an individual's location in time and social structure. Post-structuralism also offers the theoretical perspective which some scholars view as important to the development of multicultural emancipator work, although others are more doubtful.

The undesirable typecasts attitudes towards women endanger the institutional goals, making most organizations losing long term benefits. The positive influence of attitude between men and women at work are ample, these constructive effects embrace more operative teamwork, enhances job satisfaction, which is all consistent with human resource goals. Within the last decade, another group of theories became more distorted in terms of debate by exploring a poststructuralist and postmodern perspectives that dissolve the postulate of a stable gender identity. These theories claim that widespread policies and practices in the social system perpetuate discriminatory treatment of women. The most influential meanings of gender in a social space are drawn from social and cultural meanings attributed to it. The meanings thereby can be identified by gender as a category of the top social construction of sex.

Persistently, many types of research turned their consideration to spot the causes for these gender differences. A woman is primarily still seen as a homemaker in India and marriage is preferred over career as remarked by the subjects of the present study. Robeyns (2003) identified 'domestic work and nonmarket care' as an important capability and highly gendered. It involves raising children, taking care of dependents and doing household work. Robeyns viewed that the functioning will be valuable and enjoyable if done out of choice and for short periods, but could become burdensome otherwise. Gender is also taken as social, psychological and cultural construct referring not necessarily a direct product of an individual's meanings attached to the biological division of sex. These social constructions attach themselves to behaviors, expectations, roles, representations and sometimes to values and beliefs. Only the gender lenses can disclose the process of exclusion and suppression. Power is not seen here as most efficiently hierarchical, although lines of authority and accountability are significant safeguards for the exercise of power in an organizational structure.

A gender-wise breakup of data related to awards in science and technology shows a consistent marginalization of women scientists and technologists worldwide, India being no exception. According to Noble Prize official website, 2016, only 48 women have been awarded noble prize between 1901–2016 (NobelPrize.org 2017). The noble prize received by females since 1901 are- 2 in Physics, 12 in Physiology/Medicine, 4 in Chemistry, 14 in Literature, 15 in Piece and 1 in Economics. Subjects belonging to Arts, Humanities, and Social Sciences are more related to social reality and exhibit relationship with society so it is attributed to the distinctiveness to the kind of the discipline also.

Due to the differential nature of the soft discipline, women display characteristics as compassion and empathy towards students in particular. However, they accepted that they remain muddled in the social dynamics of relationships and in the pulls and pushes of social and work roles. One of the respondents spoke about the significance of access and the participation as a part of response in the in-depth interview, which says—

> "The nature of gender dynamics cannot just be addressed by referring to—if women have equal access to something as men because the problem is deeper than that . . . At the level of appearance, it might be accessible but there are constraints thrown on being a woman to use that access to participate in the process is severely disabled . . . So even if the distance to be traveled to reach a destination is equal and it is accessible to take part in the race for both, the two roads are qualitatively different with a lot of bumps and breakers for women . . . "

Faculty expressed that they should be involved before making any change in goals, problems, and opportunities as it's finally on them to teach in the most effective way. Management must ensure that these are communicated to the rest of the staff in a timely fashion. Most of the faculty denied taking an active part as they considered it as an additional burden and diversion from the main task of teaching and research. Some considered it as necessary so that faculty has a direct say in the administration and formulation of rules and regulations. They felt institutions should provide more opportunities, training and mentorships for potential leaders. In a study done by Spendlove (2007), most of the respondents perceived that academic credibility and experience of university life were crucial for effective leadership in higher education, continued with their research and teaching activities alongside their managerial roles.

Women experience a strong gender bias when being evaluated for promotions on both their level of performance as well as their potential impact. Results of a survey conducted by Boatwright and Boatwright and Egidio (2003) also demonstrated that connectedness needs, gender role, self-esteem, and fears of negative evaluation accounted for a significant amount of the variance in predicting college women's leadership aspirations. Many women perceive leadership as an endeavor of men. Results from studies done by Gerber (1988) and Boatwright and Egidio (2003) suggested same. They asserted that they have more responsibilities at home but were not ready to accept that they possess a lower degree of abilities when they were asked to compare themselves with teachers who were men.

The professional environment and the socio-cultural context are inextricably associated. Most the women interviewed, feel that do not excel sufficiently in their career due to the stereotype that women are less ambitious and lesser committed due to family responsibilities. Catalyst (2004) shows that there is hardly a difference between senior men and women when aspiring for the highest roles in an organization. Ironically, Johns (2013) argues that today men still dominate at all levels of influence in an organizational structure with significant barriers existing for women aspirations to be achieved. Men belonging to the departments of sciences found to be involved deeply in research and teaching tasks than women. Publications of men were more as compared to women faculty staff in all the departments of Science faculty. Pereira, D. and Díaz, C.'s case study (Pereira Gómez and Díaz 2016) in the context of Earth Sciences reiterates the lower representation of women in scientific publications. But the staff, in general, believed that all women who wish to seek advancement should be offered the opportunity to do so in line with the other colleagues. Zahorik et al. (2003) obtained the same finding in their investigation. Laboratory work is a prerequisite in Science and due to multiple reasons women could not afford much time for laboratory work in contrast to men. The findings of Gupta and Sharma (2002) expressed that women in academic sciences are predisposed by the prevailing socio-cultural system. Women are held back by well accepted structural barriers of long working hours, inflexible working patterns (Vianen and Fischer 2002; Davidson and Cooper 1993). Women in faculty staff found it difficult to find peers through the academic networking circles which are dominated by men; it results in lessening the efficiency through increased advising loads, anxiety for more committed work and deficiency of appropriate mentors.

Women, in general, face the problems in research, publications due to a paucity of time for having dual responsibilities at work and home. They also face discrimination at points like work environment and social climates. Family responsibilities of women are frequently found to be the reasons for gender disparity in publication rates. Intrinsic within this historical and socio-cultural process is the reality of gendered perceptions of the profession. Though women's employment is increasingly accepted in society, it is found that girls are encouraged to take a degree that would enhance her prospects of making a good match. Datta (2010) states that teaching followed by disciplines like arts and medicine are considered to be a most appropriate profession for women as they are compatible with other responsibilities of women as mother and wife.

Women, like in every profession, had to manage their careers and families. It has been observed that professional women who work outside the home perform a larger share of household work than men. Women are bound to pay equal commitment to family and job, those are considered successful are those who can handle both in a proficient manner. Consequently, there are greater chances of a career rather than the family getting compromised in this process of balancing (Scandura and Lankau 1997). Discrimination occurs in parts but comparing actual performance in academic jobs is difficult, even then there is growing concern about the differential treatment of women which is not related to performance. Some studies suggest that deficiencies are presumed even when no differences exist because of how historical roles have persisted for long (Dubno 1985; Powell 1999; Thomas and Alderfer 1989).

Women are more likely to make personal adjustments within relationships that help them in collaborative ways of working (Bass and Avolio 1994). The reason for such finding is the higher quotients of emotional sensitivity in women and it is also argued in few studies as women usually want 'multi-dimensional' lives that escort towards progress in the organization. These can be reiterated in the study conducted as most of the women in the academic faculty than men have described the plethora of adjustments that they go through in the workplace which is unusually left unnoticed by an insensitive eye. Strohschein (2016) found that men are benefitted from marriage and family whereas marriage acts as barriers for women, the benefit of men seems to be at the cost of women's freedom, opportunities and choices. It was found during our interview that those women who are multi-tasking in handling the diverse work could manage the position and so possess high ability to do a task efficiently. Most of the women have complained that the multi-tasking nature often runs contrary to performing a deep and specialized research activity.

The focus of attention is constantly shifted, much higher in the contexts of women that it becomes demotivating to pursue an effective and rigorous research. The relationship between gender and performance at the workplace is not straightforward rather it is multifaceted and complex in nature. There are several studies based on gender differences in academic lines that reveal major issues as socio-cultural background, previous socialization experiences, interpretations, and expectations of social situations. Results indicate that the configuration of professional organizations and gender-role stereotypes infiltrates into the profession and escorts to differences of performances at the workplace. One of the respondents from social sciences sums it up the following way:

> "The role played by gender in shaping one's habitus and social and cultural capital is extremely crucial yet under-examined. Even men and women have same levels of education, degrees, and other institutional requirements, cultural capital differs and that has an impact on the levels of performance, as the Head of Department, I have observed many women and men who are first generation learners or come from the lower classes, women more than men censor what they speak, struggle to socialize, can switch topics and make rarely adjustable to the changing situations with ease . . .

> . . . Higher Education is a space where, more so in social sciences, free and diverse ideas with varying terminology and accents are discussed and social practices are critiqued and debated heavily . . . the difference is cultural capital does not make a person smoothly engage with such subtle scenarios of sensitivity. Men are far more comfortably spaced than women, they socialize easier, they speak, accept and change and put a point across easier . . . it's not the same with women, they are more introvert, less open, highly insecure and hypersensitive hampering their social existence in small measures . . . "

This research moves a little deeper crossing the abstract formations into listing the capabilities that tangibly help us in dealing with gender inequality in higher education institutions. The list is backed by theoretical underpinnings, a thorough review of literature, is substantiated by empirical works, brainstormed and scrutinized in light of discussions with teachers (few of whom were the subjects who participated in the current study), in focused group discussions, and also with various experts and research scholars at various conferences and seminar interactions held on the themes of Higher Education. The inputs are proposed and cross checked with the help of various post surveys of this study in conceptualizing the nature of subjugation of women. A relevant list of capabilities developed by us below helps to relocate gender equality, focusing on the professional front. We do not concentrate on the disparity but on inequality, therefore although an equal number and representation of women and men in academia is imperative, but does not necessarily bring equality of men and women in the profession of higher education. We provide a situational discourse on how equality should also be focused on as much as a quantitative parity. In this study, we restrict ourselves to highlight the parameters of equality in a general context.

- Self-Esteem—It is the fundamental trait that contributes to the psychological well-being of an individual and also to the performance levels of individuals. Self Esteem comprises of two parts—self-confidence and self-respect. Any kinds of discrimination or any abused form of treatment would directly impact on women's self-confidence. Widening of choices, professional satisfaction, and equal status convinces the individual to deserve well-being not necessarily at the cost of freedom or interest. Any kind of academic achievement has an implicit impact on the self-esteem. It allows creativity at the workplace which is an imperative characteristic in the domain of education.

- Motivational levels—Motivation plays a vital role in achieving one's ends. It acts as a catalyst in an endeavor. It is shaped up with many internal and external factors in academia. In the mode of subjugation, women cease to possess the driving force as they have to work harder to overcome the barriers and to achieve the same equal ends that of men.
- Overall working hours spent in the organization—Due to the dual role conjured on women and the stereotypical perceptions in regard to the family, timing, and duty; Women are deprived of the both time and freedom which are fundamental requirements for research.
- Research publications—Research funding and publications are an integral part of assessing the progress and promotions in the higher education. The simple quantitative comparison of research publications can partially, if not fully, help in understanding the gender inequality.
- Administrative and decision-making posts—In a hierarchical framework power and status are biasedly associated with the positions. The representation of women in administrative works contributes to a shift in the present outlook of gender inequality.
- Research Grants—The number of grants and the amount of aid applied/sanctioned by/to women is also a significant factor in determining the reach of women relative to men. Another element which demonstrated the discriminating effect can be conceptualized by calculating a number of research grants applied to the amount sanctioned for women.
- Participation Rate—Most of the women are unable to avail the opportunity of participation in seminars/conferences/workshops due to overburden, lack of company, safety measures etc. They remain behind in social bonding and being a part of the formal/informal academic circle.

Feminist discourses have developed various examples of how a patriarchal society marginalizes women at the workplace. Gender stereotypes not only denote differences in how men and women are but also denote norms about what kind of behaviors are suitable for each of them (Eagly and Karau 2002; Heilman 2001; Rudman and Glick 2001). Empirically, Lindberg et al. (2011) demonstrates the case study of Sweden which is regarded as one of the most advanced countries in respect of gender equality; yet the dominant percentage of professors in Swedish colleges and universities were men the gender gap remains quite high. Despite the fact that women have been admitted to higher education in Sweden for 120 years, and more than 60 percent of Swedish university students are women.

A more truly gender-responsive culture would be characterized by gender equity in access, redressing structural barriers that influence the access and participation of both sexes, and women's active role in decision-making in the management and administration of higher education (Leo-Rhynie 1999, p. 10). Strategies must be explored by institutions to unite gender-responsive practices at workplace. This empirical study substantiates on the existence of barriers to achieving these functionalities desired by women, these functionalities cater to the core of the profession in higher education. Theoretically, they might have equal access to the necessary means to achieve the ends, but empirically they fall short in reaching the ends they have a reason to value (Kabeer 1999). The findings highlight the necessity for bridging this inequality by improving these particular capabilities which are beneficial for individuals as well as the institutions. The aforementioned list developed by us was in consultation with the post-research survey with faculties in various positions at the university where we have carried out the in-depth interviews, thus contributing towards operationalizing Capability Approach.

5. Conclusions

Discrimination, marginalization, and inequalities are visibly present in the social structures and are further improved and encouraged by its functioning. The cultural and psychological constructs further contribute to these imperfections, positively or negatively. The most efficient and non-coercive (not by rules, laws, regulating etc.) way of achieving gender equality in Indian Higher education context is to make the individual capable of performing those functions that would reduce or remove subjugation and raise them to equal beings. That is by improving capabilities of marginalized sections and empowering the individuals of these sections by suitable and appropriate means.

The subjugation of women can be said as the suppression of the capabilities, disabling them to be equal to men; these immaturities, containment and lack of capabilities are the barriers that hinder the functioning of women. The progress of a gender-inclusive culture must be the concern of all stakeholders of the institution. However, this affirmative perception and strong backing might diminish without an explicit gender policy to promise its execution. In stereotyping the role of women and men, there is also an element of stereotyping the whole category of gender as a single entity comprising of homogeneous individuals, but capability approach restores the uniqueness of every individual with a varying value i.e., a fractional combination of capabilities listed. This helps us to incorporate and note the ambiguity in different individual choices, preferences. This advantage can be included using the capability approach. As Sen describes the capability approach includes the ambiguities (Sen 1985), this approach is justified in relocating equality without harming their diversity, uniqueness, and individual preferences.

The aim of the study is essentially not to quantify the attributes of inequality to make them measurable, but to choose attributes which enable an effective comparative basis to address inequality. Inspecting and studying the above semi-structured interviews; one can conceptualize the oppressed capabilities of women particularly in Science and Technology thereby enabling the researchers to relocate the gender equality in the domain of higher education. The findings thus far show that an empowering milieu exists for the organization to generate a gender policy and plan of action; these actions would benefit in the formation of a gender-inclusive culture. Acting on these parameters would help in achieving gender parity in higher education, if not sufficiently but significantly. There is clearly a need to look at how reforms in the education sector are impacting women teachers' sense of personal and professional identity. These are not the prescriptive list of capabilities, but however, as a working paper, one could firmly state that they are crucial capabilities which cannot be escaped in addressing the unachieved and far way equality. Relocating the impositions of gender would minimize the oppression, discrimination and subjugation prevailing over a long period. This relocation helps in achieving balance and in attaining equality. Capability approach can act as an instrumental framework in tackling gender disparity and inequality in the Indian higher education context. Their capabilities and functionalities can be envisioned through education and empowerment. Through the elimination of gender disparity, it is also observed that it does not necessarily ensure equality, but reversely, improving and working on inequality affects the quantitative disparity by reducing it.

Author Contributions: This paper is entirely a collective effort where the study has been conceptualized and conducted as a team, where in both the authors have been present at all the stages of the study. However, if we were to judge with instrumental precision, then the design of study, analysis of extensive interviews, editing etc. have received relatively higher efforts from Dr. Tanu Shukla and the collection of data, writing the paper in the current format would have relatively greater inputs from Kalyan Kumar. Both the authors read and approved the final manuscript.

Conflicts of Interest: The authors declare no conflict of interest.

References

Alkire, Sabina. 2005. Why the Capability Approach? *Journal of Human Development* 6: 115–35. [CrossRef]
Bass, Bernard M., and Bruce J. Avolio. 1994. Shatter the glass ceiling: Women may make better managers. *Human Resource Management* 33: 549–60. [CrossRef]

Boatwright, Karyn J., and Rhonda Kaye Egidio. 2003. Psychological Predictors of College Women's Leadership Aspirations. *Journal of College Student Development* 44: 653–69. [CrossRef]

Ministry of Foreign Affairs, Government of Netherlands. 1999. Gender Equity in Education in Pakistan: Evaluation of Education Component of Social Action Program Project1 (SAPP 1). Available online: https://www.unicef.org/evaldatabase/index_14215.html (accessed on 7 July 2017).

Catalyst. 2004. *Women and Men is U.S. Corporate Leadership: Same Workplace, Different Realities?* New York: Catalyst, Available online: http://www.catalyst.org/system/files/Women%20and_Men_in_U.S._Corporate_Leadership_Same_Workplace_Different_Realities.pdf (accessed on 18 June 2017).

Datta, Smith. 2010. The Glass Ceiling: The Why and the Therefore. Vigyan Prasar. Available online: http://www.vigyanprasar.gov.in/Radioserials/1empowering%20women%20through%20s&T.pdf (accessed on 18 June 2017).

Davidson, Marilyn J., and Cary L. Cooper. 1993. *Shattering the Glass Ceiling: The Woman Manager*. London: Chapman.

Deloitte. 2013. *Status of Higher Education in South India 2013*. New Delhi: Deloitte, CII.

Donnell, Susan M., and Jay Hall. 1980. Men and Women as Managers. *Organizational Dynamics* 8: 60–77. [CrossRef]

Dubno, Peter. 1985. Attitudes toward Women Executives: A Longitudinal Approach. *Academy of Management Journal* 28: 235–39. [CrossRef]

Eagly, Alice H., and Steven J. Karau. 2002. Role congruity theory of prejudice towards female leaders. *Psychological Review* 109: 573–98. [CrossRef] [PubMed]

European Commission. 2013. *She Figures 2012, Gender in Research and Innovation. Statistics and Indicators.* Luxembourg: European Commission.

Evetts, Julia. 1994. Women and Career in Engineering: Continuity and Change in the Organisation. *Work Employment & Society* 8: 101–12.

Gerber, Gwendolyn L. 1988. Leadership roles and the gender stereotype traits. *Sex Roles* 18: 649–68. [CrossRef]

Government of India. 2016. *Educational Statistics at a Glance*; New Delhi: Ministry of Human Resource Development, Department of School Education & Literacy, Government of India. Available online: http://mhrd.gov.in/sites/upload_files/mhrd/files/statistics/ESG2016_0.pdf (accessed on 16 June 2017).

Gupta, Namrata, and Arun K. Sharma. 2002. Women Scientists in India. *Social Studies of Science* 32: 901–15. [CrossRef]

Heilman, Madeline E. 2001. Description and Prescription: How Gender Stereotypes Prevent Women's Ascent Up the Organizational Ladder. *Journal of Social Issues* 57: 657–74. [CrossRef]

Huyer, Sophia, and Nancy Halfkin. 2013. Brazilian women lead in science, technology and innovation, study shows. *Elsevier Connect*. Available online: http://www.elsevier.com/connect/brazilian-women-lead-inscience-technology-and-innovation-study-shows (accessed on 17 June 2017).

Johns, Merida L. 2013. Breaking the Glass Ceiling: Structural, Cultural, and Organizational Barriers Preventing Women from Achieving Senior and Executive Positions. *Perspectives in Health Information Management*. Available online: http://perspectives.ahima.org/breaking-the-glass-ceiling-structural-cultural-and-organizational-barriers-preventing-women-from-achieving-senior-and-executive-positions/ (accessed on 14 June 14 2017).

Kabeer, Naila. 1999. Resources, Agency, Achievements: Reflections on the Measurement of Women's Empowerment. *Development and change* 30: 435–64. [CrossRef]

Kirk, Jackie. 2008. *Women Teaching in South Asia*. New Delhi: Sage Publications.

Kulandaiswamy, Vangalampalayam C. 2005. Reconstruction of higher education in India. *The Hindu*, May 18.

Leo-Rhynie, Elsa. 1999. *Gender Mainstreaming in Education: A Reference Manual for Governments and Other Stakeholders*. London: Commonwealth Secretariat.

Lindberg, Leif, Ulla Riis, and Charlotte Silander. 2011. Gender equality in Swedish higher education: Patterns and shifts. *Scandinavian Journal of Educational Research* 55: 165–79. [CrossRef]

Ministry of Human Resource Development. 2013. *National Higher Education Mission*; New Delhi: Ministry of Human Resource Development, Government of India.

NobelPrize.org. 2017. Nobel Prize Awarded Women. NobelPrize.org. Available online: https://www.nobelprize.org/nobel_prizes/lists/women.html (accessed on 17 June 2017).

Nussbaum, Martha. 2003. Capabilities as Fundamental Entitlements: Sen and Social Justice. *Feminist Economics* 9: 33–59. [CrossRef]

Nussbaum, Martha Craven, and Jonathan Glover. 1995. *Women, Culture, and Development: A Study of Human Capabilities*. Oxford: Clarendon Press.

Pereira, Dolores. 2014. Improving Female Participation in Professional Engineering Geology to Bring New Perspectives to Ethics in the Geosciences. *International Journal of Environmental Research and Public Health* 11: 9429–445. [CrossRef] [PubMed]

Pereira Gómez, Dolores, and Capitolina Díaz. 2016. Are women properly represented in scientific publication and research? Interim results from a Spanish case study in Earth Sciences. *Episodes* 39: 52–58. [CrossRef]

Powell, Gary N. 1999. *Reflections on Glass Ceiling Effect: Handbook of Gender & Work*. Thousand Oaks: Sage Publications.

Robeyns, Ingrid. 2003. Sen's Capability Approach and Gender Inequality: Selecting Relevant Capabilities. *Feminist Economics* 9: 61–92. [CrossRef]

Rosenberg, Rosalind. 1993. *Beyond Separate Spheres: Intellectual Roots of Modern Feminism*. New Haven: Yale University Press.

Rudman, Laurie A., and Peter Glick. 2001. Prescriptive Gender Stereotypes and Backlash toward Agentic Women. *Journal of Social Issues* 57: 743–62. [CrossRef]

Scandura, Terri A., and Melenie J. Lankau. 1997. Relationships of Gender, Family Responsibility and Flexible Work Hours to Organizational Commitment and Job Satisfaction. *Journal of Organizational Behavior* 18: 377–91. [CrossRef]

Sen, Amartya. 1985. *Commodities and Capabilities*. New Delhi: Oxford University Press.

Sen, Amartya. 2005. *Development as Freedom*. New Delhi: Oxford University Press.

Spendlove, Marion. 2007. Competencies for effective leadership in higher education. *International Journal of Educational Management* 21: 407–17. [CrossRef]

Strohschein, Lisa. 2016. Do Men Really Benefit More From Marriage Than Women? *American Journal of Public Health* 106: e2. Available online: http://doi.org/10.2105/AJPH.2016.303308 (accessed on 18 June 2017).

Stromquist, Nelly P. 1993. Sex-Equity Legislation in Education: The State as Promoter of Women's Rights. *Review of Educational Research* 63: 379–407. [CrossRef]

Thomas, David A., and Clayton P. Alderfer. 1989. *The Influence of Race on Career Dynamics, Handbook of Career Theory*. Cambridge: Cambridge University Press.

UNESCO. 2010a. *Advocacy Brief: Gender Issues in Higher Education*. Bangkok: UNESCO.

United Nations. 2013. *The Millennium Development Goals Report 2013*. New York: United Nations.

Vianen, Annelies EM, and Agneta H. Fischer. 2002. Illuminating the glass ceiling: The role of organizational culture preferences. *Journal of Occupational and Organizational Psychology* 75: 315–37. [CrossRef]

World Bank. 2006. *World Development Report: Equality and Development*. Washington: World Bank.

Zahorik, John, Anke Halbach, Karen Ehrle, and Alex Molnar. 2003. Teaching Practices for Smaller Classes. *Educational Leadership* 61: 75–77.

administrative
sciences

MDPI

Article

Women and Leadership in Higher Education in China: Discourse and the Discursive Construction of Identity

Jiayi Zhao [1] and Karen Jones [2,*]

[1]   Independent Researcher, Lanzhou 730000, China; jiayi.zhao@student.reading.ac.uk
[2]   Institute of Education, University of Reading, Reading RG6 6UA, UK
*   Correspondence: karen.jones@reading.ac.uk

Received: 1 May 2017; Accepted: 15 June 2017; Published: 29 June 2017

Abstract: Prior research indicates that just 4.5 percent of mainland China's higher educational institution leaders are female. This article extends theory and research by drawing attention to identity and Discourse as an important, yet under-researched, aspect of the problem of women's underrepresentation in higher education leadership. Drawing on in-depth qualitative interviews with nine female academics in Chinese universities and informed by discursive approaches to identity and constructionist views, we analyze how women construct multiple identities, the interplay of identities, and the influence of broader societal Discourses of gender and leadership. The findings highlight the interplay between competing multiple identities, and illustrate how the women's identities are shaped and constrained by dominant historical and cultural Discourses in Chinese society, which results in identity regulation (Alvesson and Billing 2009), notably identity positioning that is congruent with social norms and conventions. A key finding is that the female academics reject the leader identity. This is true for those in middle management positions, as well as women in early career stages, who might otherwise aspire to leadership. Implications for the leadership pipeline in China's universities is discussed and recommendations are made for future research directions.

Keywords: identity; leadership; gender; Discourse; higher education; China; women

---

1. Introduction

Although women around the world face many common barriers to higher education leadership, China presents a distinct case (Zhang 2005) Since the Han Dynasty (B.C. 207–A.D. 202), Confucianism has dominated social and official ideology and is said to have attributed to the subordination of women (Mak 2013). Traditionally, under this regime, women were asked to obey 'the three obedience's and the four virtues'. The three obedience's require a woman to obey her father before marriage, her husband during married life, and her sons in widowhood; the four virtues represent physical charm, fidelity, propriety in speech, and efficiency in needlework (Cheng 2008). Traditionally, the pursuit of a career and the possibility of a high position in society was a man's job. Men were likened to being the pillar or backbone of the family. Although many women undertook waged work, historically, they occupied roles of a lesser status in the workplace (Mak 2013). After several thousand years of Chinese feudal society, it has been difficult to eliminate old ways of thinking (Zhao 2008). Although in the past few decades, particularly since the 1990s, significant social transitions have taken place in China (Zhang 2005), Chinese society continues to attribute well-defined roles to men and women (Attané 2012).

Although nowadays women's employment rates in China are amongst the highest in the world, with almost three women out of four in the labor force (Attané 2012), with many women occupying management roles and taking responsibility for promoting the construction and development of universities, relatively few women progress to senior leadership (Angeloff 2010; Sheng 2009;

Wang and Kai 2015). In higher education, a survey of presidents (the equivalent of Vice Chancellors in the UK context) in 1792 of mainland China's higher educational institutions, conducted by Renmin University of China, found that only 4.5% of leaders were female (cited in (Xue 2008)). Another study of the resumes of 7796 top-level university leaders at 1166 Chinese universities found a comparably low proportion of female leaders (Wang and Kai 2015), and a study of female leaders in a top university group, referred to as Project 985, found one or two female leaders in each institution, and some universities had none. Moreover, women were found to predominantly occupy deputy positions and serve as Communist Party leaders (Appendix A), rather than university leaders (Wang et al. 2013).

Explanations arising from prior research pinpoint a range of sociocultural barriers that may explain women's underrepresentation in leadership, specifically male-dominated networks, social stereotyping, gender discrimination in promotion and work overload due to dual work and family responsibilities (see (Zhang 2005, 2010; Huang and Aaltio 2014)). Further challenges arise for women because of dominant historical Discourses of gender and leadership. Even in contexts such as education where women often outnumber men, prototypes of leaders are predominantly male and so are the scripts that set the norms of associated attributes and characteristics for leaders (Eagly and Karau 2002). A situation of this kind fosters a masculine Discourse of leadership where leadership is viewed as male gendered, and this interplays with historical and cultural Discourses of gender that foster an idealized image of women as caring housewives and mothers (Fairhurst 2009). Since, gender plays a profound role in the formation of professional identity and acceptance within a community of practice (Nagatomo 2012), dominant Discourses of gender and leadership shape identities (Ford 2006).

It is against this background that our study, based on interviews with nine women sampled from two universities in China, analyzes how the women construct their (multiple gendered) identities, in relation to broader societal Discourses of gender and leadership. This is guided by three key questions:

1. How do female academics define their identities?
2. How do they talk about the female leader identity more generally?
3. In what ways is this talk (discourse) intertwined with larger societal Discourses of leadership and gender?

Following social constructionist perspectives (Vivien 1995), and informed by the classic literature on 'doing gender' (Butler 1999; West and Zimmerman 1987), we view (gendered) identities as talked into being and performed through interaction, influenced by historical, societal/cultural, and institutional factors, rather than being in there somewhere, an a priori identity that pre-exists talk (Van De Mieroop and Clifton 2016). Identity is treated as something we 'do' rather than something we 'have' (Fletcher 2004). Furthermore, individuals can have multiple identities throughout their life, related to social roles in professional and private spheres of life (for example, mother, wife, lecturer, leader) (Alvesson et al. 2008).

We explore identity from the perspective of discursive practices (Wiggins 2017), which allow the researcher to delve deep into the context, especially historical and cultural or political aspects and view this context as a medium for the social construction process (Fairhurst 2009). By taking a discursive and social constructionist perspective, we seek to provide a dynamic view of identity construction in the study context that reflects how individual, organizational, and socio-historical influences reflexively interrelate at a moment in time (Jaros 2012). This approach emphasizes the active role of language in the construction of reality (Lamsa and Sintonen), especially distinguishing discourse (little-d) and Discourse (big-D). Gee (1999) explains that little-d discourse refers to the micro-practices of talk, emerging in interviews, through which identities are talked into being, and big-D Discourse refers to 'the entire interlocking web of practices, structures, and ideologies: a system of understanding and exploration that prefigures which practices and interpretations are available, and how practices and structures are understood' (Kiesling 2006, p. 262). Put simply, discourses (little-d) and (big-D) are reflexively linked, since talk emerging in little 'd' discourse is affected by the larger societal Discourses available to an individual, which they enact and make relevant through talk (Jones and Jonathan forthcoming). Although individuals have some room to exercise agency, gender identity and related gendered roles are shaped and regulated by powerful Discourses in society (Alvesson and Billing 2009, p. 101; Lindsey 2015).

In this perspective, our study contributes to understanding the process by which women construct their identities, considering the multidimensionality of identities, such as the intersections between different social identities, within the context of dominant Discourses of gender and leadership pertaining to history and culture in China.

The paper begins with an outline of the theoretical framework underpinning the study, beginning with a discussion of universities, it draws on the literature on gender, identity, Discourses and leadership. Next, we explain the method adopted for the study, then we present segments of data from nine interviews with our analyses, followed by a discussion of the findings and conclusion.

2. Theoretical Framework

Historically organizations have been built upon the expectations and aspirations of men (Witz and Savage 1992), and universities are no exception (O'Connor 2014). It is said that universities are dominated by masculine Discourse (Harley 2003; Harding et al. 2010), and masculinized hegemonic structures, with the overwhelming majority of senior occupations occupied by men and definitions of excellence and merit (O'Connor 2014), and norms and values (Savigny 2014, p. 797) that benefit men but discriminate against women (Morley and Crossouard 2016). Masculinized cultures foster homosocial networks (Fletcher et al. 2007). These can resemble an exclusive gentleman's club (O'Connor 2014; Thomas and Davies 2002) and appear unfriendly (Morley and Crossouard 2016; Davies and Holloway 1995), or even hostile toward women (Williams et al. 2006). The higher up the hierarchy one goes, the more social capital appears to matter (O'Connor 2014). Precisely because Chinese society is permeated by relationships (guanxi), men benefit greatly from the social capital and opportunities that social networks provide (Lyness and Thompson 2000). Women, on the other hand, are constrained in taking part in important social networks by powerful socio-cultural barriers (Zhang 2005; Huang and Aaltio 2014; Zhang 2010). Female academics in Chinese universities are affected in many other often subtle ways (Zhang 2001). For instance, prior research suggests that women can be deterred from pursuing or accepting leadership positions because of the 'organizational culture of male-dominated senior management [. . .], power politics, and exclusive networks among male colleague' (Zhao 2008, p. 78). In consequence, the opportunity structures for males and females in Chinese universities are different and 'social prejudice against women is very strong' (Zhang 2005, p. 105).

Studies confirm that gender is especially pertinent to cultural scripts for women (Lindsey 2015), such that gender Discourse is infused with historical and cultural patterns of thought regarding the category 'women' and this may shape and constrain the identity work of women who transgress social norms by entering professions not stereotypically associated with the category 'woman'. As such, the 'doing of gender' (West and Zimmerman 1987) involves enacting specific identities through a repertoire of practices (Martin 2003), associated with stereotypical and socially constructed masculine and feminine characteristics linked to biological categories of males and females (Holmes 2007). Exactly because individuals are held accountable to their sex category 'doing gender' (West and Zimmerman 1987), and because they are validated for 'doing gender well' (Mavin and Grandy 2012, pp. 3–4), 'gender is a powerful ideological device', which produces, reproduces and legitimizes the choices and limits that are predicated on sex category' (West and Zimmerman 1987, p. 72).

The juncture between gender and identity is mediated by powerful historical and cultural scripts. Identity is shaped and constrained by social norms that one is required to abide by to be accepted by others (Ashforth 2000), shaped by the Discourses available, through culture, which individuals draw on in communications with other people (Vivien 1995, p. 123). From this perspective, Discourses and related discursive practices provide the means through which identities are crafted (Ford 2006, p. 79). For instance, Discourses, such as patriarchy, influence the identity of an individual (Collinson 2003; Halford and Leonard 2006). In consequence of masculinized cultures within higher education, 'women's academic identities are often forged in otherness, as strangers in opposition to (privileged) men's belonging and entitlement' (Morley 2010, p.38). Although individuals have some room for agency in crafting their identity, this agency is shaped by available Discourses (Jaros 2012, p. 49). Since values, norms, and rules are expected to be adhered to if one is to behave in accordance with social expectations, identity work involves some degree of identity regulation (Alvesson and Billing 2009). In consequence, individuals are constrained, to some extent, by social structures, power relations and other factors in their social context (Alvesson and Billing 2009, p. 99).

Theories of Discourse acknowledge the fact that although occupational roles are given 'off the peg', they come with cultural 'scripts' attached—patterns of belief, values, attitudes, expectations, ways of thinking, and so on (Billington et al. 1998, p. 50). Since leadership is historically rooted in the symbolic sphere of the male and represented in Discourses of hegemonic masculinity, constructing a leadership identity can be challenging for women. In Chinese culture women are highly valued for being humanistic, people-orientated, and considerate to the feelings and needs of others. By contrast, women leaders are considered 'ambitious' and 'aggressive'—an identity that is not congruent with the 'virtuous wife and caring mum' (Xian qi liang mu) Discourse that is highly valued in Chinese culture (Zhao 2008, p. 78). In Chinese culture it is customary for leaders not to 'invite others to be involved in goal setting or decision making' and to use 'status and position to make independent decisions without the input of others' (Northouse 2012, pp. 350–51). Thus, powerful cultural scripts constructed in relation to gender (Lindsey 2015) clash with traditional hegemonic masculinist Discourses of leadership that characterize leaders controlling and self-reliant individualists (Ford 2006, p. 84).

Nevertheless, it has been suggested that post-heroic developments in leadership studies that emphasize so called feminine styles of leading that are more relational, local and shared (Ford 2006; Fletcher 2004), should create a feminine advantage for women (Eagly and Carli 2003; Helgesen 2008). Although this rhetoric has been around for several years (Fletcher 2004), dominant managerial practices in higher education persist to encourage masculine Discourses of competitiveness and individuality, not feminine Discourses of empathy, supportiveness, and nurturing associated with women (Thomas and Davies 2002). Buckinshaw (2015) likens higher education communities of practice to communities of practice of masculinities, whereby hegemonic masculinities shape the learning of leadership and the doing of leadership, and effectively perpetuate masculinities. Since success and productivity is measured according to masculine norms, this has a detrimental effect on female academics in Chinese universities (Zhang 2001), just as it does in other parts of the world (O'Connor 2014; Van den Brink and Benschop 2012).

Eagly and Karau (Eagly and Karau 2002) argue that because of perceived incongruity between the female gender role and leadership role women may be evaluated less favorably as potential occupants of leadership roles and leadership behavior may be evaluated less positively when enacted by a woman. Consistent with role incongruity theory, women are more likely to experience negative reactions, such as dislike and rejection, than men for showing dominance, expressing disagreement, or being highly assertive or self-promoting (Carli 1999; Copeland et al. 1995; Rudman 1998). This can result in backlash not only on the job in leadership evaluations, but also in hiring, promotion, and salary negotiations (Brescoll 2011; Rudman and Phelan 2008; Rudman et al. 2012). Research in Chinese universities suggests that role congruity is prevalent due to social stereotyping of women and gender discrimination in promotion (Zhang 2010). Research from other parts of the world suggests women may regulate their behavior out of the fear of backlash (Brescoll 2011).

Navigating and negotiating inhospitable cultures can be exhausting work. Research with senior women in higher education in the UK confirms that considerable energy and emotional labor is expended fitting into masculine gendered leadership cultures (Burkinshaw 2015). In consequence, Alvesson and Willmott (2002) contend that in order to achieve acceptance in the work place and maintain social solidarity, people develop self-images and work orientations that are deemed congruent with the culture of their organizational context. The achievement of this goal involves considerable identity regulation and 'identity work'. This prompted Burkinshaw (2015), citing Alimo-Metcalfe (2010), to jest that the job specification for women in higher education leadership should specify they will need chameleon-like features. Goffman's (Goffman 1959) classic theory of impression management provides another framework of analysis. Goffman shows how social order is maintained by individuals through the suppression of their own desires to maintain a working consensus. Through impression management and by presenting themselves to others as 'dramaturgical', they make the performance convincing to the audience. For example, in cultural contexts where caring for the needs of others is a valued identity, research shows that women tend to categorize themselves in that way (Kondo 1990). This is of relevance to our study since traditional ideology regarding gender roles promotes images of women as housewife's and mothers in China. The view that women's work is inside the home remains strong even among women (Zhao 2008; Yang 2011).

Studies show that because women experience a heavy dual burden of domestic and waged work, this can inhibit career development (Zhang 2001) and career ambitions (Zhao 2008). This inadvertently perpetuates the idea that a 'proper academic' is male (Skelton 2004). Those women that do pursue academic career success have been found to experience psychological conflict and work overload performing both work and family roles (Zhang 2010). In addition, they have to work hard to prove themselves as capable as men (Zhang 2005). Perhaps unsurprisingly, studies reveal women experience more stress, specifically due to conflicts between work and family than their male counterparts (Zhang 2003). This raises questions of how they construct their professional identities, since 'identities are embedded in social and family life, as well as hegemonic leadership Discourse' (Ford 2006, p. 89) and historical cultural Discourses of gender. Even for women unencumbered with caring responsibilities, 'the abjected maternal body is displaced onto all women (whether they are mothers or not)' and 'conflated with the feminine' (Fotaki 2013, p. 1257).

3. Materials and Method

Adopting an inductive interpretative research strategy, the study sought to bring women in to 'dig deep' into their life-world (Berger and Luckmann 1966) to reveal aspects of their lives that may be invisible (DeVault 1996, p. 32). The data were collected through semi structured interviews because these are a form of interaction, as natural as any other (Atkinson and Silverman 1997), and benefit from following conventions participants are familiar with (Shakespeare 1996). In addition, interviews were deemed appropriate since 'talk produced in interviews can be analyzed as part of the ongoing project which is the speaker's identity work' (Taylor and Littleton 2006), and interviews can even provide an appropriate context for identity work (Taylor and Littleton 2005, p. 28).

Discursive research into professional identity is rooted in the role of language, meaning, and Discourse in the development of identification processes (Jaros 2012). As Burr (Vivien 1995) articulately puts it 'our identity therefore originates not from inside the person, but from the social realm, where people swim in a sea of language and other signs, a sea that is invisible to us because it is the very medium of our existence' (p. 53). However, language is not just a by-product, people use language to do things, such as pinpoint blame, make excuses, project themselves in a positive light, and so forth (Gill 2000, p. 175). Therefore discourse (talk) incorporates not just language but social practice, too (Gill 2000, p. 73). Expanding on the social practice perspective, Discourse is described as 'a systematic set of beliefs, ideas or knowledge and practices specific to social situations or locations' (Billington et al. 1998, p. 33). These emerge in talk and we refer to these as 'little-d' discourses. 'Big-D' Discourse can be described as systems of thought. Furthermore, professional identity is produced by Discourses, located both within the workplace and at a broader societal level (Foucault 1972; Foucault 1980). The purpose is not to report generalizable accounts of women and higher education leadership in China, but to reveal and challenge the so-called 'truths' located in cultural meanings and beliefs emerging in Discourses about women and leadership.

The sample was arrived at through a snowball sampling technique (Browne 2005). Two universities (University F and N) in the capital city of a northwest province in China were approached to begin this process. Two male deans, one from each university, provided introductions to potential participants. Nine female academics agreed to take part in the study. Following ethical approval, individual interviews were carried out in 2016, over the duration of a week, first at University F followed by University N. The researcher conducting the interviews is a native Chinese speaker and one of the authors of this paper. An interview schedule of semi-structured questions was used. This was translated into Chinese by the interviewer who is the first author of this paper. Respondents were not given a copy in advance, as this can result in rehearsed responses. The first interview was used to pilot the question schedule. No changes were required and the same method and questions were used in the interviews that followed. Nevertheless, if some words or sentences in interview questions caused comprehension barriers between languages, these words were explained thoroughly to the interviewees. The interview schedule began with initial questions about the participant's education and career trajectory to date. More in-depth questions followed to allow the participants to talk in depth about their role, how they view leaders and if they consider themselves to be a leader. This was followed by questions about their experiences and views on any dual professional and private family responsibilities they had. These interviews can be understood as social interaction between two people (Basit 2010), that allowed the researcher to approach the interviews as 'an open-ended input to identity work' (Alvesson and Willmott 2002, p. 640).

The interviews were recorded and transcription was undertaken by the researcher. They were then professionally translated into English. All personal details and information pertaining to the universities in which the participants work was anonymized. A process known as inter-rater reliability (Armstrong et al. 1997), involved reading the transcripts of all nine participants several times to assess consistency with regards to English translations and to provide a form of auditing (Lincoln and Guba 1985). This was repeated at subsequent stages of analysis to check reliability and validity, with regard to participant's understanding and coherence, for example (Gill 2000, p. 189). Through immersion in the data the researchers also gained familiarization with the material (Gill 2000). The material was then subjected to thematic coding (Yin 2014). The process was iterative as it involved cycles of inquiry back and forth between theory and the empirical data throughout the process (Strauss and Corbin 1990). Various dimensions of identities emerged, which reflect the different career experiences, life histories and attitudes of the women, which we explored further, guided by discursive analysis to pinpoint not only Discourses but also subject positions, positioning and subjectivity, in order to explore ideological aspects of Discourse and its influence on subjectivities (Wiggins 2017, p. 33).

Table 1 provides information about the sample. All the women began their careers as teachers (instructors/lecturers). They represent women at different career stages and with different levels of experience of leadership, ranging from very minimal early career committee roles to middle management level roles. Among these nine participants there is one Dean (head of school), one Associate Dean, two Department Directors, and one Section Chief. Four of the women are instructors/teachers with additional responsibilities as Secretary of the Youth League Committee (Appendix A).

Table 1. Profile of research participants.

Name	Position	Brief Profile
Respondent D	Dean	53 years old; Bachelor's degree; works at University F; married; has an adult son.
Respondent S	Associate Dean	50 years old; Master's degree; works at University F; married; has an adult son.
Respondent O	Department Director	49 years old; Doctor's degree; works at University N; married; has a high school daughter.
Respondent F	Department Director	42 years old; Master's degree; works at University F; married; has a high school son and a baby boy.

Table 1. *Cont.*

Name	Position	Brief Profile
Respondent L	Section Chief	34 years old; Master's degree; works at University F; married; has a baby girl.
Respondent R	Teacher (Instructor or lecturer) and Secretary of the Youth League Committee	29 years old; Master's degree; works at University N; single; no children.
Respondent Y	Teacher (Instructor or lecturer) and Secretary of the Youth League Committee	37 years old; Master's degree; work at University N; married; has a primary school boy.
Respondent X	Teacher (Instructor or lecturer) and Secretary of the Youth League Committee	28 years old; Master's degree; works at University N; single; no child.
Respondent W	Teacher (Instructor or lecturer) and Secretary of the Youth League Committee	28 years old; Master's degree; works at University N; married; pregnant.

There are two systems in Chinese universities: the management or administration system, and the teaching system. These are independent of each other and teachers in the administration system and the teaching system undertake different types of work. First, the administration system focuses on the management of school administrative issues. Participants in this study working in the administrative system include the Section Chief and the four instructors—although they give a few lessons to students, their titles belong to the administrative level (for example, Section Chief, Division Chief, Director-General, and Minister, etc.). Second, participants working in the teaching system devote most of their energy to teaching. They include: the Dean, Associate Dean, and Department Directors. Their titles belong to Teacher professional titles (for example, Assistant, Lecturer, Associate Professor, and Professor). Regarding the mixed sample of women, the focus was placed on leadership experiences at different levels of higher education, ranging from teachers to a dean. Following Northouse, leadership is defined as: 'a process whereby an individual influences a group of individuals to achieve a common goal' (Eagly and Carli 2003, p. 5). The two universities are located in an important industrial city which acts as a transportation hub. The population of this city was approximately 3.69 million in 2015, and it has thirteen higher educational institutions (http://www.tjj.lanzhou.gov.cn). The two universities are typical of universities in the northwest of China. They have over fifty-five thousand students over three thousand teaching and administrative staff in total, so are well-known locally.

4. Analysis and Findings

Segments of narrative from the interviews follow to illustrate our analysis of the data. Since the term manager/management appears interchangeably with the term leadership in the narrative, it follows that use of these terms may be called into question. It would be futile for us, as discursive scholars, to embark on a lengthy discussion on this, as leadership from a discursive perspective is in effect a set of 'language games' not in the strictest linguistic sense (Fairhurst 2009, p. 1609), but grounded in the everyday realities of individuals who aspire to lead or be led (Kelly 2008). From this perspective, what is defined as leadership or management is not of concern, it is the context, especially historical and cultural or political aspects that are of interest to our analyses. In what follows, we begin to set out our analyses by exploring the interplays of multiple identities and Discourses of gender, followed by a more in-depth study of the 'leader' identity, then we present our analyses of respondents' discourse concerning female leadership and the broader societal Discourses of gender and leadership that are invoked.

4.1. How Do Female Academics Define Their Identities?

First, our analyses reveal the interplay and dynamics of multiple identities, derived from different social roles performed by the women in private and professional realms of their lives. Although the respondents do not share the same portfolio of identities (e.g., wives, mothers, teachers, managers or leaders), they all invested in the articulation of their own particular multiple identities, and the interplay and relative importance of each identity. This is illustrated in an excerpt from Respondent O, a Department Director: 'I am a good mother, then a good teacher, and last a good manager.'

While each identity (e.g., mother, teacher, manager) appears to be distinctive to the other, there is a clear interplay between each of these identities. Notably, the presentation of such accounts in sequential order and within a particular temporal structure, highlights that certain things need to be known first (Wiggins 2017, p. 124). Most prominent in the data is the notion that to be a successful leader or manager, and to achieve legitimacy in that role, one must first be recognized as a good teacher, as illustrated in another segment from the previous respondent:

> I think I should be a good teacher, because in university, your ability in teaching matters a lot. Only if you have a good ability of teaching, other staff are willing to respect your management (Respondent O, Department Director).

Such utterances reflect the professional path shared by respondents, since all of them began their career in higher education as teachers (lecturers/instructors). However, identities should not simply be likened to job roles, as synergies, and interplays between identities arise, not least because the accomplishment of a legitimate identity in one realm is perceived to act as a precursor to success in another. As such, the accomplishment of legitimacy as a leader (or manager) interplays with other identities, such as that of a teacher.

The second theme that resonates with all the respondents to our study is a Discourse of gender that illustrates the strong role of socio-political ideology in shaping identities in ways that reflect idealized images of women as mothers and housewives (Nagatomo 2012). This is explored in detail in a segment from an interview with Respondent Y:

> I take care of the daily chores all by myself. Because my husband is an intellectual who needs much quiet time, it means that his thoughts cannot be easily interrupted. Hence, I have to do more housework. I think men should do great things, and women should get small things done. This is my principle of doing things [...] At noon I go back home to cook, and then in the morning I get up at 6:00 a.m. to prepare for breakfast. For example, there are seven kinds of soup and a variety of dishes for breakfast in one week because I think breakfast is the most important. Then lunch and dinner.

There are a number of features to this narrative. First, use of a discursive strategy referred to as 'category entitlement' (Wiggins 2017) functions to produce categories to which women and men are bound. In this segment sex categories determined who might or might not be expected to engage in household chores. However, the segment is not simply about housework, rather, it accords with the 'virtuous wife and caring mum' (Xian qi liang mu) Discourse promoted through socio-political ideology in China, and it provides insight into gender hierarchies and identity. The husband is characterized as an 'intellectual' and his intellectual needs take priority over those of the woman who is portrayed as passive and lacking in agency. Specifically, the term 'I have' (to do more housework) indicates she has no choice in this matter. However, she resolves this with an assessment that 'men should do great things' and 'women should get small things done'. The detailed account of daily chores that follows discursively functions to support the speaker's entitlement to tell the account and reinforce her identity as accurate, since if a person claims an identity they must effectively do that identity to be believable (Wiggins 2017). Throughout the segment a male/female dichotomy is reinforced in line with broader Discourses of gender. Another example of traditional ideological Discourse pertaining to women's role in the private sphere of life is provided by Respondent D, a Dean, who explained: 'personally, I didn't want to do this job, because as a woman, family is the most important thing.' She reinforces her statement concerning the importance of family in a segment about domestic duties:

> I do all the housework, my husband was born in Gansu province, so he does not have the consciousness of doing housework, but if I arrange some work for him he will do it anyway. Generally, in my view, household is the most important thing for a woman. Happiness of the family is most important of all (Respondent D).

One consequence of this discourse is that women may be perceived as less committed in professional spheres of life. Indeed, some respondents subscribed to this view, as illustrated by Respondent W: 'If the female is tethered by her family role, she would definitely cut down the time and efforts for her career. However, the male faces a different situation.'

The third theme that resonates with all respondents is that they discursively distance themselves from leadership as a professional identity. Having explored this phenomena in more depth, we identified two key strategies used by respondents, which we refer to as 'downgrading leadership' and 'rejecting leadership'. For instance, although several of the respondents hold formal positions that involve leadership (e.g., giving direction, decision-making, social influence, etc.), and/or management (e.g., managing courses, staff, budgets, resources etc.), they frequently downgrade or reject that identity. The discursive strategies used to downgrade or reject leadership appear interchangeably and intermittently throughout the interviews. In what follows we illustrate this in segments from an interview with Respondent F, a Department Director.

Respondent F worked in a corporate role for ten years where she rose to secretary of the board. After gaining her Master's degree she decided to become a university teacher. That was over ten years ago, and she was promoted to her current position as a Director of a Department a year ago. She describes the promotion as 'not that complicated' [. . .] there was a vacancy, so I became director'. The promotion, therefore, is described in oblique terms and its significance downplayed. By contrast, this is followed by an assessment offered not by the respondent herself, but by her family: 'they think that my present job is exceptionally great.' Extreme words such as 'exceptionally' discursively function to emphasize a point; in this instance the point is: 'my present job is exceptionally great'. However, she attributes this statement to her family, and in doing so evades taking ownership of the statement herself. Female modesty is congruent with idealized images of women in China and it has been documented elsewhere as an important factor in women's reluctance to self-promote (Rudman 1998). Interestingly, however, she is the only respondent to explicitly refer to herself as 'being a leader' but, thereafter, she denies herself this identity. In the following segment, she describes how she views her current role:

> As the director of the department of Human Resources Management, my responsibility is to do the tasks which are assigned by the superior, to arrange the courses for students, and to coordinate and manage the teachers' arrangements. That is not exactly management, more like coordination. Plus, I'm responsible for making and amending the syllabus. So far, I spend 20% of my energy on managing the whole department.

There are a number of features to this narrative. First, the respondent's professional status as a Director is reaffirmed, but she positions herself as lacking in agency in this role. Tasks are 'assigned', and she is passive in that process in relation to her 'superior'. The classification of tasks involved in Directing a Department is further downplayed in the assessment that follows. The term 'not exactly' (management) discursively functions to minimize the significance of this role. Following this the term 'management' is further downgraded to 'coordination'. Outright rejection of the leader identity follows again in response to a question about her personal experiences:

> Actually I don't need to answer this question, because I never treat myself as a leader. There is no such social status for me. I am a teacher, and only a teacher . . . all the women or female leaders I met, all of them, including me, have such feelings. I think it is normal.

In common with other respondents, she discursively constructs the teacher identity in relation to other social identities, but once more rejects the leader identity:

> I still prefer to be addressed as teacher or my name. Actually, we work for people, instead of being a leader . . . it's important to have a good attitude, and put you into others' shoes. Do not regard yourself as leader and [think] everyone must follow your leadership . . . There is no such social status for me. I am a teacher and only a teacher (Respondent F, Department Director).

Following the first assessment 'I still prefer to be addressed as a teacher', the evaluation ('I am a teacher and only a teacher') serves to strengthen the argument and preference structure for the teacher identity, which is upgraded above that of leader. Lists and contrasts serve to add rhetorical strength to an argument and can be used to manage accountability and identities. Furthermore, discursive devices such as minimization—'there is no such social status for me' function to downplay the significance or importance of something, in this instance the respondent's identity as a leader, which she rejects as 'there is no such social status for me' (Wiggins 2017). Shifting between author and narrator of this complicated discourse regarding various subject positions, she adds further rhetorical strength to the argument, by accounting for this assessment in oppositional terms—the importance of having 'a good attitude' and of putting 'you into others' shoes', is depicted as contrasting with the alternative unappealing reality that 'everyone must follow your leadership' which can be located within normative heroic leadership Discourse. Claiming dislike of this style of leadership, she claims a subject position that is more appealing in the traditional cultural context of China—'I am a teacher and only a teacher'. Alvesson and Billing (Alvesson and Billing 2009) suggest that by emphasizing the relative importance of one identity compared to another, an individual may not view themselves as a fully legitimate member of the social group to which they dis-identify (Alvesson and Billing 2009). In this instance, the teacher identity is given prominence and the leader identity is clearly rejected. O'Connor (2014), suggests that universities, with their homosocial male dominated organizational cultures, promote the view that leadership is a masculine pursuit, since not only is the language and voices of leadership male, but the working practices, networks and promotion routes are predisposed to benefit men. These processes can make it difficult for women to claim legitimacy in leadership roles. Women internalize negativity, discrimination, exclusion and othering as feelings of fraudulence. Added to this, women have fewer role models of the same gender to identity with (Singh et al. 2002), and this can lead to them feeling like an outsider in the organization (Bagilhole and White 2013).

We have presented a segment to illustrate through fine grained analyses the common theme of downgrading or rejecting a leadership identity. In what follows we shift attention from respondents' descriptions of their own identities to explore how they talk about male and female leaders more generally.

4.2. How Do They Talk about the Female Leader Identity More Generally?

Respondents' descriptions of leaders (Table 2), drawn from across the interviews, reflect gender stereotypes—normative essentialist definitions of gender and masculine and feminine leadership. The dichotomy between male and females is one dimensional—men are described as unemotional whereas women are the direct opposite—emotional. According to this stereotype, men are rational and women sensitive, and so forth. Evidently, this dichotomy leaves no room for a man to display emotions or for a woman to be rational. Naturally, this stereotypical view can constrain men, as well as women, to do gender (West and Zimmerman 1987) and enact leadership in a way that is congruent with gender stereotypes.

Table 2. Words used by respondents to describe male and female leaders.

Male	Female
Objective	Emotional
More time and energy to do work	Understand
Rational	Sensitive
Reasonable	Influence by emotions
Steel	Water
Bold	Confront the tough with tenderness
Dedicate	Delicate
Vigorous	Patient
Resolute	Female traits
Decisive	Considerate

Table 2. *Cont.*

Male	Female
Have a whole view of the work/Focusing on the overall situation and solving problems more quickly Not easily influenced by emotions	Pay more attention on the details/focusing on the details/Meticulous Sentimental Be good at teaching Soft/blandness Solicitude Responsible Diligence Endeavour Weak

These discourses of gender stereotypes significantly emphasize traditional societal Discourses of gender and leadership that permeate Chinese culture. We explore how this discourse (little-d) and Discourse (big-D) is intertwined in greater detail in what follows.

4.3. In What Ways Is This Talk Intertwined with Larger Societal Discourses of Leadership and Gender?

In each of the interviews numerous accounts of male and female leaders highlight the influence of dominant Discourses of leadership and gender. The discourse (little-d) is more complex since it reveals many contradictions and tensions. For instance, although the respondents unanimously claim that 'men and women are equal' (Respondent D), a key theme in the interviews is that their descriptions invoke difference and inferiority in relation to female leaders. This discourse reflects dominant historical and cultural Discourses concerning gender and leadership that prevail in China, and elsewhere. In the majority of cases, difference is attributed inherent traits or personality characteristics. For example, Respondent R, said: 'the different genes result in male's rationality and female's sensibility, which no one can change'. Although, generally, there is consensus among respondents that women can be successful leaders, especially with 'training' and 'experience', this came with the proviso that:

> When a female takes a role in management, it's important to control her emotion well. From my work experience in past few years, I don't think females can often manage it well. If a female can do it [manage her emotions] better, she can be an excellent manager (Respondent F).

A second theme is that of invoking difference in a way that highlights women's relative advantage over male counterparts. For example, Respondent X said:

> Males are much more vigorous, resolute, and decisive. Because they consider things from a different angle, they focus on the overall situation and solving problems more quickly. Females are meticulous and patient, and they focus on details. They solve the problem with systematic guidance and they are very good at dealing with everything in a soft way.

Another similar example, from Respondent S is that men are 'rigorous, decisive, and bold at work' and women are 'more gentle, tender, and more considerate'. While this discourse emphasizes feminine styles of leadership (Ford 2006; Fletcher 2004) and difference, women are not inferior. Many other examples of this permeate the transcripts. In each instance, female leaders are typically considered 'more delicate and more considerate' (Respondent Y). In addition, 'Female leaders have their own methods of dealing with work and might in some aspects work better than male leaders' (Respondent L). Overall, by emphasizing Discourses of gender that promote the essentialist view of women as possessing unique feminine qualities (Eagly and Carli 2003; Helgesen 2008), respondents emphasized that: 'women have their own advantages. Being sensitive and being rational have their respective advantages' (Respondent O). Indeed, many believed a female leader 'should exert her leadership charisma through some female traits' (Respondent W).

These discursive strategies function to highlight women's unique qualities in leadership, but still men are believed to have a relative advantage:

> I worked over twenty years, and met more male leaders. On the one hand, male leaders are objective [. . .] There are some advantages for men to be leaders. Firstly, he has more time and energy to do work; secondly, he is rational and reasonable instead of easily being influenced by emotions. Thirdly, [. . .] it is easier for men to make orders. In our university, there are more female teachers, usually speaking, they are more likely to follow the male leaders' instructions. It is true, though I don't know the exact reasons.

This discourse about women leaders, although not specifically relating to themselves, provide insights into self-understandings of how to be a woman (Alvesson and Billing 2009). Indeed, some respondents provided examples that reflect a Discourse of women's difference, and in some instances inferiority, in relation to themselves. For instance, Respondent D revealed: 'I don't have the courage and willpower like a man, as a woman I am more emotional and soft hearted.' Providing a different insight an excerpt from Respondent R reveals how gender and leadership Discourse influences not only her views, but also her actions:

> Even in my student management work, I prefer to assign a job to a boy student instead of girls. Our college has more than 30% boy students and more than 60% girls. Girls are obviously in the majority, but I still would rather assign a job to a boy student. The reason is that I think boy students can do a more satisfying job than girls.

The comparisons between men and women leaders (and boys/girls) in these segments take a grammatical form that involves setting up a hierarchy of who 'does' difference, when they 'do' difference and what 'doing' difference means. Once more, not only does this theme in the data highlight the negative aspect of being a woman, it reinforces the male/female dichotomy. On the one hand, the discourse brings out the so-called caring side of women while, on the other hand, it maintains a deficit version of women; that is, women are somehow deficient in relation to male norms of leadership.

5. Discussion and Conclusions

This article has explored how female academics in higher education in China construct their (gendered) identities. We considered the multidimensionality of identities important to our analyses, as many of the women in our study simultaneously performed roles as teachers, managers, or leaders while also being wives and mothers. In addition, we considered the influence of powerful historical and cultural Discourses.

First and foremost, the findings show that the women describe a multiplicity of identities drawn from private and social realms of life. Notably the findings highlight the interplay and tensions between competing multiple identities, and reveal how those identities are shaped and constrained by dominant Discourses concerning gender in Chinese society. Notably this results in identity regulation (Alvesson and Billing 2009, p. 99), notably identity positioning that is congruent with social norms and conventions (Lindgren and Packendorff 2008). A key theme is that the women do not identify as leaders, despite undertaking roles that involve leadership. This is an important finding since the rejection of an identity is an indication of not belonging to a particular social group (Alvesson and Billing 2009, p. 98). This may be due to the leader identity breaking too closely with traditional ideas of femininities, which can be problematic for women (Billing 2011). The extent to which we view identity as free choice or as an unjust social outcome is debatable. On the one hand, personal identity is not fixed once and for all (Alvesson et al. 2008; Alvesson 2010; Stewart and McDermott 2004), and there is scope for resistance and change within higher education in China. However, it has long been established that social expectations shape the doing of gender (West and Zimmerman 1987) in ways that are congruent with social and cultural expectations (Eagly and Karau 2002), and those women that deviate from social expectations are likely to experience repercussions (Brescoll 2011; Rudman and Phelan 2008; Rudman et al. 2012). Fundamentally, even though identity should not be reduced to simply to gender variables, 'the male norm indicates that gender identity is a major identity signifier' (Billing 2011, p. 300). This means the process of doing gender and doing leadership does not simply involve individual micro-level identity work; rather, identities are shaped by a range of factors at meso (organizational) and macro (societal) levels (Billing 2011, p. 303), since constructions of 'femininities and masculinities permeate social life, and guide and constrain people's behavior' (Alvesson and Billing 2009, p. 18). On the point of meso-level factors, it has been said that the academy is a 'source of oppression and a location for exploring liberation and empowerment' (Morley 1994, p. 202). Our study shows that the Chinese higher education context continues to be marked by gendered norms. This has implications for the career advancement of female academics and consequences for reversing the underrepresentation of women in senior leadership in universities in China. However, this situation should not be viewed as irreversible. Senior leaders in higher education can potentially shape the internal culture of their organizations and influence the wider higher education context (O'Connor 2014).

A second key contribution of this article is that the data provides unique insights into the discursive construction of male and female leaders more generally in the higher education context in China, specifically illustrating how culture and language both construct and reflect gendered meanings (Alvesson and Billing 2009). Most cultures have 'systems of meanings and norms prescribing different activities and characteristics for women and men (Alvesson and Billing 2009, p. 50). It is of note that the findings highlight the constructs of feminine and masculine are positioned as opposites in the descriptions of female and male leaders, and the masculine is generally privileged (Alvesson and Billing 2009), while the feminine is given a lesser or deficit status. Traditional Discourses of gender and leadership that permeate Chinese culture were found to be strongly reflected in the discourse invoked as part of the respondents' descriptions of female leaders as sensitive and emotional and male leaders as rational, decisive, unemotional, and so forth. In terms of practical implications, the findings suggest that initiatives that seek to address the underrepresentation of women in leadership are likely to be undermined in the absence of understanding how career opportunities are shaped by discursive practices (Tannen 1995; Sturges 1999; Lämsä and Sintonen 2001) and dominant Discourses (Ford 2006).

While this article contributes to understanding key issues surrounding women and leadership in China's universities, which may be relevant in other cultural contexts, we acknowledge there are limitations to this study. First, we interviewed nine women from two universities. A larger sample from a broader range of higher education contexts could reveal a diversity of views regarding male and female leaders. Second, the interviews were conducted at a single point in time and do not capture the temporal nature of identity work. A further limitation of our study is that only four of the women were in formal leadership positions, although the remaining five respondents had some experience of leadership through their work with the Youth League Committee. Future research could involve longitudinal research, perhaps following newly appointed female academic leaders. Comparative studies with other national contexts could also prove fruitful. Lastly, although our study concerned women in higher education in China, future studies could explore men and masculinities to understand gendered structures and open up opportunities to challenge the masculine norm.

In conclusion, an individual acquires and learns various identities, by way of their sense of belonging or membership to social categories and groups (Alvesson and Billing 2009, p. 98). Although the women in this study reject or downgrade their identity as a leader, they could be viewed as mediating larger societal Discourses of gender and leadership, since they have learnt how to position themselves within those Discourses in ways that are congruent with social and cultural norms and expectations. From this perspective, it could be argued these women are forging new ways of doing leadership and doing identity work. While they may appear to be complicit in perpetuating dominant Discourses, they have found ways to navigate those Discourses. As such the circumstances through which they have forged an academic career may be viewed as emancipatory and part of the change process, at least as a first step on a longer journey.

Author Contributions: K.J. and J.Z. conceived and designed the study; J.Z. performed the interviews; K.J. analyzed the data; J.Z. contributed to the introduction, methods and findings sections; K.J. wrote the paper.

Conflicts of Interest: The authors declare no conflict of interest.

Appendix A

(1) Chinese universities are established, managed, and led by the government as an affiliate organization to the government. University staff belong to the administrative level; senior managers of the school are not only the school leaders, but also officials. University presidents are the top chief executive and academic officer in charge of all affairs. As universities are led by the government, the presidents of universities are appointed directly by the government. In the selection and appointment of principals, the government values the political identity and academic status of the president candidates. That is to say, firstly, the candidate must be a member of the Communist Party of China. Secondly, the academic ability, administrative capacity and management ability of the candidates is taken into consideration (Wang et al. 2013; Li 2007).

(2) The term 'homosocial' is defined (Sedgwick 2015, p. 1) as 'social bonds between the same sex' in 'Between Men', a groundbreaking study of men's relationships and their impact on women.

(3) 'Guanxi' is a term that refers to the deeply embedded system of relationships, personal connections, contacts and networks cultivated between people that are important for career success. These are formed over time and are based on trust and reciprocity (Huang and Aaltio 2014).

References

Alimo-Metcalfe, Beverly. 2010. An investigation of female and male constructs of leadership and empowerment. *Women in Management Review* 25: 640–48. [CrossRef]

Alvesson, Mats. 2010. Self-doubters, strugglers, storytellers, surfers and others: Images of self-identities in organization studies. *Human Relations* 63: 193–217. [CrossRef]

Alvesson, Mats, and Yvonne Due Billing. 2009. *Understanding Gender and Organizations.* Thousand Oaks: Sage.

Alvesson, Mats, and Hugh Willmott. 2002. Identity regulation as organizational control: Producing the appropriate individual. *Journal of Management Studies* 39: 619–44. [CrossRef]

Alvesson, Mats, Karen Lee Ashcraft, and Robyn Thomas. 2008. Identity matters: Reflections on the construction of identity scholarship in organization studies. *Organization* 15: 5–28. [CrossRef]

Angeloff, Tania. 2010. China at work (1980–2009): Employment, gender, and migrations. *Travail, Genre et Sociétés* 1: 79–102. [CrossRef]

Armstrong, David, Ann Gosling, John Weinman, and Marteau Theresa. 1997. The place of inter-rater reliability in qualitative research: An empirical study. *Sociology* 31: 597–606. [CrossRef]

Ashforth, Blake. 2000. *Role Transitions in Organizational Life: An Identity-Based Perspective.* Abingdon: Routledge.

Atkinson, Paul, and David Silverman. 1997. Kundera's immortality: The interview society and the invention of the self. *Qualitative Inquiry* 3: 304–25. [CrossRef]

Attané, Isabelle. 2012. Being a woman in china today: A demography of gender. *China Perspectives* 5: 5–15.

Bagilhole, Barbara, and Kate White. 2013. An outsider in academia. In *Generation and Gender in Academia.* Basingstoke: Palgrave Macmillan.

Basit, Tehmina N. 2010. *Conducting Research in Educational Contexts.* London: Continuum International Publication Group.

Berger, Peter, and Thomas Luckmann. 1966. *The Social Construction of Knowledge: A Treatise in the Sociology of Knowledge.* Soho: Open Road Media.

Billing, Yvonne Due. 2011. Are women in management victims of the phantom of the male norm? *Gender, Work & Organization* 18: 298–317.

Billington, Rosamund, Jennifer Lorna Hockey, and Sheelagh Strawbridge. 1998. *Exploring Self and Society.* Basingstoke: Palgrave Macmillan.

Brescoll, Victoria L. 2011. Who takes the floor and why: Gender, power, and volubility in organizations. *Administrative Science Quarterly* 56: 622–41. [CrossRef]

Browne, Kath. 2005. Snowball sampling: Using social networks to research non-heterosexual women. *International Journal of Social Research Methodology* 8: 47–60. [CrossRef]

Burkinshaw, Paula. 2015. *Higher Education, Leadership and Women Vice Chancellors, Fitting into Communities of Practice of Masculinities*. Basingstoke: Palgrave Macmillan.

Butler, Judith. 1999. *Gender Trouble*. New York: Routledge.

Carli, Linda L. 1999. Gender, Interpersonal Power, and Social Influence. *Journal of Social Issues* 55: 81–99. [CrossRef]

Cheng, Liying. 2008. The key to success: English language testing in china. *Language Testing* 25: 15–37. [CrossRef]

Collinson, David L. 2003. Identities and insecurities: Selves at work. *Organization* 10: 527–47. [CrossRef]

Copeland, Catherine L., James E. Driskell, and Eduardo Salas. 1995. Gender and reactions to dominance. *Journal of Social Behavior and Personality* 10: 53.

Davies, Celia, and Penny Holloway. 1995. Troubling transformations: Gender regimes and organizational culture in the academy. In *Feminist Academics: Creative Agents for Change*. London: Taylor & Francis Ltd., pp. 7–21.

DeVault, Marjorie L. 1996. Talking back to sociology: Distinctive contributions of feminist methodology. *Annual Review of Sociology* 22: 29–50. [CrossRef]

Eagly, Alice H., and Linda L. Carli. 2003. The female leadership advantage: An evaluation of the evidence. *The Leadership Quarterly* 14: 807–34. [CrossRef]

Eagly, Alice H., and Steven J. Karau. 2002. Role congruity theory of prejudice toward female leaders. *Psychological Review* 109: 573. [CrossRef] [PubMed]

Fairhurst, Gail T. 2009. Considering context in discursive leadership research. *Human Relations* 62: 1607–33. [CrossRef]

Fletcher, Joyce K. 2004. The paradox of postheroic leadership: An essay on gender, power, and transformational change. *The Leadership Quarterly* 15: 647–61. [CrossRef]

Fletcher, Catherine, Rebecca Boden, Julie Kent, and Julie Tinson. 2007. Performing women: The gendered dimensions of the uk new research economy. *Gender, Work & Organization* 14: 433–53.

Ford, Jackie. 2006. Discourses of leadership: Gender, identity and contradiction in a uk public sector organization. *Leadership* 2: 77–99. [CrossRef]

Fotaki, Marianna. 2013. No woman is like a man (in academia): The masculine symbolic order and the unwanted female body. *Organization Studies*. [CrossRef]

Foucault, Michel. 1972. *The Archaeology of Knowledge and the Discourse on Language*. London: Tavistock.

Foucault, Michel. 1980. *Power/Knowledge: Selected Interviews and Other Writings, 1972–1977*. New York: Pantheon Books.

Gee, James Paul. 1999. *An Introduction to Discourse Analysis: Theory and Method*. Abingdon: Routledge.

Gill, Rosalind. 2000. *Discourse Analysis*. Thousand Oaks: Sage Publications.

Goffman, Erving. 1959. *The Presentation of Self in Everyday Life*. Garden City: Doubleday and Company Inc.

Halford, Susan, and Pauline Leonard. 2006. Place, space and time: Contextualizing workplace subjectivities. *Organization Studies* 27: 657–76. [CrossRef]

Harding, Nancy, Jackie Ford, and Brendan Gough. 2010. Accounting for ourselves: Are academics exploited workers? *Critical Perspectives on Accounting* 21: 159–68. [CrossRef]

Harley, Sandra. 2003. Research selectivity and female academics in uk universities: From gentleman's club and barrack yard to smart macho? *Gender and Education* 15: 377–92. [CrossRef]

Helgesen, Sally. 2008. *The Female Advantage*, 4th ed. Oxford: Blackwell Publishing.

Holmes, Mary. 2007. *What Is Gender? Sociological Approaches*. London: Sage Publications Ltd.

Huang, Jiehua, and Iiris Aaltio. 2014. Guanxi and social capital: Networking among women managers in china and finland. *International Journal of Intercultural Relations* 39: 22–39. [CrossRef]

Jaros, Stephen. 2012. Identity and the workplace: An assessment of contextualist and discursive approaches. *Tamara Journal of Critical Organisation Inquiry* 10: 45.

Jones, Karen, and Clifton Jonathan. Forthcoming. Rendering sexism invisible in workplace narratives. A narrative analysis of female entrepreneurs' stories of not being talked to by men. *Gender, Work & Organization*.

Kelly, Simon. 2008. Leadership: A categorical mistake? *Human Relations* 61: 763–82. [CrossRef]

Kiesling, Scott F. 2006. Hegemonic identity-making in narrative. In *Discourse and Identity*. Cambridge: Cambridge University Press, pp. 261–87.

Kondo, Dorinne K. 1990. *Crafting Selves: Power, Gender, and Discourses of Identity in a Japanese Workplace*. Chicago: The University of Chicago Press.

Lämsä, Anna-Maija, and Teppo Sintonen. 2001. A discursive approach to understanding women leaders in working life. *Journal of Business Ethics* 34: 255–67. [CrossRef]

Li, Zhuang. 2007. Study on the Principal Responsibility System under the Leadership of Party Committees in Universities. Master's Dissertation, Party School of the CPC Central Committee, Beijing, China. (In Chinese)

Lincoln, Yvonna S., and Egon G. Guba. 1985. *Naturalistic Inquiry*. London: Sage Publications Ltd.

Lindgren, Monica, and Johann Packendorff. 2008. Woman, Teacher, Entrepreneur On Identity Construction in Female Entrepreneurs of Swedish Independent Schools. In *Women Entrepreneurship and Social Capital: A Dialogue and Construction*. Copenhagen: Copenhagen Business School Press, pp. 193–223.

Lindsey, Linda L. 2015. *Gender Roles: A Sociological Perspective*. New York: Routledge.

Lyness, Karen S., and Donna E. Thompson. 2000. Climbing the corporate ladder: Do female and male executives follow the same route? *Journal of Applied Psychology* 85: 86. [CrossRef] [PubMed]

Mak, Grace CL. 2013. *Women, Education, and Development in Asia: Cross-National Perspectives*. Abingdon: Routledge.

Martin, Joanne. 2003. Feminist theory and critical theory: Unexplored synergies. In *Studying Management Critically*. London: Sage Publications, pp. 66–91.

Mavin, Sharon, and Gina Grandy. 2012. Doing gender well and differently in management. *Gender in Management: An International Journal* 27: 218–31. [CrossRef]

Morley, Louise. 1994. Glass ceiling or iron cage: Women in uk academia. *Gender, Work & Organization* 1: 194–204.

Morley, Louise. 2010. Hyper modernization and Archaism: Women in Higher Education Internationally. In *Gender Change in Academia: Re-Mapping the Fields of Work, Knowledge, and Politics from a Gender Perspective*. Wiesbaden: Springer, pp. 27–42.

Morley, Louise, and Barbara Crossouard. 2016. Gender in the neoliberalised global academy: The affective economy of women and leadership in south asia. *British Journal of Sociology of Education* 37: 149–68. [CrossRef]

Nagatomo, Diane Hawley. 2012. The Impact of Gender on the Professional Identity of Seven Female Teachers of English in Japanese Higher Education. *Ochanomizu University* 8: 213–226.

Northouse, Peter G. 2012. *Leadership: Theory and Practice*. Los Angeles: Sage.

O'Connor, Pat. 2014. *Management and Gender in Higher Education*. Manchester: Manchester University Press.

Rudman, Laurie A. 1998. Self-promotion as a risk factor for women: The costs and benefits of counterstereotypical impression management. *Journal of Personality and Social Psychology* 74: 629. [CrossRef] [PubMed]

Rudman, Laurie A., and Julie E. Phelan. 2008. Backlash effects for disconfirming gender stereotypes in organizations. *Research in Organizational Behavior* 28: 61–79. [CrossRef]

Rudman, Laurie A., Corinne A. Moss-Racusin, Julie E. Phelan, and Sanne Nauts. 2012. Status incongruity and backlash effects: Defending the gender hierarchy motivates prejudice against female leaders. *Journal of Experimental Social Psychology* 48: 165–79. [CrossRef]

Savigny, Heather. 2014. Women, know your limits: Cultural sexism in academia. *Gender and Education* 26: 794–809. [CrossRef]

Sedgwick, Eve Kosofsky. 2015. *Between Men: English Literature and Male Homosocial Desire*. New York: Columbia University Press.

Shakespeare, Pamela. 1996. *Aspects of Confused Speech: A Study of Verbal Interaction between Confused and Normal Speakers*. Hong Kong: Open University.

Sheng, Yunlong. 2009. 'Glass ceiling' in professional development of female faculty viewed from analysis of the faculty structure. *Collection of Women's Studies* 1: 26–31.

Singh, Val, Savita Kumra, and Susan Vinnicombe. 2002. Gender and impression management: Playing the promotion game. *Journal of Business Ethics* 37: 77–89. [CrossRef]

Skelton, Christine. 2004. Gender, career and 'individualisation'in the audit university. *Research in Education* 72: 87–102. [CrossRef]

Stewart, Abigail J., and Christa McDermott. 2004. Gender in psychology. *Annual Review of Psychology* 55: 519–44. [CrossRef] [PubMed]

Strauss, Anselm, and Juliet Corbin. 1990. *Basics of Qualitative Research*. Newbury Park: Sage, vol. 15.

Sturges, Jane. 1999. What it means to succeed: Personal conceptions of career success held by male and female managers at different ages. *British Journal of Management* 10: 239–52. [CrossRef]

Tannen, Deborah. 1995. The power of talk: Who gets heard and why. *Harvard Business Review* 73: 138–48.

Taylor, Stephanie, and Karen Littleton. 2005. Narratives of Creative Journeys: A Study of the Identity Work of Novices in Artisitc and Creativity Fields. Paper presented at Narrative, Memory and Knowledge Conference, University of Huddersfield, Huddersfield, UK, April 9.

Taylor, Stephanie, and Karen Littleton. 2006. Biographies in talk: A narrative-discursive research approach. *Qualitative Sociology Review* 2: 22–38.

Thomas, Robyn, and Annette Davies. 2002. Gender and new public management: Reconstituting academic subjectivities. *Gender, Work & Organization* 9: 372–97.

Van De Mieroop, Dorien, and Jonathan Clifton. 2016. *Life Stories*. Amsterdam: John Benjamins.

Van den Brink, Marieke, and Yvonne Benschop. 2012. Slaying the seven-headed dragon: The quest for gender change in academia. *Gender, Work & Organization* 19: 71–92.

Vivien, Burr. 1995. *An Introduction to Social Constructionism*. London: Routlegde.

Wang, Yin-han, and Kai Yu. 2015. A survey of the female leaders of chinese universities. *Fu Dan Education Forum* 3: 21–26.

Wang, Yinhan, Yue Qi, and Yu Kai. 2013. Women Leaders of Higher Education: Female Executives in Leading Universities in China. *Cross Cultural Communication* 9: 40–45.

West, Candace, and Don H. Zimmerman. 1987. Doing gender. *Gender & Society* 1: 125–51.

Wiggins, Sally. 2017. *Discursive Psychology*. London: Sage Publications Ltd.

Williams, Joan C., Tamina Alon, and Stephanie Bornstein. 2006. Beyond the 'chilly climate': Eliminating bias against women. *Thought Action* Fall 2006: 79–96.

Witz, Anne, and Mike Savage. 1992. The gender of organization. In *Gender and Bureaucracy*. Edited by Mike Savage and Anne Witz. Oxford: Blackwell, pp. 3–62.

Xue, Fei. 2008. Women's Status in Higher Education: Where are Women President's in Chinese Universities? Ph.D. Thesis, University of Oslo, Oslo, Norway.

Yang, Rui. 2011. Self and the Other in the Confucian Cultural Context: Implications of China's Higher Education Developmentfor Comparative Studies. *International Review of Education* 57: 37–355. [CrossRef]

Yin, Robert K. 2014. Case Study Research: Design and Methods, 5th ed.London: Sage.

Zhang, Lili. 2001. Stress and Coping among Women Academics in Research Universities of China. Ph.D. Thesis, The University of Hong Kong, Hong Kong, China. (In Chinese)

Zhang, Lili. 2003. A probe into stresses on female academics in research universities. *Tsinghua Journal of Education* 24: 44–50.

Zhang, Lili. 2005. The particular career experiences of chinese women academics. In *Women's Studies in China: Mapping the Social, Economic and Policy Changes in Chinese Women's Lives*. Seoul: Ewha Womans University Press, pp. 71–114.

Zhang, Lili. 2010. A study on the measurement of job-related stress among women academics in research universities of china. *Frontiers of Education in China* 5: 158–76. [CrossRef]

Zhao, Ke. 2008. Life Cycle and Career Patterns of Academic Women in Higher Education in China Today. Masters Dissertation, The University of Oslo, Oslo, Norway.

administrative
sciences

MDPI

Review

An Overview of the Current State of Women's Leadership in Higher Education in Saudi Arabia and a Proposal for Future Research Directions

Azzah Alsubaie and Karen Jones *

Institute of Education, University of Reading, Reading, Berkshire RG6 6UA, UK;
a.h.h.alsubaie@student.reading.ac.uk
* Correspondence: karen.jones@reading.ac.uk

Received: 5 September 2017; Accepted: 28 September 2017; Published: 12 October 2017

Abstract: Despite the predominance of perspectives on women's leadership, which consistently emphasize the underrepresentation of women in virtually every sphere of political and economic life in countries around the world, very little is known about women's leadership, especially in higher education, in the Kingdom of Saudi Arabia (KSA). This has resulted in a gap in the literature, since higher education is one area of employment where Saudi women have made progress, and in spite of complex social, religious, cultural and organisational barriers, some have broken through the glass ceiling into higher education leadership. One goal of this paper is to highlight, through a synthesis of existing literature, the current state of women's higher education leadership in Saudi Arabia. The second goal of this paper is to propose new directions for future research to address the current dearth of empirical work on women's leadership in higher education in Saudi Arabia. This may be relevant to other regions of the Middle East and elsewhere.

Keywords: Saudi Arabia; women; higher education; leadership research

1. Introduction

Despite the predominance of perspectives on women's leadership, which consistently emphasize the underrepresentation of women in virtually every sphere of political and economic life in countries around the world, very little is known about women and leadership, especially in the context of higher education, in the Kingdom of Saudi Arabia (KSA) (Abalkhail 2017). Akin to academic imperialism (Dupre 1994), much of the literature concerning women and leadership (including higher education contexts), predominantly emerges from scholarship in western contexts. When Saudi Arabian women are the centre of attention, it is usually in non-academic articles that 'promote stereotypical images of Saudi women as exotic and erotic' (Hamdan 2005, p. 61), or as shrouded victims of oppression (Shannon 2014). Yet, Saudi Arabia is more complex than such articles imply and a fascinating case to study. Within this deeply conservative society, modernity, juxtaposed with tradition (Gorney 2016), and 'gender politics and religion', are all intertwined (Al-Rasheed and Azzam 2012, p. 7). On the one hand, women are redefining the boundaries of what modernity and economic empowerment means (Gorney 2016). Indeed, the country has witnessed some noteworthy improvements in women's status in social, political, and economic life over the past two decades. But those improvements contrast sharply with fierce criticism from activists and the media of legislation and practices that curtail women's rights (Shannon 2014). These criticisms arise first and foremost because Saudi Arabia is one of the most gender segregated countries in the world. Secondly, under male guardianship (mahram), policy, every woman must obtain permission from a male guardian—usually her husband or father, but possibly even her brother or son—to access education, to travel, work and to obtain medical treatment, to gain permits, and so forth (Forsythe 2009, p. 396). This can create challenges for women who wish to pursue a career as they must obtain permission from their male guardian. Added to this, once in the workplace, women contend with an array of complex laws, rules, and social practices, which impact on their day-to-day working practice and freedom of movement (Abalkhail 2017).

Although research concerned with women and leadership in higher education in Saudi Arabia is limited, one goal of this paper is to highlight, through a synthesis of existing literature, the current state of Saudi Arabian women's higher education leadership in Saudi Arabia. A second goal of this paper is to propose directions for future research. We believe this is a novel contribution that will be relevant to those in the academic community, as well as PhD candidates formulating proposals for research, and existing doctoral researchers undertaking studies of the region. It may also be of interest to policy makers and government bodies in the Middle East, particularly those who sponsor research. In addition, although the focus of the paper is on women native to Saudi Arabia, many of the issues discussed will be relevant and, therefore, of interest to Western women or women from neighbouring countries who seek or are in leadership roles in higher education in the KSA.

The paper opens with a brief explanation of the methods and materials used in this desk-based study. This is followed by an historical profile of the KSA, focusing on the development of education for females, then women's participation in higher education, to provide insight into this unique and complex culture, and women's position within it. Next, we outline gender gaps in Saudi Arabia. After that, we focus on women's leadership in higher education, then we explore barriers to leadership, first drawing on empirical evidence from the Middle East, then more specifically Saudi Arabia. We briefly draw comparisons with evidence from Western contexts. This brings us to the second goal of this paper, to propose new directions for future research. The paper closes with concluding comments.

2. Materials and Methods

The paper is based on desk-based research that involved searching academic online databases and use of the google search engine to source material. We assessed the scope, content, accuracy, as well as the authority and relevance of the articles, reports and web-based material used in this paper following guidance for finding, retrieving and evaluating journal and web based information (Graham 2007; Metzger 2007). Most sources were from peer reviewed journals. We supplemented those with reports on the region, where appropriate.

We were particularly committed to providing a platform for local studies conducted in Saudi Arabia or the Gulf Cooperation Council (GCC) states, which are often rendered peripheral to mainstream literature from western contexts in scholarly journals. In this sense, we offer a novel contribution that seeks to privilege and legitimate local studies (Milligan 2016), rather than giving centre stage to the mainstream, Western-focused literature, which predominantly reflects and privileges European, Canadian and north American cultures, for example. However, we have drawn on the mainstream literature, in places, to explore if any of the obstacles to women's leadership bear a resemblance to barriers identified in Saudi Arabia.

In terms of our positionality as researchers and our expertise in the study context, it is important to relay that the first author of this paper is a native Saudi Arabian woman who is a doctoral researcher in the UK, with research interests in educational leadership and management in Saudi Arabia. She is also a well-known liberal journalist in Saudi Arabia. As a 'cultural insider', with lived experience of the social, legislative and political conditions that impact on women, she is reflexive about her degree of social proximity and personal standpoint on the issues facing women in the Kingdom. The second author of this paper is a UK academic with expertise in women's leadership, and experience in the supervision of doctoral research in educational leadership and management in the KSA and other GCC states. She is reflexive of her position as a cultural outsider and the dilemmas this presents understanding 'others' (England 1994).

3. An Historical Profile of Saudi Arabia—Women and Education

An appreciation of the historical socio-economic and political conditions of Saudi Arabia is essential to understanding women's position in Saudi society (Hamdan 2005, p. 42). Within this deeply conservative nation, gender politics and religion are inextricably linked (Al-Rasheed and Azzam 2012). While Saudi Arabia is governed by a monarchy, with a Council of Ministers nominated by the King who formulate and implement policies, the constitution is governed by strict interpretation of Islamic law (Mobaraki and Söderfeldt 2010), one of the main characteristics of which pertains to 'the power struggle between the 'ulamā [religious scholars] and the state' (Mai 2000, p. 95). Women are frequently at the centre of discussion and debate between the two. We explore this first in the case of education for females.

At the formation of the modern state of Saudi Arabia in 1932, it was a poor country with just 12 schools and 700 students, educating only boys (Alamari 2011). The discovery of oil in 1938 led to exponential wealth creation, which by the 1940s enabled some elite families to travel to other countries. As they did so, their views on girls' education changed, causing many to enrol their daughters in informal schools upon their return to Saudi Arabia (Altorki 1986). In 1953, the Ministry of Education was founded, with public schools for boys opening for the first time (Al-Munajjed 1997). It was King Faisal and his wife Iffat Al Thunayan who zealously lobbied for education for girls, but they faced fierce objection from religious scholars (Hamdan 2005). In 1956, the first private school for girls opened in Jeddah, in spite of continuing opposition from factions of religious scholars ('ulamā') who claimed education would corrupt girls' morals and destroy the foundations of the Saudi Muslim family (Geel 2016). Although King Faisal and his wife fervently supported women's rights, it took some time to convince the public, and it was only through the use of Islamic teachings that this was achieved (Hamdan 2005). Hamdan (2005), citing Lacey (1981, p. 368), explains how the King would respond to resistance by asking 'is there anything in the Holy Qur'an which forbids the education of women? He also stated: 'We have no cause for argument, God enjoins learning on every Muslim man and woman'. Illustrative of the power of religious scholars, it was only after they were reassured that the girls schooling was in accordance with Islam that they gave their approval, and only then that conservative families sent their girls to school (Al-Munajjed 1997). In 1960 education for girls was expanded with a school in Riyadh (Al-Rawaf and Simmons 1991). While this era marks the beginning of formal education for girls, it also represents the beginning of gender segregation (Geel 2016), and the extensive development of women-only public spaces (Doumato 2009; Hamdan 2005; Geel 2016), which has caused Saudi Arabia to be dubbed the most gender segregated nation on Earth (Gorney 2016).

Gradual acceptance of school education led to the development of higher education. The first university, King Saud University, was established in 1957 and a further six universities opened over the following twenty years, together with the establishment of the Ministry of Higher Education in Saudi Arabia (Alamari 2011). Higher education was made available to women from 1962 and in 1970 the first college for women was established to provide female teachers (Alaugab 2007). This was followed by many more public and private universities and colleges for women (Al Alhareth et al. 2013). However, it was only in 2002 that the administration of education for females was taken over by the Ministry of Education. Prior to 2002, education for females was administered by the Department of Religious Guidance to ensure it did not deviate from its original purpose to 'make women good wives and mothers, and to prepare them for 'acceptable' jobs such as teaching and nursing that were believed to suit their nature' (Hamdan 2005, p. 44).

4. Women's Participation in Higher Education

Despite fervent objection to education for females and concerns that it would be useless and even dangerous, education has increased dramatically over the past few decades (Hamdan 2005). This is particularly the case since King Abdullah ascended the throne in 2005 (Pavan 2016). In fact, there are currently 36 universities across the country (Ministry Of Education 2017). E-learning has also gained popularity, especially among women unable to access mainstream higher education provision (Al Alhareth et al. 2013). In accordance with cultural conventions, men and women are segregated in education and subjects are more limited for women (Hamdan 2005). This is because it is socially unacceptable for women to pursue certain careers and they are forbidden from studying some subjects in Saudi Arabia (Mobaraki and Söderfeldt 2010). To overcome these limitations, many families send their daughters abroad to study the specialisms closed to them (Hamdan 2005). However, over the past decade some restrictions have been lifted, for example, since 2007 women have been permitted to study law (Meijer 2010), and the door was opened for the first woman to gain a Master's degree in archaeology in 2009 (Al-Sudairy 2017).

Aligned with the philosophy of gender segregation, there are some universities for men, such as King Fahad University of Petroleum and Minerals and the Islamic University. Universities for women include Princess Nora bint Abdul Rahman University, which entrusted the first female as rector, making a female equal to male counterparts at other Saudi universities for the first time in the nation's history (Almansour and Kempner 2016). The university is also staffed entirely by women (Meijer 2010; Al-Sudairy 2017). In recent years, some co-ed universities have been created, although men and women are still segregated into sections (campuses), one for men and one for women, and they study separately. There is only one university where segregation does not occur, allowing both male and female students to study together, that is, the King Abdullah's University of Science and Technology (Ministry Of Education 2017).

Over the past decade, the government has put in place reform plans to diversify revenue from oil and gas. Gargantuan investment in education further demonstrates this is a top policy priority for the government. For instance, a five-year education plan announced in 2014 was estimated to be worth 80 billion riyals or $21.33 billion to the education sector (Reuters 2014). Much of this investment was directed to higher education. In 2005, the King Abdullah Sponsorship Programme (KASP) was established (Taylor and Albasri 2014). This programme offers Saudi students a range of opportunities, which include studying abroad in western countries such as the United Kingdom and USA. Drawing on the Saudi statistical yearbook for the years 2012–2013, Manail (2015) reports there were approximately 150,109 males and 49,176 females (roughly a 3:1 ratio) studying abroad. Current statistics from the Ministry of Education Statistics Center (2017) indicate the number of females undertaking a PhD in a western country is 5165. This figure equates to 41.91% of Saudi students who study for a PhD in a western country. It is now widely agreed that many Saudi women have made phenomenal advancements in education, as witnessed in the exponential rise in the number of women accessing higher education to gain graduate and postgraduate degrees (Hamdan 2005; Islam 2014; Khan and Varshney 2013; Parveen 2014; Ministry of Higher Education 2010).

5. Gender Gaps

Despite significant progress in the areas outlined thus far, much more needs to be done for women to achieve gender equality in Saudi Arabia. As women's rights is deemed a marker of progress, considerable attention has been given to the nation's gender gap (Shannon 2014). Evidence from the Global Gender Gap Report, produced annually by the World Economic Forum (2016), ranks the KSA 141 out of 144 countries in the World for gender parity, and third lowest among 18 countries in the Middle East and North Africa region. The gender gap extends to many areas of a woman's life (Table 1), and presents a generally gloomy, but somewhat mixed picture. For instance, on the one hand, the country is ranked 105 for educational attainment, but, reflecting the advancements in women's education outlined in this paper, it has also been ranked as the fifth most improved country in the world for its education. Presenting an even more polarized picture, although it is ranked almost at the lowest end of the scale for economic participation and opportunities for women, a more promising 57th position is achieved for labour force participation among those with advanced degrees. Still, despite the fact that more educated women are making advancements in the labour force, it is of concern that the KSA is ranked lowest in the world when it comes to women achieving a high income (US $12,736 or more) (World Economic Forum 2016). A report from the OECD (2016) notes Saudi Arabia has the largest gender gap in employment rates at all levels of educational attainment, across all OECD and partner countries. The report highlights that women educated to tertiary level have less than half the employment rate of similarly educated men.

Table 1. Global gender gap index (World Economic Forum 2016).

Key Indicators	Rank
Global Gender Gap Index	141
Economic participation and opportunity	142
Educational attainment	105
Health and survival	128
Political empowerment	121
Rank out of	144

Nevertheless, some Saudi women have enjoyed career success, as illustrated by labour force statistics which show an increase from 14% in 1990 to 21% in 2016 in women's employment (World Economic Forum 2016). Albeit that this is in a limited sphere of sectors, as Saudi women are predominantly restricted to careers in sectors such as health care and education (Al-Ahmadi 2011). To overcome the limited career choices available, many Saudi women pursue success through entrepreneurship (Azzam 1996; Welsh et al. 2014).

6. Women and Higher Education Leadership

Reflecting the rise in educated women in Saudi Arabia, one area of employment where women have made strong progress is higher education. The number of female lecturers increased from 4700 in 2003/2004 to approximately 19,600 in 2008/2009. That corresponds to an increase of 7200 to around 48,800 male lecturers over the same period (Al Alhareth et al. 2015, p. 11). Precisely because women make up a reasonably good proportion of higher education faculty, and education is segregated by gender, this should create opportunities for women who aspire to higher education leadership, particularly in female only universities (Alomair 2015). However, female academics tend to hold lower level positions (Al-Ohali and Al-Mehrej 2012; Jamjoom and Kelly 2013). Thus, in common with other countries, the rise in educated women and female faculty is not matched by the proportion of women in higher education leadership.

It is particularly shocking, since education is one of the few careers available to women, that more women have not advanced into educational leadership. One key explanation is that historically women have been prevented from occupying positions of leadership in Saudi Arabia due to strict cultural conventions and legislative restrictions. In fact, historically, according to Smith (1987, p. 34), the education system itself subjugated women to 'ensure that at every level of competence and leadership there will be a place for them that is inferior and subordinate to the positions of men.' Significant to the reversal of this situation is a ruling announced by the king of Saudi Arabia, King Abdullah bin Abdul-Aziz on 23 February 2009 that granted Saudi women the freedom to be leaders. Underlining the King's commitment to advancing women's leadership and specifically women's role in educational leadership, the King immediately announced that the first woman to be appointed to a leadership position would be Deputy Minister of Education. Subsequently, a wide range of government policies has begun to reverse the deficit of women leaders. A significant example is the Shura Council, which appointed 30 women members in 2015. It is also of note that the women were not excluded to a female only area, instead they participated among men and were received by the King and his Crown Princess (Al-Sudairy 2017). Another milestone is the right from 2015 for women to be nominated in municipal elections. Nine hundred women put themselves forward for the first elections, resulting in 37 women holding seats (Al-Sudairy 2017).

Still, women are a long way from achieving parity with men, both in the workplace and in social spheres of life. Reports indicate that just 3.2% of women that hold senior leadership positions in the Middle East and North Africa (MENA) region (Pande and Ford 2011; Patel and Buiting 2013), and the figure of 1% has been reported from Gulf Cooperation Council (GCC) countries (Bahrain, Kuwait, Oman, Qatar, Saudi Arabia, and the United Arab Emirates (UAE)) (Sperling et al. 2014).

Table 2 illustrates statistics specifically relating to women's leadership in higher education. The highest position reported is the role of dean at Princess Nora Bint Abdul Rahman University (a female only university). The second highest position is vice (deputy) dean at a co-ed university. There are 12 women vice deans (presidents) in other universities, such as King Abdullah University of Science and Technology, or vice (deputy) deans for women's sections (campuses), such as King Faisal's and King Saud's Universities. Some universities are considered women's colleges (sections or campuses) because the deanship is subsumed under the Presidency of Academic Affairs. The dean's responsibilities are restricted to women only. However, there are several deans' faculties where women have more responsibilities for women and men. For instance, at Jizan University the Dean of Community Service and Sustainable Development is responsible for both women and men, as is the Dean of the Arts and Design. Women have made stronger advancements in gaining positions as vice (deputy) dean of colleges (campuses), as shown in table one. Most of their responsibilities are for girls' colleges and campuses. Thus, within those institutional contexts, women have crossed boundaries to roles previously designated only for men. Although the number of women in higher education leadership is still finite, this marks an important turning point for women's leadership in Saudi Arabia.

Table 2. Saudi female leaders in higher education (Ministry Of Education 2017)[1].

Position	N (%) Women	N (%) Men
Director of university	1 (3.1%)	33 (3%)
Vice President	12	128 (9.3%)
Dean	61	330 (18.4%)
Deputy dean of faculty	228	542 (42%)
Total	302	1033(29.2%)

In the section that follows we draw on empirical research from the region to explore key barriers to women's leadership in the Middle East and, more specifically, Saudi Arabia, which we compare to evidence from Western contexts.

7. Barriers to Leadership

7.1. Evidence from the Middle East

A small but growing strand of studies concerned with women's careers and, more specifically, women in leadership and management has emerged from the Middle East in the past decade. This includes, for example: Jordan and Oman (Metcalfe 2006) Bahrain (Metcalfe 2006, 2007); Lebanon (Sidani et al. 2015; Tlaiss 2014; Tlaiss and Dirani 2015); Saudi Arabia, Kuwait and the UAE (Abalkhail and Allan 2016) as well as comparative studies within Middle East states (Metcalfe 2008). This body of work highlights a wide range of factors that are fundamental to understanding the underrepresentation of women in leadership (and the workplace) in the region. In particular, combined studies by Metcalfe (2006, 2007, 2008, 2011) and a systematic review by Kauser and Tlaiss (2011) highlight cultural practices that guide interpretations of women's right to work and define gender role expectations. In particular, studies show that traditional gender hierarchies and patriarchal organisational structures benefit men by providing access to important individual and family networks (Metcalfe 2007). That is not to say

---

[1] Data sourced from information provided by universities, accessed through the Ministry of Education in Saudi Arabia website.

women cannot benefit from *Wasta*, meaning 'a social network of interpersonal connections, rooted in family and kinship ties' (Abalkhail and Allan 2016, p. 162). Indeed, this can provide women with connections to gain professional opportunities, and it is the easiest route to gain professional influence; however, women must rely directly on male family members to facilitate wider social connections (Doumato 2010). Within patriarchal structures, masculine leadership traits flourish while women suffer from age-old gender stereotypes that view women as best suited to roles as mothers and wives (Sidani et al. 2015).

7.2. Evidence from Saudi Arabia

Empirical evidence from professional workplace settings in Saudi Arabia suggests that Saudi female managers are as effective as their male counterparts, and they even score slightly higher than men (Al-Shamrani 2015). Still, professional women in Saudi Arabia face many challenges in the workplace. Hodges (2017) categorizes these as social, religious, cultural and organisational. Generally, across various industries women suffer from:

> 'lack of mobility; the salience of gender stereotypes; gender discrimination in the workplace' limited opportunities for growth, development, and career advancement; excessive workload caused by a lack of family-work balance; and gender-based challenges related to dealing with pregnancy'. (Al-Asfour et al. 2017, p. 184)

Focusing specifically on higher education in Saudi Arabia, Abalkhail (2017) explored the challenges and opportunities for women and leadership in interviews with 22 women in two Saudi higher education institutions. The findings reveal that despite possessing higher qualifications, and having longer experience than their male counterparts, the participants believed that men were given preference in recruitment processes for leadership roles. They attributed this to cultural reasons and power linked to religious views. The findings suggest that gender segregation impedes women from participating in strategic meetings and restricts access to important information and resources. Discriminatory practices in promotion and lack of training were also reported. Nevertheless, participants believed education and support from male family members can facilitate the path to leadership.

Other research in Saudi Arabia highlights that participation in the public sphere, such as academic conferences, is challenging for female academics due to family obligations and cultural issues related to transportation and international travel. In fact, the authors of the study note the women exhibited 'extraordinary will' and had to overcome many impediments to participate in the public sphere (Almansour and Kempner 2016, p. 883).

Most prior empirical work is small scale and qualitative, therefore, the findings from a quantitative study with 78 faculty members in three universities in the Riyadh region of Saudi Arabia provide useful additional insights (Alsubaihi 2016). The findings confirm those by Abalkhail (2017), by highlighting that women suffer from limited opportunities for engagement in strategic decision making, especially due to centralized decision making and the limited powers granted to women leaders. Similary, Almansour and Kempner (2016) cite several papers presented at a symposium at King Faisal University in 2006, that raise concerns about the exclusion of women deans from important decisions and meetings (Alsayeg 2006; Almobaireek 2006; Bobshait 2006, cited in Almansour and Kempner 2016). Research also highlights lack of empowerment, and personal challenges that create obstacles to leadership for women in higher education (Alsubaihi 2016).

Other critical problems for women leaders include financial, cultural and empowerment issues (Abukudair 2012, cited in Almansour and Kempner 2016). Additionally, Almengash (2009) notes poor standards for leadership, such as inadequate guidelines, poor job descriptions as well as multiple male and female department directors, which results in communication problems, poor coordination and conflict.

7.3. Comparison of Barriers to Leadership in Western Contexts

Many of the findings from studies in the Middle East, including Saudi Arabia, bear an uncanny resemblance to the significant barriers to leadership experienced by women in other parts of the world (Morley 2013a; Reilly and Quirin 2015). More specifically, for example, studies in Western contexts similarly highlight obstacles such as masculinized organisational cultures (Benschop and Brouns 2003; Leathwood and Read 2009), which bind men together into a hierarchy in which they can flourish (Fenton 2003). Patriarchal cultures that privilege masculine leadership traits often lie beneath the misrecognition of women's leadership capabilities (Morley 2013b), and low perceptions of their capabilities as leaders (Benschop and Brouns 2003). The qualities expected for leadership become normalized in recruitment processes, putting women at a disadvantage (Grummell et al. 2009). Homosociality silences and excludes women from social and professional networks (Fotaki 2013). Other obstacles include limited role models, mentoring and leadership training and development for women (Morley 2013a). Studies in western contexts also point to bias in performance evaluation (Fletcher et al. 2007). Thus, women in the western world experience marginalization and devaluation (Fotaki 2013) in many comparable ways to women in the Middle East. Extensive research also shows that women suffer the double burden of family obligations (Probert 2005), and even for women without such responsibilities, 'the abjected maternal body is displaced onto all women (whether they are mothers or not)' and 'conflated with the feminine' (Fotaki 2013, p. 1257).

While women in Saudi Arabia experience many of the same barriers as women in other parts of the world, their situation is profoundly more complex as they are caught in a unique mix between religion and culture (Al Alhareth et al. 2015).

8. Proposed New Research Directions

There is a dearth of contextually based research on women's careers in Arab countries, especially in Saudi Arabia (Abalkhail 2017). The limited evidence that is available clearly shows that women face many challenges that prevent them from achieving equitable status with men in the workplace. However, shifts in policy and new initiatives to support women's leadership in Saudi Arabia have the potential to bring about change. Much more research is needed to understand the current state of women's leadership in the country and to monitor the impact of new policies and initiatives. Fundamentally, research in the Arab region needs new directions. The very small stream of studies concerned with women and leadership, including those conducted in higher education, focus predominantly on the challenges women face (Alomair 2015). Furthermore, it is often assumed that studies from one Arab state are applicable to another, when in fact although the GCC states share many commonalities, each nation has its own unique characteristics that are deserving of scholarly attention (Sidani and Gardner 2000). Future research must also account for the heterogeneity that exists within Saudi Arabia, by exploring not only the main urban areas of the country but also regions that are more traditional and rural. In the discussion that follows, we revisit key debates identified in the literature and propose new directions for future empirical work.

First and foremost, within Arab states, gender politics and religion are intertwined (Al-Rasheed and Azzam 2012). Conservative views rooted in local interpretations of Islamic law have fuelled debates about women's education and women's leadership, among many other topics in recent years (Al-Rasheed 2013). Some commentators claim it is enshrined in the Holy Qur'an that women should not be leaders (Vidyasagar and Rea 2004). Apoplectic clashes between liberal reformers and conservative 'ulamā' have become notorious in the media (Meijer 2010). The arguments put forth by conservative commentators act as a powerful obstacle to women's full participation in leadership. However, it is important to note, as Hamdan (2005) argues, that it is cultural practices, which result in strict patriarchal interpretations of Islam, not the Islamic religion per se, that contribute to gender inequality in Saudi Arabia. This results in dominant discourses, which have power because they are held to represent knowledge and truth (Foucault 1972). Deconstruction of these dominant discourses, associated texts and narrative, would allow new meanings and counter discourses to emerge. Studies of law and interpretations of Islam in Saudi society may also throw new light on the debates surrounding women's suitability for leadership.

Secondly, gender segregation has a significant impact on all aspects of professional life in Saudi Arabia (Elamin and Omair 2010). However, the notion that this is detrimental to women's career advancement is contested. At one end of the debate, Doumato (2000) argues that gender segregation is a major factor in women's underrepresentation in the workforce. Combined studies by Metcalfe (2006, 2007, 2008, 2011) suggest that gender segregation has given rise to gender based occupations, sustained patriarchal organisational structures, and it is the cause of limited professional support and mentoring for women. However, contrasting perspectives include the view that gender segregation can give women a professional advantage as they do not have to compete with men in women only spaces (Hamdan 2005).

It is important to note that 'the practice of seclusion of Arab Muslim women is a comparatively recent phenomenon. Historically Muslim Arab women participated in all aspects of life politically, socially, and economically' (Hamdan 2005, p. 45). Al-Rasheed (2013) attributes changing practices to Islamic nationalism[2] and oil wealth (2012). She argues that since the 1980s, in particular, restrictive interpretations of Islam have been used, not only to further limit women's visibility in public space, but to emphasise women's emotionality so as to discredit women as being suited to public and state positions. Like Le Renard (2008), Al-Rasheed (2013) argues that wealth created through the oil industry diminished the need for women's salaries as a means of sustaining the family and, subsequently, women not working became a symbol of wealth and moral standing. In addition, she points out that fatwas[3] on women, requiring them to deal with minute aspects of their appearance and lifestyle, became notorious with the rise in oil wealth (Al-Rasheed 2013, p. 120). This caused many Saudi women to view themselves as protected 'jewels' and gain a reputation as 'educated but idle women' (Al-Rasheed 2013, p. 23). Furthermore, oil wealth marginalized women because it made 'controlling women affordable' and 'separating them from the public sphere very affordable' through gender segregation and the exponential development of women only banks, universities and other public spaces (Al-Rasheed and Azzam 2012, p. 7). Further research is needed to fully understand the impact of gender segregation in Saudi Arabia, not just on women and their careers but on men, businesses and institutions, the economy, and society itself. Taking a constructionist approach, researchers may expose power relations between men and women by exploring gender segregation discourse, policy and/or practice.

Thirdly, a significant and highly controversial legislative obstacle to women's advancement into leadership is the male guardianship system. It has been described as one of the most humiliating of all experiences (Fatany 2013). Under guardianship law, a female is considered a minor throughout her life. This means she is not able to make decisions about herself (Quamar 2016). Since personal status law dictates that 'an unmarried adult is the ward of her father, a married women is the ward of her husband and a widowed woman is the ward of her sons' (Mobaraki and Söderfeldt 2010), females live under a male guardian for life (Quamar 2016). Therefore, men are responsible for female family members and their permission is required when a woman wishes to travel (Al Alhareth et al. 2015). In addition, women are required to have a male guardian to accompany them when travelling outside Saudi Arabia, although many do travel without a male guardian (Al-Rasheed and Azzam 2012). Vidyasagar and Rea (2004, p. 262) argue that the constitution prevents gender equality by restricting women's freedom to travel, to access education and to work under guardianship rules (p. 262). Added to this, Saudi Arabia is the only country in the world to prohibit women from driving, hence, women are severely restricted

---

[2] Al-Rasheed and Azzam (2012, p. 5) explains 'Religious nationalism is actually about constructing community, very much like nationalism. It is based on certain mythologies about the family, the nation as a family and the place of women in the family and in the nation.'

[3] A fatwā is an Islamic legal pronouncement, issued by an expert in religious law (mufti) (The Islamic Supreme Council of America 2017).

in their freedom of movement, especially travelling for work purposes (Mobaraki and Söderfeldt 2010). This has resulted in fierce criticism from commentators.

Thus, two royal decrees, announced in 2017, mark a significant turning point for women's liberation in Saudi Arabia. The first royal decree will relax the country's guardianship laws. It is anticipated to come into force by the end of 2017. The second royal decree, announced in September 2017, will reverse the driving ban placed on women. It is expected to be implemented in June 2018. While the announcement to relax guardianship laws generated positive responses, many observers remain cautious about whether the proposed changes will be implemented effectively in practice. Still, proposed changes in guardianship law offer women a ray of hope that systematic injustices pertaining to their freedom of movement will be lifted. Future research will be needed to monitor the extent to which changes in guardianship law are implemented in practice. Large scale quantitative studies would provide evidence of this and help to identify problems that may impede progress. Longitudinal research will be necessary to track change over time. In addition, understanding how changes in guardianship law impacts on women qualitatively through exploration of their lived experience may also prove fruitful for researchers and policy makers. Future research will also be needed to understand the impact of the ruling allowing women to drive, on women's lives and work, as well as the economy.

Fourth, traditional ideology appears to be having a powerful influence on social attitudes toward women. Empirical research in Saudi Arabia confirms that Saudi men have developed more 'traditional attitudes towards working females', in recent years. Saudi men strongly believe 'the premise that men are dominant, independent, competitive and capable of leadership and women are submissive, dependent, caring and good for domestic tasks and child rearing' (Elamin and Omair 2010, p. 758). If is of concern that these studies contradict earlier research in the region (Mostafa 2003, 2005), which had reported that attitudes towards women who work were becoming less traditional. Elamin and Omair (2010) suggest the return to traditional values may be associated with Saudi Arabia's strict Islamic teachings and cultural values. Despite advancements in women's education, women are, therefore, expected to give priority to their family not a career (Al-Ahmadi 2011). Although this can cause some women to abandon their goals and become satisfied with staying at home and waiting for marriage, many women have learnt to use 'legitimate' religious language, which cannot be challenged to achieve their goals (Hamdan 2005). In depth narrative studies, combined with fine grained socio-linguistic analyses or analytical approaches such as discursive psychology, as well as discourse analysis may take this research in new directions.

Fifth, many forms of discrimination present additional barriers to women's career advancement in Saudi Arabia (Al-Ahmadi 2011). In addition to discrimination in the hiring process, the profound social and cultural barriers that exist (Al-Ahmadi 2011; Alomair 2015) can influence a woman's decision to pursue leadership. Added to this, debates surrounding women's leadership can cause people to question women's leadership abilities. Other barriers concern perceptions of women's impartiality and independence, which are considered key qualities of leaders (Northouse 2015). This is often of concern to employers in Saudi Arabia because cultural convention dictates that a woman will impart discussions and even workplace practices to her father or husband (Al Alhareth et al. 2013). Since this can result in women not being considered independent or impartial compared to their male counterparts in the workplace, employers may be deterred from giving women the opportunity to be the leaders (Al Alhareth et al. 2013). The research community has a role to play countering traditional myths and prejudices by highlighting the contribution that women leaders make in the workplace and society.

Finally, new initiatives such as 'Saudi vision 2030' and 'Saudi female leaders' announced in April 2016 by the Chairman of the Council of Economic and Development Affairs, include 'The National Transformation Plan 2020' (Saudi Vision 2017). The National Transformation Plan's goal is to increase the percentage of women in leadership positions by 2020. The plan includes a multitude of initiatives to support this goal, such as training programmes for women leaders, reforms and legislation, which can help to improve the condition of women's lives. Future research should include evaluation of the impact of the new national transformation plan on women in Saudi Arabia. Research is needed to establish if the Saudi vision for women's empowerment is being accomplished and how it can be extended. Research is also needed to understand the nature of initiatives to support women in the Saudi context, and how women experience and benefit from various kinds of interventions, such as mentoring, networking, training and so forth. Longitudinal research would track the impact on women's careers over time. Research in the region also needs to take new directions that incorporate constructivist and constructionist approaches to understand the subjective experience of women, to explore how women construct their identity, as well new novel studies into identity work and/or identify regulation, which will be particularly pertinent during these times of change.

9. Conclusions

Saudi Arabia is a country that is in the midst of social change (Alyami 2016); yet, key aspects of change such as women's participation in waged work, and especially women's leadership, have received limited attention from the academic community. In this paper, we provided an overview of the current state of women's leadership, focusing on the higher education context, and discussed proposals for future research directions. New policies and initiatives that aim to improve women's freedom of movement, their participation in the workplace and in leadership, provide the academic community with a rich source of research material.

History has witnessed a gargantuan shift in attitudes towards education for Saudi females over the past five decades, which despite the severe restrictions placed on Saudi women has resulted in the percentage of women graduating from higher education reaching record levels (Abalkhail and Allan 2015). Many women have carved out successful careers in higher education and other sectors. This strongly suggests that many Saudi Arabian women want to have the same career opportunities as women in other parts of the World. If government policies and plans for women's advancement in the workplace and into leadership mirror successes achieved in education, Saudi Arabian women may reap the benefits over the coming years. This should be viewed as a work in progress, to which the academic community can contribute through empirical research and scholarly work.

Author Contributions: Karen Jones conceived and designed the study, Azzah Alsubaie and Karen Jones performed the research and wrote the paper.

Conflicts of Interest: The authors declare no conflict of interest.

References

Abalkhail, Jouharah M., and Barbara Allan. 2015. Women's Career Advancement: Mentoring and Networking in Saudi Arabia and the UK. *Human Resource Development International* 18: 153–68. [CrossRef]

Abalkhail, Jouharah M., and Barbara Allan. 2016. "Wasta" and women's careers in the Arab Gulf States. *Gender in Management: An International Journal* 31: 162–80. [CrossRef]

Abalkhail, Jouharah M. 2017. Women and leadership: Challenges and opportunities in Saudi higher education. *Career Development International* 22: 165–83. [CrossRef]

Abukudair, E. 2012. The Challenges Facing Women Leaders in Higher Education Institutions in the Kingdom of Saudi Arabia. *Saudi Journal of Higher Education* 7: 87–124.

Al Alhareth, Yahya, Neil McBride, Mary Prior, Mike Leigh, and Catherine Flick. 2013. Saudi Women and E-Learning. Paper presented at the Pixel International Conference: The Future of Education, Florence, Italy, June 13–14. Available online: http://conference.pixel-online.net/foe2013/common/download/Paper_pdf/142-ELE15-FP-Alhareth-FOE2013.pdf (accessed on 22 August 2017).

Al Alhareth, Yahya, Ibtisam Al Dighrir, and Yasra Al Alhareth. 2015. Review of Women's Higher Education in Saudi Arabia. *American Journal of Educational Research* 3: 10–15. [CrossRef]

Al-Ahmadi, Hanan. 2011. Challenges facing women leaders in Saudi Arabia. *Human Resource Development International* 14: 149–66. [CrossRef]

Alamari, Majed. 2011. Higher Education in Saudi Arabia. *Journal of Higher Education Theory and Practice* 11: 88–91.

Al-Asfour, Ahmed, Hayfaa A. Tlaiss, Sami A. Khan, and Rajasekar James. 2017. Saudi women's work challenges and barriers to career advancement. *Career Development International* 22: 184–99. [CrossRef]

Alaugab, Abdullah Mohammad. 2007. Benefits Barriers and Attitudes of Saudi Female Faculty and Students toward Online Learning in Higher Education. Unpublished Ph.D. thesis, University of Kansas, Lawrence, KS, USA.

Almansour, Sana, and Ken Kempner. 2016. The Role of Arab women faculty in the public sphere. *Studies in Higher Education* 41: 874–86. [CrossRef]

Almengash, Sarah. 2009. Administrative organisation in the female students' divisions in Saudi Universities: Problems and suggested solutions. *Educational Science Journal* 17: 149–201.

Almobaireek, W. 2006. Administrative Organisation in Girls Divisions in Saudi Universities. Paper presented at the Symposium of Administering Girls Divisions: Challenges and Ambitions, Dammam, Saudi Arabian, March 6–8.

Al-Munajjed, Mona. 1997. *Women in Saudi Arabia Today*. New York: St. Martins Press.

Al-Ohali, Mohammad, and Hamad Al-Mehrej. 2012. Faculty Salary and Remuneration. In *The Kingdom of Saudi Arabia. Paying the Professoriate: A Global Comparison of Compensation and Contracts*. Abingdon: Routledge, pp. 278–87.

Alomair, Miznah O. 2015. Female Leadership Capacity and Effectiveness: A Critical Analysis of the Literature on Higher Education in Saudi Arabia. *International Journal of Higher Education* 4: 81–93. [CrossRef]

Al-Rasheed, Madawi. 2013. *A Most Masculine State: Gender, Politics and Religion in Saudi Arabia*. Cambridge: Cambridge University Press, ISBN 9780521122528.

Al-Rasheed, Madawi, and Maha Azzam. 2012. *The Prospects and Limits of Women's Mobilization in Saudi Arabia*. London: Chatham House.

Al-Rawaf, Haya Saad, and Cyril Simmons. 1991. The Education of Women in Saudi Arabia. *Comparative Education* 27: 287–95. [CrossRef]

Alsayeg, N. 2006. Roles of Deans at Girls Divisions in Saudi Arabian Universities from Their Point of View. Paper presented at the Symposium of Administering Girls Divisions: Challenges and ambitions, Dammam, Saudi Arabian, March 6–8.

Al-Shamrani, Mohammed S. 2015. An Empirical Study of Male and Female Leadership Styles in a Segregated Work Environment in the Kingdom of Saudi Arabia. Unpublished Ph.D. thesis, University of Hull, Hull, UK.

Alsubaihi, Shroog Ibrahim. 2016. *Challenges for Women Academic Leaders to Obtain Senior Leadership Positions in Higher Education in Saudi Arabia*. Ann Arbor: ProQuest Dissertations Publishing. [PubMed]

Al-Sudairy, Hend T. 2017. *Modern Woman in the Kingdom of Saudi Arabia: Rights, Challenges and Achievements*. Newcastle-upon-Tyne: Cambridge Scholars Publishing.

Altorki, Soraya. 1986. *Women in Saudi Arabia: Ideology and Behaviour among the Elite*. New York: Colombia University Press.

Alyami, Rfah Hadi. 2016. *Saudi Women's Education and Work Opportunities: Equity Matters*. Reading: University of Reading. Available online: http://centaur.reading.ac.uk/59581/3/19000042_%20Alyami_s2.pdf (accessed on 1 September 2017).

Azzam, Maha. 1996. Gender and Politics of Religion in the Middle East. In *Feminism and Islam: Legal and Literary Perspectives*. Edited by Mai Yamani. New York: New York University Press, pp. 217–30.

Benschop, Yvonne, and Margo Brouns. 2003. Crumbling ivory towers: Academic organizing and gender effects. *Gender, Work & Organisation* 10: 194–212. [CrossRef]

Bobshait, A. 2006. Skills in Managing Girls Divisions and Obstacles of Application Confronting Women Leaders. Paper presented at the Symposium of Administering Girls Divisions: Challenges and Ambitions, Dammam, Saudi Arabian, March 6–8.

Doumato, Eleanor Abdella. 2000. *Getting God's Ear. Women, Islam, and Healing in Saudi Arabia and the Gulf*. New York: Columbia University Press.

Doumato, Eleanor Abdella. 2009. Obstackles to Equlity for Saudi Women. In *the Kingdom of Saudi Arabia, 1979–2009: Evolution of a Pivotal State. A Special Edition of Viewpoints*. Washington: The Middle East Institute.

Doumato, Eleanor Abdella. 2010. Saudi Arabia. In *Women's Rights in the Middle East and North Africa: Progress Amid Resistance*. Edited by Sanja Kell and Julia Breslin. New York: Freedom House, Lanham: Rowman and Littlefield.

Dupre, John. 1994. Against Scientific Imperialism. *Philosophy of Science Association Proceedings* 2: 374–81. [CrossRef]

Elamin, M. Abdallah, and Katlin Omair. 2010. Males' attitudes towards working females in Saudi Arabia. *Personnel Review* 39: 746–66. [CrossRef]

England, Kim V. L. 1994. Getting Personal: Reflexivity, Positionality, and Feminist Research. *The Professional Geographer* 46: 80–89. [CrossRef]

Fatany, Samar. 2013. Modernizing Saudi Arabia. North Charleston: Create Space Independent Publishing Platform, ISBN 978-1482509984.

Fenton, Natalie. 2003. Discrimination of Female Academics: Equality will not be Achieved without the Right Resources and Laws. Availabe online: https://www.theguardian.com/education/2003/apr/01/highereducation.educationsgendergap (accessed on 10 October 2017).

Fletcher, Catherine, Rebecca Boden, Julie Kent, and Julie Tinson. 2007. Performing women: The gendered dimensions of the UK new research economy. *Gender, Work & Organisation* 14: 433–53. [CrossRef]

Forsythe, David P. 2009. *Encyclopedia of Human Rights*. Oxford: Oxford University Press, vol. 1.

Fotaki, Marianna. 2013. No woman is like a man (in academia): The masculine symbolic order and the unwanted female body. *Organisation Studies* 34: 1251–75. [CrossRef]

Foucault, Michael. 1972. The discourse on language (L'ordre du discourse). In *The Archaeology of Knowledge Andthe Discourse on Language*. Edited by Michael Foucault. NewYork: Pantheon Books, pp. 215–37.

Geel, Annemarie van. 2016. Separate or together? Women-only public spaces and participation of Saudi women in the public domain in Saudi Arabia. *Contemporary Islam* 10: 357–78. [CrossRef]

Gorney, Cynthia. 2016. The Changing Face of Saudi Women. *National Geographic* February: 110–33.

Graham, Ann-Maree. 2007. Finding, retrieving and evaluating journal and web-based information for evidenced-based optometry. *Clinical and Experimental Optometry* 90: 244–49. [CrossRef] [PubMed]

Grummell, Bernie, Dympna Devine, and Kathleen Lynch. 2009. The careless manager: Gender, care and new managerialism in higher education. *Gender and Education* 21: 191–208. [CrossRef]

Hamdan, Amani. 2005. Women and education in Saudi Arabia: Challenges and achievements. *International Education Journal* 6: 42–64.

Hodges, Julie. 2017. Cracking the walls of leadership: Women in Saudi Arabia. *Gender in Management: An International Journal* 32: 34–46. [CrossRef]

Islam, Samira Ibrahim. 2014. Saudi women: Opportunities and challenges in science and technology. *Education Journal* 3: 71–78. [CrossRef]

Jamjoom, Fatima B., and Philippa Kelly. 2013. Higher Education for Women in the Kingdom of Saudi Arabia. *Higher Education in Saudi Arabia* 40: 117–25.

Kauser, Saleema, and Hayfaa Tlaiss. 2011. Middle Eastern women manager: Participation, barriers, and future prospects. *Journal of International Business Economy* 12: 35–56.

Khan, Sami A., and Deepanjana Varshney. 2013. Transformational Leadership in the Saudi Arabian Cultural Context: Prospects and Challenges. In *Culture and Gender in Leadership: Perspectives from the Middle East and Asia*. Edited by James Rajasekar and Loo-See Beh. London: Palgrave Macmillan, pp. 200–27.

Lacey, Robert. 1981. *The Kingdom: Arabia and the House of Sa'ud*. New York: Harcourt Brace Jovanovich.

Le Renard, Amélie. 2008. Only for women: the state, and reform in Saudi Arabia. *The Middle East Journal* 62: 610–29. [CrossRef]

Leathwood, Carole, and Barbara Read. 2009. *Gender and the Changing Face of Higher Education: A Feminized Future?* New York: SRHE/Open University Press.

Mai, Yamani. 2000. *Changed Identities: The Challenge of the New Generation in Saudi Arabia*. London: Chatham House Royal Institute of International Affairs.

Manail, Anis Ahmed. 2015. Outward Mobility of Saudi Students: An Overview. *International Higher Education* 83: 19–20.

Meijer, Roel. 2010. The Gender Segregation (ikhtilāṭ) Debate in Saudi Arabia: Reform and the Clash between 'Ulamā' and Liberals. *Journal for Islamic Studies* 30: 2–32. [CrossRef]

Metcalfe, Beverly Dawn. 2006. Exploring cultural dimensions of gender and management in the Middle East. *Thunderbird International Business Review* 48: 93–107. [CrossRef]

Metcalfe, Beverly Dawn. 2007. Gender and HRM in the Middle East. *International Journal of Human Resource Management* 18: 54–75. [CrossRef]

Metcalfe, Beverly Dawn. 2008. Women, management and globalization in the Middle East. *Journal of Business Ethics* 83: 85–100. [CrossRef]

Metcalfe, Beverly Dawn. 2011. Women, empowerment and development in Arab Gulf States: A critical appraisal of governance, culture and national human resource development (HRD) frameworks. *Human Resource Development International* 21: 131–48. [CrossRef]

Metzger, Miriam J. 2007. Making sense of credibility on the Web: Models for evaluating online information and recommendations for future research. *Journal of American Society for Information Science and Technology* 58: 2078–91. [CrossRef]

Milligan, Lizzi. 2016. Insider-outsider-inbetweener? Researcher positioning, participative methods and cross-cultural educational research. *Compare: A Journal of Comparative and International Education* 46: 235–50. [CrossRef]

Ministry Of Education. 2017. Electronic Services. Available online: https://www.moe.gov.sa/ar/Pages/default.aspx (accessed on 31 August 2017).

Ministry of Education Statistics Center. 2017. Students enrolled abroad by grade 2–7. Available online: http://departments.moe.gov.sa/PlanningInformation/RelatedDepartments/Educationstatisticscenter/EducationDetailedReports/Docs/table7-2.html (accessed on 1 September 2017).

Ministry of Higher Education. 2010. *Women in Higher Education, Saudi initiatives and Achievements*. Riyadh: Ministry of Higher Education.

Mobaraki, Aeh, and Björn Söderfeldt. 2010. Gender Inequity in Saudi Arabia and Its Role in Public Health. *Eastern Mediterranean Health Journal* 16: 113–18. [PubMed]

Morley, Louise. 2013a. *Women and Higher Education Leadership: Absences and Aspirations*. London: Leadership Foundation for Higher Education.

Morley, Louise. 2013b. The rules of the game: Women and the leaderist turn in higher education. *Gender and Education* 25: 116–31. [CrossRef]

Mostafa, Mohamed. 2003. Attitudes towards Women Who Work in Egypt. *Women in Management Review* 18: 252–66. [CrossRef]

Mostafa, Mohamed. 2005. Attitudes Towards Women Managers in The united Arab Emirates: The Effects of Patriarchy, Age, and Sex Differences. *Journal of Managerial Psychology* 20: 522–40. [CrossRef]

Northouse, Peter G. 2015. *Leadership: Theory and Practice*. Thousand Oaks: Sage Publications Ltd.

OECD. 2016. *Education at a Glance 2016: OECD Indicators*. Paris: OECD Publishing. [CrossRef]

Pande, Rohini, and Deanna Ford. 2011. Gender Quotas and Women Leadership: World Development Report. Available online: http://www.worldbank.org/ (accessed on 1 September 2017).

Parveen, Musrrat. 2014. Saudi feminization: Dynamical phases of Saudi women in the field of education and employment. *Journal of American Science* 10: 52–66.

Patel, Gita, and Sophie Buiting. 2013. Gender Differences in Leadership Styles and the Impact within Corporate Boards. The Commonwealth Secretariat, Social Transformation Programmes Division. Available online: http://www.cpahq.org/cpahq/cpadocs/Genderdiffe.pdf (accessed on 1 September 2017).

Pavan, Annalisa. 2016. Higher Education in Saudi Arabia: Rooted in Heritage and Values, Aspiring to Progress. *International Research in Higher Education* 1: 91–100. [CrossRef]

Probert, Belinda. 2005. 'Just couldn't fit it in': Gender and unequal outcomes in academic careers. *Gender, Work & Organisation* 12: 50–72. [CrossRef]

Quamar, Md. Muddassir. 2016. Sociology of the Veil in Saudi Arabia: Dress Code, Individual Choices, and Questions on Women's Empowerment. *Digest of Middle East Studies* 25: 315–37. [CrossRef]

Elizabeth C. Reilly, and J. Bauer Quirin, eds. 2015. *Women Leading Education across the Continents: Overcoming the Barriers*. Plymouth: Rowman & Littlefield.

Reuters. 2014. Saudi Arabia Approves $21 bln Five-Year Education Plan -SPA. Available online: http://www.reuters.com/article/saudi-education-idUSL6N0O53HU20140519 (accessed on 31 August 2017).

Saudi Vision 2017. *Vision 2030 Kingdom Saudi Arabia*. Available online: http://vision2030.gov.sa/en (accessed on 3 October 2017).

Shannon, Kelly J. 2014. 'I'm glad I'm not a Saudi Woman': The First Gulf War and US encounters with Saudi gender relations. *Cambridge Review of International Affairs* 27: 553–73. [CrossRef]

Sidani, Yusuf M., and William L. Gardner. 2000. Work values among Lebanese workers. *The Journal of Social Psychology* 140: 597–607. [CrossRef] [PubMed]

Sidani, Yusuf M., Alison Konrad, and Charlotte M. Karam. 2015. From female leadership advantage to female leadership deficit: A developing country perspective. *Career Development International* 20: 273–92. [CrossRef]

Smith, Dorothy. 1987. *The Everyday World as Problematic*. Toronto: Toronto University Press.

Sperling, Julia, Chiara Marcati, and Michael Rennie. 2014. GCC Women in Leadership: From the First to the Norm. McKinsey & Company. Available online: http://www.mckinsey.com/~/media/McKinsey%20Offices/Middle%20East/Latest%20thinking/GCC_Women_In_Leadership_FINAL.ashx (accessed on 22 August 2017).

Taylor, Charles, and Wasmiah Albasri. 2014. The Impact of Saudi Arabia King Abdullah's Scholarship Program in the US. *Open Journal of Social Sciences* 2: 109–18. [CrossRef]

The Islamic Supreme Council of America. 2017. What is a Fatwas? Available online: http://www.islamicsupremecouncil.org/understanding-islam/legal-rulings/44-what-is-a-fatwa.html (accessed on 22 August 2017).

Tlaiss, Hayfaa A. 2014. Betweenn the traditional andthe contemporary: careers of women managers from a developing Middle Eastern Country Perspective. *The International Journal of Human Resource Management* 25: 2858–80. [CrossRef]

Tlaiss, Hayfaa A., and Khalil M. Dirani. 2015. Women and training: An empirical investigation in the Arab Middle East. *Human Resource Development International* 18: 366–86. [CrossRef]

Vidyasagar, Girija, and David M. Rea. 2004. Saudi Women Doctors: Gender and Careers within Wahhabic Islam and a 'Westernised'work Culture. *Women's Studies International Forum* 27: 261–80. [CrossRef]

Welsh, Dianne HB, Esra Memili, Eugene Kaciak, and Aliyah Al Sadoon. 2014. Saudi Women Entrepreneurs: A Growing Economic Segment. *Journal of Business Research* 67: 758–62. [CrossRef]

World Economic Forum. 2016. The Global Gender Gap Report. Available online: http://www3.weforum.org/docs/GGGR16/WEF_Global_Gender_Gap_Report_2016.pdf (accessed on 31 August 2017).

MDPI

St. Alban-Anlage 66

4052 Basel

Switzerland

Tel. +41 61 683 77 34

Fax +41 61 302 89 18

www.mdpi.com

Administrative Sciences Editorial Office

E-mail: admsci@mdpi.com

www.mdpi.com/journal/admsci

MDPI
St. Alban-Anlage 66
4052 Basel
Switzerland

Tel: +41 61 683 77 34
Fax: +41 61 302 89 18

www.mdpi.com

MDPI

ISBN 978-3-03897-265-5

www.ingramcontent.com/pod-product-compliance
Lightning Source LLC
Chambersburg PA
CBHW051314020426
42333CB00028B/3341